MASS
CONSUMPTION
AND PERSONAL
IDENTITY

MASS CONSUMPTION AND PERSONAL IDENTITY

EVERYDAY ECONOMIC EXPERIENCE

Peter K. Lunt and
Sonia M. Livingstone

OPEN UNIVERSITY PRESS
Buckingham • Philadelphia

Open University Press
Celtic Court
22 Ballmoor
Buckingham
MK18 1XW

and

1900 Frost Road, Suite 101
Bristol, PA 19007, USA

First Published 1992

A catalogue record of this book is available
from the British Library

Library of Congress Cataloging-in-Publication Data

Lunt, Peter K. (Peter Kenneth), 1956–
   Mass consumption and personal identity: everyday economic
experience/Peter K. Lunt and Sonia M. Livingstone.
     p.   cm.
   Includes bibliographical references and index.
   ISBN 0–335–09672–7 (hardback)
   ISBN 0–335–09671–9 (paperback)
   1. Consumption (Economics). 2. Shopping. 3. Self-perception.
4. Social Values. I. Livingstone, Sonia M. II. Title.
HC79.C6L86 1992
339.4'7'019–dc20   91–45914
                                            CIP

94-692

Typeset in 9.5/11.5pt Sabon
by Graphicraft Typesetters Ltd, Hong Kong
Printed in Great Britain
by Biddles Ltd, Guildford and Kings Lynn

We dedicate this book to Joseph

CONTENTS

ACKNOWLEDGEMENTS

This book is based on research that we carried out jointly, firstly at the Department of Experimental Psychology and Nuffield College, Oxford University, then at the University of Kent at Canterbury, and finally at University College and the London School of Economics, London University. We wish to thank Nuffield College, Oxford and the University of Kent at Canterbury for their financial help with the empirical research reported in this book. Some of the empirical material and data analysis which is reported in this book has appeared elsewhere (see articles by Livingstone and Lunt, and by Lunt and Livingstone in the References).

The research project was conceived and designed equally by both authors, and we each conducted the interviews, discussion groups and statistical analyses. We wrote the preliminary draft of the book by dividing up the chapters, with Peter Lunt writing Chapters 2, 5, 7 and 8, and Sonia Livingstone writing Chapters 1, 3, 4 and 6. However, each of the chapters has been discussed and thoroughly revised and rewritten by both authors.

When we were making these revisions, John Baxter, Phil Brown, Mark Casson, Helga Dittmar, Angela Livingstone, Rodney Livingstone and Naomi Tadmor, among others, offered helpful comments and criticisms for which we are most grateful. We also thank Benjamin Livingstone and Ann Milne for their practical help in conducting this project. Finally, we thank all those people who agreed to be interviewed or to complete our lengthy questionnaire, for the book is based on their personal experiences, which they generously shared with us and from which we have learnt much.

EVERYDAY EXPERIENCES OF MASS CONSUMPTION

ONE

This book is about people and their money. We ask what money means to people and what role it plays in their everyday lives. We consider how people spend or save their money, what they buy and why, whether they talk about money and to whom, what they think of consumerism, credit cards, shopping and people's feelings about changes in consumption. It is often said that we live in an age of consumerism – what does this mean for people's everyday experience and sense of identity?

When we began this project, we received several kinds of reactions from our colleagues and friends. The first reaction was that we had picked a trivial and uninteresting subject. How could there be anything significant in the inanimate objects people filled their houses with, or the fact that we now use credit cards instead of cash? Surely getting into debt is simply a matter of not having enough money, going shopping a matter of personal taste and fashion, talking about money just a form of social chit chat? We would respond in two ways. First, the study of the (apparently) trivial is not in itself trivial, for while our everyday lives consist in just such a series of experiences – chatting to our friends, watching television, cooking a meal, going shopping – it is through such activities people produce and reproduce significant social divisions such as those of gender or class and significant economic structures such as those of the credit system or the leisure industry. Secondly, as social science has long argued, social patterns which appear trivial and obvious are revealed to be complex and multifaceted on further analysis. We hope to show, for example, how people's relations to inanimate objects provide a context for their relations with other people, how credit cards and cash have different implications for control over one's finances and hence for what we buy and why, how getting into debt is a matter of attitudes and values as well as income and outgoings, and so on. Despite the apparent naturalness and normality of our everyday lives, it is not in fact obvious why a washing machine has become a necessity, why, for many, borrowing – legal and routine – is seen as a source of shame, why driving down the motorway to the shopping mall is a great way to spend a Saturday morning, why well-washed, second-hand clothes are seen as dirty, or why we feel truly individual when selecting the latest fashions from the chain store.

The second reaction we received about our project was that we had chosen the most important subject for our times. Surely more couples argue about and separate over money than anything else, and it is a greater taboo to ask about someone's income or debts than to ask them about sex. Many believe that consumption has become our major leisure activity, that dreaming about, planning and shopping for goods and then arranging them in our homes, is a supreme source of pleasure. From this it follows that goods no longer enable us to do something else but rather provide satisfaction simply by our possessing them. Moreover, one can argue that people cannot create authentic identities and relationships when social relations are modelled on material systems of exchange, dominated by the balancing of giving and taking, by the signalling of social worth through material possessions, and by the investment of personal meanings in inanimate objects. If goods symbolize social status, it is the practices which constitute social relations that give them their social meaning. If money problems dominate private arguments, then it is the way we as a society organize private relationships and domestic space which gives these problems their potency. However, these everyday practices may be liberating as well as determining, for not only may they reinforce and reconstitute social inequalities and economic pressures, but they may also provide spaces in which alternative, oppositional or local meanings may be negotiated.

The third kind of reaction we received to our proposed project was that the way people handled their money was becoming a social problem. A study of mass consumption was seen to address concrete, practical problems facing society which require exploration and, perhaps, resolution. The 1980s saw a boom in house prices, in the use of consumer credit, in personal borrowing and debt, in the availability of consumer goods, in advertising, and so forth. Yet we still know very little of the impact these changes have had on people's lives. Nor do we understand the role, if any, that everyday practices have played in bringing about such changes. Consequently, we cannot yet judge whether, for whom, and according to what criteria, such economic changes should be seen as advantageous or problematic, nor can we make wholly satisfactory recommendations about how, for example, the credit system should be regulated or debt advice provision be targeted.

Finally, some asked what everyday economic experience had to do with social psychologists – surely economic phenomena are for economists to study. Another version of this argument is that economic phenomena concern the facts – what people actually do – rather than people's accounts, beliefs and explanations about what they do, which are what social psychologists usually study. If only it were so simple: in relation to personal finances especially, we have very little access to what people do except through their reports, and reported actions are embedded in belief systems. It has proved extremely difficult to discover how money is managed within the domestic sphere, between husbands and wives or parents and children (Pahl, 1989). Summary statistics issued by building societies or credit card companies are inadequate to tell us by whom, for what purposes and how everyday economic transactions are conducted. They certainly do not tell us what such transactions mean, and yet such nebulous terms as consumer satisfaction, confidence or normative expectation are used to explain and predict, in so far as they are predictable in this way, such recent economic 'facts' as the consumer boom, adaptation to new technologies or the dramatic growth in personal debt. Finding out what people really do is complexly tied up with how people understand and report their practices.

It is becoming a truism in the social sciences that the economic, social, psychological and historical are all intricately bound up together. This is not simply a fashionable claim for interdisciplinary studies, but rather a basic research orientation according to which we assume – and try to show – that, for example, family relations or domestic habits or generational differences are all affected by the economic context not just of the individual or family but also of the wider society. Thus people's everyday lives depend both on their income and outgoings and on the economic processes of inflation, credit regulation, advertising, pricing policy, unemployment, and so forth. Conversely, we also assume that people's everyday lives affect their income and outgoings – they may work harder if expectations about the standard of living rise, they may accept lower incomes through part-time work if norms dictate they should stay at home with their children, they may get into debt if the category of socially defined necessities expands – and in turn these must affect broader economic processes. If attitudes change to accept organic food or environmentally friendly products despite their greater cost, if satellite dishes are rejected in favour of cable television because of their visible social message, if the concept of credit is successfully detached from the moral connotations of being in debt, then the meanings of economic practices, which are themselves partly determined by a variety of social and psychological factors, as we show in this book, will have broader implications.

Our main focus in this book is on the everyday experience of a wide range of issues that surround mass consumption. We are concerned with the felt reality of present consumer arrangements, with ordinary beliefs about how daily life is and should be, with the relations between goods and identity, consumption and pleasure, budgeting and control. We have tried to ground our arguments firmly in the accounts people gave us of their lives, and yet also to analyse these accounts in the context of the different social conditions from which these accounts originated, conditions which varied by gender and generation, social class and personal life history.[1]*

We used a variety of methods in the research project: a detailed and lengthy survey questionnaire, a series of personal interviews covering financial life histories, a series of focus group discussions, and a number of paper and pencil tasks, all designed to elicit people's experiences of money and possessions in their everyday lives. These methods varied in how far they were open-ended and receptive to issues or ideas raised by the respondents and how far they were more directive, drawing on theory and previous research. While any one method has its limitations, we hoped that the combination of different methods would provide some compensation for these limitations and give us a satisfactory picture of people's experiences of mass consumption. The data which resulted allowed us to conduct both qualitative and quantitative analyses and, again, it is through their combination that these are most useful. The discussions and interviews were audio-taped and transcribed. The questionnaires were coded and analysed on the computer. All details of these analyses, together with further details of the samples that are given below, can be seen in the Appendix.

The main source of data came from the questionnaire that was completed by 279 people who varied in gender, age, social class, income and family status. Of these 279 respondents, 62 per cent were women and 38 per cent were men. They ranged in age from 18 to 82 years, with an average age of 44 years. The sample varied in social class, but was predominantly lower middle class/upper working class. All of the respondents were kept anonymous and all the data were treated in confidence. Throughout the book, where individuals are described in detail or are named, all names have been changed, and any identifying details either omitted or altered.

The size of the survey sample, while large enough to draw useful statistical conclusions and comparisons, was limited by available resources, for we decided to concentrate on obtaining a large quantity of information from our respondents rather than extending the size of the sample at the cost of the richness and complexity of information obtained. We particularly wanted to obtain both detailed quantitative information about people's circumstances and resources and to provide space for them to add to this information in an unstructured format if they wished. In all, we asked nearly 400 questions of each respondent, covering a wide range of issues and taking an hour or more to complete.

Despite our best efforts, caution is needed when interpreting our findings, for we note that the sample contains rather more women than men, more middle and upper working class than lower working class or very poor people, though it covers the entire age span fairly. We encountered particular problems in measuring household or joint resources and expenditure as only one member of a couple completed a questionnaire, so again caution is needed (Pahl, 1989). The research was conducted in the south of England and is therefore not simply generalizable to people living in different socioeconomic conditions. Finally, but

---

* Superscript numerals refer to numbered notes at the end of the book.

importantly, we emphasize that the present research has not been concerned primarily with extreme poverty (or extreme wealth): most of the sample who were in debt were not suffering much poverty, nor were they generally experiencing house repossession, unemployment, significant illness, or other events associated with major financial problems. Rather, the study concerns the everyday economic experiences among the majority of 'ordinary' people who vary from the fairly poor to the fairly well-off, and caution should be exercised in generalizing to other social groups.

We designed the questionnaire to cover a range of issues which, according to previous literature or our pilot research, we judged relevant to everyday economic experiences. We were influenced mainly by the recent literature on mass consumption stemming from the fields of economic psychology, cultural anthropology and cultural studies, and our own basic orientations within social psychology and symbolic interactionism will also be apparent.

First, we asked a number of questions about respondents' demographic situation – their sex, age, occupation, partner's and parents' occupations, their children, their housing situation, and so forth. Next, we asked in some detail about their financial situation and, if appropriate, that of their partners: what sources of income did they have and how much, what did they spend on regular outgoings, what savings accounts, bank accounts and credit cards did they have, what did they owe and how much did they repay, and did they save money or have savings? We asked what major life events they had experienced recently, and since the way that people cope with problems might mediate their impact, we asked about their coping strategies when faced with problems, both general and financial. We were interested in whether people were satisfied with various aspects of their lives, about whether they felt in control of their lives, and we asked a range of questions pursuing this issue of control – did they know what money they had in the bank or what their bills would be, for example. We asked how they organized their money, whether they budgeted, how they paid for goods, when and where they shopped and whether they enjoyed shopping. As well as all these microeconomic practices, we were concerned about how people understood these practices. Thus we asked both generally about their attitudes towards saving and borrowing and about the morals and values they felt they lived by, for example, how they balanced desire for security against desire for pleasure. More specifically, we asked about their beliefs about what counts as debt, what leads to financial problems, how to economize or budget, what they felt they had learnt about money from their own lives, and so on. We asked about the pleasure of possessions, about their material desires and about their sense of what was necessary to them – where they drew the line between necessities and luxuries. Finally, we asked about the social role of money in their lives – whether they talked or argued about money and with whom, what possessions they thought their peers owned in comparison to themselves, how well off they felt compared to their parents and their children and why, whether they saw themselves as beating or cheating the system or as using money and goods as a way of fitting in and participating in society.

A series of small focus group discussions pursued more general beliefs and concerns about mass consumption, covering issues such as views on the present use of credit, the relation between credit and debt, the balance of responsibility between individuals and society, perceptions of social change, and so on. Through these wide-ranging discussions, we explored some of the social myths and representations about economic experience and social change.

Finally, the more personal and individual aspects of everyday experience were addressed through in-depth interviews based on telling a financially oriented life story. Respondents described their upbringing, their parents' attitudes to money, their own financial independence when they started work, the role of money and possessions in their relationships and marriages, the attitudes to their children, and so forth. Through these interviews, the complex interdependence of expectations, decisions, beliefs, resources, needs and wants, and social and family relations was explored.

MASS CONSUMPTION AND CONSUMER CULTURE

TWO

There has been considerable interest recently within the social sciences – psychology, sociology, anthropology, gender studies and economics – in material culture and mass consumption, allowing for a critical appraisal of the impact of consumerism on the lives of ordinary people. In the early 1980s, there was a growth in unemployment and the mid-1980s saw an enormous increase in personal debt. These social problems, among others, became the focus for social science research and for widespread public concern, questioning the supposed freedoms which mass consumption gives to the individual. The 1980s also saw a sustained political attack on elite institutions in society, together with increasing priority being given to the individual consumer. This involved raising the economic potential of working people and broadening markets, widening the availability of credit, and stimulating home ownership and share ownership. The political right and left came together in a demand for citizens' rights (Held, 1991), many of which were primarily consumers' rights. Not only did the home consumer market grow during the last decade, but also its salience and political importance grew considerably. This renewed the debate over citizens' freedoms: Do these moves really empower the individual or disadvantaged social groups? Is consumer culture a form of oppression or liberation? What are the consequences of the growth in material standards of working people and has this brought any increase in involvement in society? As we shall see, there have been various attempts by the left to appropriate the diversity in consumer culture that has become such a powerful symbol of Conservative politics, seeing this diversity as providing spaces for resistance or subversion in everyday life.

Mass consumption: The classic inheritance from Marx and Simmel

In *Capital*, Marx (1976) argued that working people have limited political power because they have limited access to and control over the production process. Capitalism separated the producer from the thing produced, and the process of production took on a logic of its own, developing into an ever more institutionalized process, driven by conditions of centralized economic resources and maximum exploitation of labour. Marx saw this as leading to such terrible material conditions for working people and such polarization between workers and capitalists that the workers would eventually revolt. It was a contradiction of capitalism that its increasing organization of the workforce would enable the revolution of organized labour. However, the processes which Marx suggested were inevitable have not taken place. The development of late capitalism has been to move away from large-scale forms of production requiring massive organized labour, thereby fragmenting the production process and the mass organization of labour. The question arises as to whether this new form of consumer society dissipates the political potential of labour or opens another area of potential opposition, resistance and revolt in the power of the consumer. The character of the power and self-determination afforded to the consumer by mass consumption and the forms of resistance which consuming may encode, is a central concern of theories of consumption. One theme of this book, therefore, will be to examine the processes by which people resist commercialization and establish identities in opposition to market pressures.

The rupture of producers from the goods they produce was analysed by Simmel in *The Philosophy of Money* (1990), which focused on the role of money in the standardization of commodity values. Marx had argued that the value of a commodity is not an inherent property of things, but the result of evaluations made about them by people. Simmel argued that we attribute value to objects which we desire and which resist our attaining them. Desire of goods and their associated valuation thus involves a separation of objects from people. In modern society, this separation can only be overcome by purchasing goods. Buying goods means involvement in the exchange system and the consequent sacrifices we have to make in terms of labour and money to obtain goods. Thus, the economic value of an object is measured in terms of what we have to sacrifice to obtain it, where the instrument of the exchange process is money.

Simmel analysed the cultural, social and psychological implications of money being the instrument of exchange. Money becomes a single standard by which all things can be measured and therefore compared. Simmel suggested that money abstracts the calculation from exchanges and makes buying the common form of exchange rather than barter (Parry and Bloch, 1989). As a consequence, money becomes a threat to the moral order because it becomes the sole measure of value for objects. While moral orders work through assigning objects to categories according to moral principles, money changes all that, for there are no moral categories of goods in the abstraction of monetary value. Thus money at once reduces dependency ties based on cultural relations and expands the potential exchange relations:

> On the one hand, money makes possible the plurality of economic dependencies through its infinite flexibility and divisibility, while on the other it is conducive to the removal of the personal element from human relationships through its indifferent and objective nature (Simmel, 1990, p.297).

In an extension of Marx's notion that capital becomes the model for all forms of social relations in capitalist societies, Simmel argued that money moved people from a form of social relationships based on emotions and imaginative thinking to a set of relations based upon calculation. Money rationalized the social relations in the exchange process and thereby became a model for social relations generally. Thus money enabled the rational exchange of commodities, and permitted new personal freedoms through the breaking down of traditional forms of exchange. However, because it became a model for social relationships, money also threatened people's freedom to develop emotional relationships. A major theme of this book is the question of how involvement in material culture conditions people's beliefs and relationships. Modern theories of consumption have been concerned with whether moral orders are dominated by market relations or whether people can in some way resist the spread of the exchange model into their social relationships.

Money as an instrument of exchange changes the level of dependence between people that exists in less abstract exchange systems (see also Douglas and Isherwood, 1978). Because money allows the anonymous exchange of goods without dependency ties, it erodes traditional dependency ties within communities, and so market relations tend to take over communities and undermine existing cultural ties. At the same time, capital makes exchange with other communities possible and this trade undermines the culture from without through its external relations. The advance of capital gives people new responsibilities in the exchange relation but breaks their traditional community-based responsibilities; in this way, capitalism has constructed individual responsibilities as opposed to communal responsibilities. The individual is therefore alienated and fragmented because the system of capital at once produces the individual through exchange relations and dissolves cultural ties.

Simmel observed how in capitalist societies consumption spread from the production of heavy engineering to cover aspects of domestic life. The products of capitalism became more diverse and abstract and the emerging middle classes had access to more and more diverse goods (Miller, 1987). On a psychological level, individuals could now make any comparison they liked between things. They were no longer limited by the classification of objects according to traditional meaning systems. For Simmel, therefore, the modern condition involved new freedoms characterized by the potential for more abstract thinking in the classification and evaluation of things balanced by the loss of a secure, traditional cultural identity. Modern consumption theories must consider whether this diversity also allows more real expression of personal choice. In contrast, Gramsci (1971) interpreted the diversity in mass consumption as an expression of the lack of coherence of working-class political consciousness, arguing that diversity leads to the fragmentation of the working class and the consequent dissolution of its revolutionary potential. For Gramsci (1971), the working class needed the insight of intellectuals to see through the mirage of choice in mass consumption to the underlying ideology of the hegemony of class relations, for, as Althusser (1971) argued, ordinary thinking is merely an echo of ideology. Capitalism had constructed the individual by first undermining traditional cultural forms and then offering the diverse consumption of mass culture. On this view, individual identity is an artefact of ideological processes which mystify the true economic processes of domination. The individual is distracted from the realities of their domination in the class system by the illusory freedoms of personal choice.

Marx was concerned with consumption only in so far as he saw the desire for goods as a fetish which clouds political consciousness by introducing false choices and concerns and by mystifying actual processes of exploitation. In this, he influenced the critical theory of the Frankfurt school (e.g. Adorno and Hork-heimer, 1973), which regarded popular culture as vacuous, not affording possibilities of real intellectual thinking, and as the site of the manipulation of the working classes by capital. Thus, until recently, the expansion of popular culture was seen as the process through which capital produced the false identity of individualism in order to manipulate the masses. A key question posed mass consumption theory in late capitalism is how to assess the contribution of popular culture and how to unravel its political implications.

Critiques of Marx: Cultural anthropology and mass consumption

The centrality of money

Parry and Bloch (1989) question the central role that Marx and Simmel gave to money in the progress of capitalism against traditional culture by examining a growing body of anthropological studies on the impact of money on 'traditional' worlds. Capitalism has developed into a global economic system that seems to have gobbled up all local cultures in the creation of world markets. This implies that the spread of the market system and its characteristic form of monetary exchange has the capacity to overcome what Parry and Bloch term the characteristic 'moral economies' of traditional societies.

Parry and Bloch (1989) critically reappraise Bohannan's (1959) study of the impact of the introduction of money into the exchange system of the Tiv of northern Nigeria. The Tiv had a complex exchange system which operated with three separate sets of commodities (subsistence products, brass rods and women). The system of exchange differed for each type of good and it was regarded as highly significant when goods were traded between categories of goods. The introduction of Western money converted this complex and culturally embedded system into the more parsimonious monetary system. With money as the standard by which all goods can be valued, the traditional segmentation of goods into different categories based on cultural criteria was lost, and, with it, the role such a system played in maintaining local culture.

Parry and Bloch question Bohannan's analysis, pointing out that even after the introduction of money, some things could not legitimately be bought and sold in the Tiv economy (e.g. land). Thus, the local culture limited the spread of monetary exchange so that money could not become the measure of all things and all things could not become commodities (and hence, the changes brought about by money may be stopped short of being total). Further, the introduction of money into Tiv society was promoted by some sections, notably the young, who saw it as a way of subverting the power held in the old exchange system by the elders, and thus the reception of commoditization depends upon the complex relations of interest in the culture. In fact, most cultures are not in the position where anything can be exchanged for anything else, for there are usually cultural constraints on the spread of monetary valuation achieved by creating classes of objects which are culturally defined as outside the commodity sphere (Kopytoff, 1986).

Commercial exchange and social relations

Does money produce a characteristic cognitive set in people involved in monetary exchange? Parry and Bloch argue that various forms of money and market exchange predate capitalism, that cultures vary in the way they adopt monetary systems and that money can be given different meanings in the same culture. Thus, rather than money creating a world view, existing world views affect the way monetary systems operate. The culturally diverse meanings of money express the different functions which money performs. Thus there is not one process of monetary exchange but many. As one study within Western culture also found, 'money did come with different labels attached to it and . . . it was spent for different emotional purposes' (Wilson, 1987, p.199). While challenging Marx's mechanistic and economic determinism, this approach may become relativist, unless culturally negotiated meanings of money are analysed not as a separate system but in terms of transactions and transformations within a cultural context (Parry and Bloch, 1989).

The social meanings of goods

Instead of seeing the commodity as a product of the production system with associated monetary value, the meanings of things are transformed as things travel through systems of production, exchange and ownership. They thereby overcome the reduction of all goods to their exchange value and their relation to production (Appadurai, 1986). Marx contrasted the commodity and the gift, placing gifts in the realm of the social and commodities outside the social in a realm of calculated exchange. Just as Mauss (1966) and Bourdieu (1984) have shown that gift-giving is an exchange imbued with the properties of economic exchange, so Appadurai argues that the exchange of commodities is imbued with social, cultural, personal and political meaning. Hence, money does not make abstract independent exchange the norm. Appadurai (1986) reasserts the cultural dimension of modern capitalist societies, for these are too often represented simply as economic exchange systems which emphasize the commodity as produced for monetary exchange to the neglect of the cultural, social, personal and political meanings of things.

Consumption and alienation

For Marx, the unhappy consciousness of the masses was an inevitable result of people's inability to recognize the social and oppressive nature of production because of the effective workings of an ideology that presents a variety of competing world views that overwhelm authentic human interests. Miller (1987) argues that Marx was so profoundly affected by the awful material conditions of workers in early capitalism in northern England that he did not foresee the gradual improvement in material conditions of the working classes as capitalism developed or the various social, political and economic changes such as the trade union movement, the development of social democratic politics and the growth of the consumer market. Through these processes, the antagonism between capital and labour has been reduced while the worker has gained rights as consumer and citizen.

The feminist critique of the capitalist system of redistribution

> Dividing production from consumption at the door of the household may make very good sense of men's lives. They work when they are outside the home. Inside the home they *are* generally consuming. But it makes no sense of women's lives. Their activity in the home is not just consumption (Bruegel, 1983, p.80).

The Marxist analysis of the economic position of women was concerned only with their relation to the mode of production, and the family was seen simply as the institution that provided workers for the production system. Class domination cannot be linked to patriarchy just through an analysis of the mode of production, for this reduction to production precisely misses the site which has most economic impact on women, that of redistribution within the household (Wilson, 1987; Pahl, 1989; Moore, in press).

Theories of consumption

There is no one dominant theory of mass consumption, but rather a range of theories drawing on different disciplinary traditions, taking as their starting point different aspects of the critique of Marx's approach. We will consider each theory in some detail below, because each offers valuable insights, concepts and organizing frameworks, which together provide a resource for our analysis of the empirical research on everyday economic experiences which we present in subsequent chapters.

Cultural diversity in economic systems

The focus then is on the range of cultural meanings which surround monetary transactions, and not on the kinds of problems of monetary theory which have conventionally preoccupied the economist (Parry and Bloch, 1989, p.1).

Parry and Bloch (1989) discuss anthropological evidence for cultural variation in thinking, talking about and using money. They argue that concepts and systems of production and exchange are culturally constructed. Consequently, there are no economic concepts and mechanisms which predate, lie outside or are in any other sense prior to culture.

However, despite the dependency of production and exchange on cultural diversity, Parry and Bloch argue that there are some abstract features of culturally grounded exchange systems, particularly that exchange systems are geared to the reproduction of cultural forms which operate on time-scales beyond the life-scales of the individuals in the society. Market exchange is a short-term transaction that works systematically to reproduce cultural relations and the cosmic order. Cultural relativity lies in what the cosmic order consists of, which exchange mechanisms exist and the nature of the connections between short-term market relations and long-term cultural relations.

Rather than seeing the economic as a domain devoid of moral content, Parry and Bloch (1989) discuss anthropological studies which show how monetary exchange is imbued with moral value. For example, Carsten (1989) examined how money is transformed from a subversive and threatening force into something which has moral value through its connection with gender. Malay fishermen engage in commercial exchanges with comparative strangers so as to distance money from kin relations. The men then hand the money over to the women who remain uncontaminated by contact with the exchange system. The women then decontaminate the money by cooking it, thereby converting it into something safe and nourishing. Thus the household as the site of cultural relations is buffered from the monetary exchange system through gendered economic and domestic practices. The activities within the household preserve the long-term cultural system and are supported and maintained by segmenting off the commercial and using it as a resource.

There is always the danger of pollution of the cultural by the commercial, where pollution might be the diversion of individuals entirely into the commercial so that they do not invest in the cultural or where the cultural becomes distorted to fit the needs of the commercial. Many activities, including individual motivations, can be interpreted as attempts to preserve culture while exploiting commerce. The individual is thus not only a constituent of the commercial world but also the guardian of the moral and cultural order. However, Parry and Bloch are pessimistic in their suggestion that long-term moral concerns have disappeared from modern capitalism, seeing modern Western capitalism as an example of a society where long-term cultural and moral concerns have succumbed to the short-term economic ones. Following Marx, they see economic exchange as the model for all social relations. Unlike Marx, they maintain that long-term moral concerns do not disappear but rather become redefined in monetary terms, 'The values of the short term order have become elaborated into a theory of long term reproduction' (Parry and Bloch, 1989, p.29). In modern Western culture what is normally a subordinated domain has become the basis of the encompassing order – a theory in which it is *only* unalloyed private vice that can sustain the public benefit. 'Western ideology has so emphasised the distinctiveness of the two cycles that it is unable to imagine the mechanisms by which they are linked' (Parry and Bloch, 1989, p.30).

The social nature of commodities

Taking my lead from Veblen, Douglas and Isherwood, and Baudrillard, I suggest that consumption is eminently social, relational and active rather than private, atomic or passive (Appadurai, 1986, p.31).

Appadurai (1986) analyses the trajectories of goods, showing how they cannot be reduced to production for exchange value. Value is encoded in commodities and so analysis should focus on the things exchanged rather than the process of exchange. The meanings of goods go beyond any simple conception of their monetary value and include their forms, the way they are used, and their trajectories or social lives in given social contexts. Situations ground things, giving them meaning, rather than there being a category of goods with 'commodity' characteristics. Situations vary in how far they construct objects as commodities. Appadurai breaks this down into the commodity phase of the social life of things, the commodity candidacy of things and the commodity context into which things can be placed. A thing can be in a commodity state or not, with different time-cycles for the transformation from non-commodity to commodity. There can be varying criteria and standards for the exchange of a thing in different situations: social situations make salient the classification, value, meaning, rules and practices for the exchange of things. Under certain circumstances (international trade and extreme hardship), these situational factors do not operate, but they are typical of the everyday exchange of objects. 'Regimes of value' describe the different degree to which a given thing has an agreed value in exchange: when a commodity has a globally agreed value, this transcends local, culturally grounded boundaries and dislocates the meaning of a thing from the local system.

Appadurai complexifies the notion of the commodity to show that an object becomes a commodity at the intersection of a variety of temporal, cultural and social factors. It is characteristic of modern society that a greater proportion of the objects we come into contact with have a phase of their lives as commodities. Appadurai suggests different types of commodities: some goods are intended as commodities and only come into existence as such, some things are intended for other uses but become commodities, and some things were commodities and are no longer. The social lives of commodities can be understood as a series of narratives which depict the paths and diversions through which a good travels, including moving in and out of the commodity state. The paths vary from agreed, prescribed paths to *ad hoc* deviations, and the flow of any particular good follows both formalized and informal directions, echoing the tendency of capitalism to increase standardization while commoditization is constrained by informal resistance (Kopytoff, 1986).

The social life of things is illustrated by the *kula*, a pre-industrial, translocal, non-monetized exchange system that operates in the Massim group of islands near New Guinea (see Appadurai, 1986). Two kinds of valuable objects, decorated necklaces and armshells, are exchanged for one another. As the valuables move from place to place, changing hands as they go, they acquire specific biographies and reputations along their journey, or *keda*. The *keda* describes both the journey of the valuables and the sociopolitical relationships among the men who make up the paths. Most abstractly, *keda* refers to the path to wealth, power and reputation, both reflecting and constituting social partnerships and power relations. Recent reinterpretations of the *kula* have usually revolved around this notion of trajectory and around 'tournaments of value', social occasions where the value of a commodity is formally negotiated. An example would be an art auction. The unusual nature of these occasions, with their ludic, ritual and reciprocal dimensions, demarcate them from normal exchange situations and mark their importance. It is not simply the purchasing power of those involved which distances them from everyday exchange, but the manner of their involvement in the valuation of commodities and value of commodities.

How does demand work in this world of goods? Following Baudrillard (1988), Appadurai argues that demand emerges from the social practices around commoditization rather than from human needs. Some cultures resist the maximization of purchasing in relation to their needs. Appadurai cites, as an example, Gell's work on the Muria Gonds, which shows that they do not consume goods available to them according to their wealth and the market because they value economic egality and sociality. Goods do not fall simply into the two classes of luxury and necessity. Rather luxuries are defined socially in terms of being restricted to elites, being difficult to obtain, encoding multiple meanings, requiring special knowledge to be consumed and being related to processes to do with the person. These goods require a basis of necessity goods in the background and therefore stimulate demand for necessities: 'Demand is thus neither a mechanical response to the structure and level of production nor a bottomless natural appetite. It is a complex social mechanism that mediates between short and long term patterns of commodity circulation' (Appadurai, 1986, pp.40–1).

Commodity appropriation and consumption work

If the rift between objects and people is an inevitable dimension of capitalism, it may be overcome by the ways that people appropriate goods. Miller (1987) examines the progressive dimension of objectification whereby externalities are brought back into subjective experience through various transformations of objects. In the case of goods, they are external at the point of commoditization, when the goods are bought, but they are brought back into an authentic mode by being tailored to local needs:

> Although the subject may at certain periods appear lost in the sheer scale of its own products, or be subject to the cultural mediation of a dominant group, and thus fail to perceive these cultural forms as its own creations, the tendency is always towards some form of reappropriation through which the external can become part of the progressive development of the subject (Miller, 1987, p.180).

Human values enter into the commodity system when people transform an inalienable commodity into an alienable object in their local culture. This appropriation is a result of the improving material conditions of working people in late capitalism, for it requires that people have money and leisure time. When shopping for goods we immerse ourselves in the vast array of goods which Marx highlighted at the start of *Capital* but on acquiring the goods we transform them into cultural objects:

> This is part of a long and complex process, by which the consumer works upon the object purchased and recontextualizes it, until it is often no longer recognizable as having any relation to the world of the abstract and becomes its very negation, something which could neither be bought nor given (Miller, 1987, p.190).

Cultural Studies and the modern consumer

> . . . a reassessment and revalorization of popular cultural forms and popular experience, of the meanings consumption produces (Nava, 1991, p.164).

Many critics now offer a valorization of the consumer as a balance to Marx's preoccupation with production, addressing the question of how far the developments of late capitalism have dissolved the contradictions of capitalism. In particular, have the material conditions of working people advanced far enough for them to live a cultured life and do the opportunities afforded by popular culture constitute grounds for authentic existence or the reduction of alienation? One answer has been to valorize the diversity of ways of existing within popular culture, countering the notion derived from critical theory (Held, 1980) that popular culture is a mechanism for the spread of ideology, and suggesting that popular culture provides a site where commodities can be appropriated for cultural meanings. With emerging environmental concerns and the collapse of socialism in Eastern Europe, consumerism has become a 'highly visible cult whose imagery permeates the physical and cultural territory it occupies. Modern identities and imaginations are knotted inextricably to it' (Nava, 1991, p.157).

Nava examines the intellectual context of the manipulationist thesis, that the masses are exploited by capitalism and kept passive through the ideology expressed in popular culture, was emphasized by the Labour Party in the post-war period, which rejected consumerism, and by the celebration of traditional working-class culture by writers as diverse as Hoggart (1957) and Eliot (1948). In *1984*, Orwell portrayed the 'proles' as complete dupes of the ideological elite. When social critics such as Marcuse (1964) did talk about consumerism, they saw it as a mechanism of social control, and in the feminist movement the commodity was perceived as the site of women's oppression by writers such as Frieden (1965). In the context of the Cold War, the notion of manipulation also took hold of the right, and the view that advertising was a form of manipulation, for example, became the norm in such work as Packard's *The Hidden Persuaders* (1957).

Mennell (1985) shows how in the domain of food, the manipulationist thesis was popular with both left- and right-wing critics. He argues that both the right and the left in the interwar years agreed about the character of mass passivity and ignorance but attributed this to different causes. The right blamed the masses who, by virtue of increased wealth, had endangered the elite structure of society which had created great gourmet dishes. The left blamed the culture industry for producing bland, mass-produced foods which appealed to the in-fantile proclivities of the masses. Thus the right could argue that 'the incursion of the ignorant, too easily pleased *nouveaux riches* into Paris and London restaurants undermined the standards of cooking, and was the first sign of the collapse of the informed gastronomic public opinion within which critical con-sensus once existed' (Mennell, 1985, p.318). Mennell also explores the exten-sion of critical theory to the food industry which manipulates gastronomic taste by fetishistic preference for a restricted range of foods and an appeal to the regressive state of childhood in processed foods full of sugar and lacking fibre.

In contrast, Cultural Studies has approached consumerism in a different way, attempting to give respect to popular culture and the consuming practices of ordinary people. This meant moving away from the dominant intellectual view of the consumption of popular culture as manipulated and mindless. A key element was feminist writings which valorized women's experience, under-mining earlier perceptions of women as victims and examining what is reward-ing, rational and sometimes liberating about popular cultural forms such as soap operas (Radway, 1984; Livingstone, 1990) and women's magazines (Winship, 1987; McRobbie, 1989): 'What all these texts have in common is a legitimizing of the consumer and of the commodities and cultural forms that are *actively* con-sumed by him or her' (Nava, 1991, p.166).

Cultural Studies is built upon a critical reaction to the manipulationist theses and in particular on the questioning of the emphasis on economics and the apparent breakdown of social structure based on class lines. The popular appeal of Thatcherism and more recently the appeal of consumerism in Eastern Europe have made this an urgent challenge for the left. Experiences of consumption may reflect forms of resistance and political consciousness. Material resources may be used to resolve problems of contradictory class positions and divided loyalties, simultaneously immersing oneself in consumption and rejecting it.

For example, Hebdige (1979) argued that underprivileged, marginalized youths used clothes as codes to distance themselves from the status quo. Thus style rather than traditional class position is used to create identity. When examining the appropriation of American culture by British youths, Hebdige suggested that:

> American popular culture – Hollywood films, advertising images, packaging, clothes and music – offers a rich iconography, a set of symbols, objects and artifacts which can be assembled and re-assembled by different groups in a literally limitless number of combinations (Hebdige, 1988, p.55).

The new consumer culture creates the opportunity for working out diverse and novel identities using the variety of commodities available. This has broader social, cultural and political implications:

> Consider the proliferation of models and styles, the increased product differentiation which characterises post Fordist production . . . We can see mirrored there, too, wider processes of cultural diversity and differentiation, related to the multiplication of social worlds and social 'logics' typical of modern life in the West . . . These allow the individual some space in which to reassert a measure of choice and control over everyday life and 'play' with its more expressive dimensions (Hall, 1988, p.56).

The economic conditions which created the consumer market through modern production methods vastly increase the diversity of goods available to the consumer. This explosion in goods provides the material conditions which overwhelm traditional identities based on social class position, allowing for a growing individual freedom from social determinism. Mennell (1985) presents an extensive analysis of the growth in diversity of foods available to increasing numbers of people through the development of the retail and catering industries.

Post-industrial society

We have discussed the implications of the present conditions of late capitalism for theories of mass consumption without yet considering the status of late twentieth-century capitalism itself. Has it taken on a form so different from the mass society of modernism that it can be considered a form of post-modern society? Or is the basic form of society still a version of capitalism, albeit a late capitalism which is more diverse in surface appearance but none the less essentially structured upon the same lines as classic capitalism?

Recent economic changes have resulted in new technology, more flexible work practices and greater consumer choice, with a correspondent reduction of the traditional working classes and an increase in the lower middle classes (Hall,

1988). Economically, there has been an expansion of the global economy. Culturally, there has been a fragmentation of working class into a plural popular culture and the consequent decline in traditional collective solidarities. On a personal level, the shift has been away from identities based on social class position towards identities based on lifestyle and mode of consumption.

One characterization of the British economy is in terms of Fordism (Murray, 1988; Gardner and Sheppard, 1989), which involves mass standardized production of uniform components and products, mechanized production techniques, the deskilling of human labour through the breakdown of tasks into their component parts and the use of management science techniques and flowline assembly methods. Fordism has various significant weaknesses. It is based on authoritative staff relations and rigid, inflexible workplace relations which have exacerbated industrial unrest. Mass production depends on the whims and desires of a mass market. Further, production-driven economy is essentially speculative, and the Fordist industrial method has been prone to sudden loss in demand. These weaknesses became particularly salient with the opening up of the consumer market.

Initially, post-modernism, or post-Fordism, was used to refer to a new epoch. Later debates instead use post-modernism as a development within rather than after capitalism (Featherstone, 1991). Post-Fordism involves the use of new technology to transform distribution and assembly methods, the shift from economies of scale to economies of scope and the shift to innovation. All these changes depend upon new technology to obtain rapid information about product demand and to allow designers to encode changes into the production process, while the use of such technology depends on the production process being changed to one of flexible specialization using small batch manufacture. The questions for mass consumption theories concern the cultural implications of such technological and manufacturing changes.

The historical development of consumer society

Both criticisms of Marx and ideas about post-industrial society assume that the social practices of mass consumerism did not occur in the nineteenth century (and therefore Marx could not foresee the possibilities which consumerism had to offer the ordinary person). However, historians argue that a consumer revolution occurred in eighteenth-century England (McKendrick et al., 1982). During this century, the acquisition of objects as commodities became a possibility for larger sections of society than ever before, and many objects which had previously only been available through inheritance became available through purchase as commodities. Thus consumerism and commoditization were spreading through society before Marx's writings. The spread of the consumer society could be seen in the emerging network of shops and the shortening life-span of products: 'Where once material possessions were prized for their durability, they were now increasingly prized for their fashionability. Where once a fashion might last a lifetime, now it might barely last a year' (McKendrick et al., 1982, p.1). There was a growing market in magazines for consumer fashions, whereas people previously depended on word of mouth and rumour. The work of retailers in creating these possibilities was also highly visible. Thus, while the *desire* to consume was not new . . . the ability to do so was' (McKendrick *et al.*, 1982, p.2) Before then:

> The barriers to a consumer society were . . . numerous and effective. To overcome them required changes in attitude and thought, changes in prosperity and standards of living, changes in commercial technique and promotional skills, sometimes changes in the law itself. Above all it required the commercialisation of society (McKendrick *et al.*, 1982, p.2).

The changes in attitude were not restricted to any narrow conception of taste but linked to major political, intellectual and social issues as well as economic realignments. One significant consequence of the growth of consumerism was the commercialization of leisure, to be seen in increases in the consumption of food (particularly beef), spending on housing, interest in fashion, a boom in books, music, entertainment and holidays, and a rapid growth in leisure resorts. The growth in consumer-related uses of print was an important mechanism in this process, for printing made self-instruction possible through self-help manuals and pamphlets as well as books, while the complex social structure of the society promoted emulation and the new economic potential promoted upward mobility. It was through these printed works that the ideas and tastes of a small elite could permeate society.

In a historical analysis of eating habits in Britain and France from the Middle Ages to the present day, Mennell (1985) emphasizes that the current diversity in eating habits and the broader availability of foods to a greater proportion of society is part of a process that has been going on over the course of history. There is a dynamic, similar to that proposed by Simmel for fashion (but see Campbell, 1987), whereby elite groups adopt differentiating eating habits, which are in time appropriated by the lower classes and are further transformed when the elite adopt new habits. This cycle continues but the upshot is a genuine increase in standards of food for more and more people.

Mass consumption as social activity

Changes in production, marketing and commercial practices now operate to construct new forms of consumption activity, indeed, to construct the consumer. Baudrillard (1988) examines new forms of shopping as providing a context in which people experience shopping as a social activity. The shopping mall or shopping centre especially creates a fantasy world in which desires and identities are created. On this view, production processes again determine consumption patterns, albeit in new forms. The ever-powerful reach of capital has spread beyond the production of the commodity to include also the creation of the modern consumer, evidencing a progressive imperialism in which economic exchange provides the context for, and indeed the model of, social relations and personal identities.

There is no doubting the profusion and display which is evident in the modern shopping context. In their presentation of commodities as display, shops offer goods in a celebratory context by analogy with a feast – the celebration of surplus and the social display of wealth: 'almost every clothing store or appliance store presents a gamut of differential objects, which call upon, respond to, and refute each other' (Baudrillard, 1988, p.31). Consumption choice is not to be understood as the individual shopper satisfying a need but as a mode of involvement with, and celebration of, the organization of goods. The consumer is swept up in a psychological chain reaction which consists of apprehending the diverse display as a meaningful category system:

Few objects today are offered alone, without a context of objects to speak for them. And the relation of the consumer to the object is consequently changed: the object is no longer referred to in relation to a specific utility, but as a collection of objects in their total meaning. Washing machine, refrigerator, dishwasher, have different meanings when grouped together than each has alone ... The arrangement directs the purchasing impulse towards networks of objects in order to seduce it and elicit, in accordance with its own logic, a maximal investment, reaching the limits of economic potential (Baudrillard, 1988, p.31).

The shopping mall combines in practice things which are traditionally in opposition: the design of the commodity and the design of the shop; the small shop and the large shop; the slow pace of antiquity with the fast pace of modernity; open nine to five and open all hours; the anarchy of the old city and the order of the modern; money as exchange and credit as exchange:

Clothing, appliances, and toiletries thus constitute object paths, which establish inertial constraints on the consumer who will proceed logically from one object to the next. The consumer will be caught up in a calculus of objects, which is quite different from the frenzy of purchasing and possession which arises from the simple profusion of commodities (Baudrillard, 1988, p.31).

Baudrillard argues that the basic organizing concept in the shopping mall is ambience: the manipulation works by creating ambience rather than by encoding factors which have specific psychological effects on the shopper's decisions. The shopping mall affords the opportunity of participation in the currency of modern society: exchange (implying a contrast with the structure of Athenian democracy where the currency of participation was argument). The shopping mall is a public forum – the site of participation in late capitalist society as formulated through commoditization. The consumer culture is a new form of the manipulation of the ordinary person by the exchange system. When the family goes to the shopping mall together at the weekend, the mall provides a form of leisure, of structuring time, and a site for constructing family relations of gender and generation. Our identities and experiences are produced by the experience of participation in the cultural forum of late capitalism – the shopping mall:

> We have reached the point where 'consumption' has grasped the whole of life; where all activities are sequenced in the same combinatorial mode; where the schedule of gratification is outlined in advance, one hour at a time; and where the 'environment' is complete, completely climatized, furnished and culturized ... Work, leisure, nature, and culture all previously dispersed, separate, and more or less irreducible activities that produced anxiety and complexity in our real life, and in our 'anarchic and archaic' cities, have finally become mixed, massaged, climate controlled, and domesticated into the simple activity of perpetual shopping (Baudrillard, 1988, pp.33–4).

Gender relations in mass consumption

Critiques of the economic role of the household emphasize the enormous variability of household forms, attacking the idea that households can be understood in terms of their position in the process of production and social reproduction (Moore, in press). However, the observation of diversity is compatible both with the notion of individual freedom and with the notion of an elaborate commercial manipulation. This dichotomy may be overcome by mapping the relations between different components of the economy: 'The question thus shifts from "where is the household?" to "what are the significant units of production, consumption and investment in this region/group/people?" and "what are the major flows and transfers of resources between individuals and units?"' (Guyer and Peters, 1987, p.208. Cited in Moore, in press).

Just as Appadurai holds that, as things have a social life, the economic aspects of culture can be analysed in terms of the transformations of things, Moore suggests that gendered aspects of the economic activity of the household can be analysed in terms of the patterning of resource flows and processes of redistribution, replacing the 'big' question of freedom vs ideology. The romantic view of the household as a retreat from the system of exchange, where people are free to overcome the meanings of commodities in the exchange system, is challenged by recognizing that the household is only semi-autonomous, being located in a network of relations which relates domestic units to more abstract social economic structures right up to the global economy.

Within the household, gender inequalities are consistent and widespread – women contribute a larger share of their income to the household than men, women engaged in productive and reproductive labour work longer hours than men, women are less well educated and less well nourished, and they have less access to economic resources, even to their own earnings (Pahl, 1989). This unequal redistribution of money and commodities depends not only on access to material resources (for some things, like getting husbands to do housework, cannot be bought; Hartmann, 1981), but also on the ways that power and ideology frame domestic negotiations over gender identity:

> One result of the rapprochement between feminist theorising and mainstream anthropology/economics has been the emergence of a view of the household which sees it as a locus of competing interests, rights, obligations and resources which often involve household members in bargaining, negotiating and possibly even conflict (Moore, in press).

Researchers have attempted to model the household in terms of contractual relations or bargaining systems, examining the ways in which the discursive nature of domestic negotiations, which generate the meanings of rights and needs within the household, determine the allocation of resources. The encoding of power relations in gender ideologies of, for example, motherhood or the breadwinner, constrain the strategies that individuals employ in negotiating their access to resources (Whitehead, 1981). And through such negotiations, the gender ideologies are themselves reproduced.

As the allocation of resources within the household is managed through contested definitions of rights and needs, as played out according to gender ideologies, domestic discourse must be examined. Fraser (1989) identifies three levels of discourse concerning needs: the struggle to establish the legitimate status of a need and place it on the agenda; the struggle over the definition of the need and its satisfaction; the struggle over satisfying the need by obtaining the resources to satisfy it. Ways of making claims are culturally framed, drawing on accepted argumentation, conventional voices, and conventional definitions of needs and rights. Discourse connects with wider social structures in several ways. For example, the use of resources at one level affects the working of the economy at other levels (as in the availability of women in the workforce), and through ideology and social representations some discourses are dominant and some dominated, whatever the individual's skill in framing arguments.

The system of redistribution connects different levels of social organization: because the system of production is gendered, the system of redistribution must be gendered, and the introduction of market forces is reflected in changing social organisations which are gendered through the process of redistribution (Moore, in press). For example, Mandinka society (as described by Moore, in press) has a sexual division of labour in which women grow rice, a lowland crop, while men grow upland crops of groundnuts, millet and maize. When development agencies in the 1960s introduced pump irrigation, men gained the rights over irrigated land even though women used to control rice production. The relief agencies acted as if households operated a joint utility function, not realizing that previously there was a sexual division in rights over the low lands, and so women's land rights were signed away by their husbands to a collective for which the women were then obliged to work:

> Definition of land types has consequences for labour control, and changes in the nature of labour allocation and control gives new meaning, both

practically and discursively, to what it means to be a wife, a husband, and a dependent. Thus social identities are fully engaged in the processes of bargaining and negotiation that shape access to economic resources, as well as the direction of resource flows both within the household and beyond. Such resource flows are the outcome of the system of redistribution, and it is through processes of redistribution that social identities are themselves reproduced (Moore, in press).

Mass consumption and personal identity

The material conditions of consumer society constitute the context within which people work out their identities. People's involvement with material culture is such that mass consumption infiltrates everyday life not only at the levels of economic processes, social activities and household structures, but also at the level of meaningful psychological experience – affecting the construction of identities, the formation of relationships, the framing of events. The social psychological research which we present in the following chapters demonstrates, on the one hand, how people 'manage' the pressures of modern consumerism and, on the other, how personal identity is fundamentally social, for modern consumer culture creates the need to have, to discover, an identity. Processes of identity formation as we understand them in contemporary society do not predate the social changes we have examined in this chapter but are intimately bound up with changing material conditions. As Giddens (1991) has pointed out, the modern condition entails both opportunities and dangers for the individual. The material conditions within which and in response to which we form our identities are not benign. They both afford possibilities for personal development and they threaten that development – increased freedoms go hand in hand with increased responsibilities.

Giddens implies that we have moved away from traditional forms of relationship, forms which were stable, uncontestable and faithfully reproduced from one generation to the next, offering little opportunity for personal development but a high degree of security. However, we need not argue that the possibilities for personal development under modern consumption are new in order to argue for its significance. Indeed, it is a myth of modern consumerism that only the new is significant, putting pressure on research to claim new forms of social relationship. Rather, we can argue for evolving forms, transformations, breaks and continuities which are significant in their meanings and their social effects.

The focus of our enquiry into mass consumption and personal identity is the way in which the response of ordinary people to their economic circumstances involves the negotiation of personal identities in terms of needs, rights and responsibilities in everyday economic affairs. The construction of personal identities draws on conventionally given class, gender, cultural and generational identities as well as on individual biographical and family experience. The identities which result reflect and are reflected in people's feelings of security, their notions of their needs and desires, their feelings of pleasure and involvement, their moral judgements and explanations for social and economic processes, their response to social influence and the way they conduct their social relationships. They give meaning to everyday economic activities and experiences. These diverse aspects of personal identity are constructed through responding to the challenge, opportunities and problems which modern consumer culture presents to the individual.

THREE | SAVING AND BORROWING

Old style thrift has gone out of fashion. The attitude is, 'I want it and I want it now' (Governor, Bank of England, quoted in the *Sunday Times*, 17 June 1990).

Far too many people aspire to a champagne lifestyle on a beer income (Brian Walden, former Labour MP, quoted in the *Independent*, 15 April 1990).

Home life ceases to be free and beautiful as soon as it is founded on borrowing and debt (Ibsen, *A Doll's House*).

Everyday finances

In this chapter, we ask about people's management of their money, focusing on borrowing, saving, budgeting, credit and debt. Who is living at, above or within their means? Does this depend on demographic, economic or psychological factors? How can we account for variation in management within the same income groups? How do people make their financial calculations?

Everyday financial decisions are embedded in a moral and cultural context which influences desire, links possessions with identities and actions with judgements, provides for pleasure in consumption, and generally gives significance to everyday practices. In present-day Britain, the Protestant work ethic, according to which, crudely speaking, saving is right (the result of industriousness and hard work) and borrowing is wrong (the result of idleness and profligacy), is still strong, although its future, bound up with changes in employment structures, is uncertain (Furnham, 1990). Thus it is often assumed that borrowing is somehow morally bad even, though, in practice, the use of credit is widespread and levels of borrowing are high.

In this chapter, we consider people's strong sense of being under pressure as consumers, examining some of the ways they respond to this. We then analyse different patterns of personal financial management, focusing on the diverse roles which spending, saving and borrowing play in people's lives, weaving together the interview and discussion material with statistical findings from the questionnaire.

Developments in consumer credit, debt and saving

Recent rapid growth in consumer credit and in personal debt problems has received widespread popular attention in the media and in everyday conversation over the last decade and has been documented through a range of economic indicators (see, for example, Hartropp et al., 1987; Parker, 1988; Leigh-Pemberton, 1989; Berthoud and Kempson, 1990). Consumer credit has been growing in Britain by at least 10 per cent in real terms nearly every year since 1977 (Hartropp et al., 1987). In 1988, 15.3 million people had a Visa card and 12.2 million had an Access card, figures which have increased over four-fold since the mid-1970s. Two-thirds of all adults now possess some kind of plastic money card (Social Trends, 1991).

The amount of outstanding personal debt (excluding mortgages) reached £48.2 billion in December 1989, three and a half times the amount outstanding in March 1982 (Social Trends, 1991). This represents some 14 per cent of annual household disposable income (compared to 8 per cent in 1981: Social Trends, 1989). In 1989, household expenditure exceeded household income for the fourth successive year (Social Trends, 1991).

In 1990, 76,300 households were in mortgage arrears of 6–12 months, with 18,800 in arrears of more than 1 year (Social Trends, 1991). In 1987, 22,900 properties were repossessed by building societies (compared to 4200 in 1981) and there has been a substantial increase in the number of people using the Citizens Advice Bureaux (Social Trends, 1989). The situation has been worsening consistently over the 1980s and 1990s. There have been public calls for tightening up lending agreements, shop practices and advertising restrictions, and for increasing debt advice provision.[1]

In recent years, household saving, expressed as a percentage of household disposable income, has fallen from around 4 per cent in the 1970s to a negative 2 per cent by the late 1980s (Social Trends, 1991). In other words, household expenditure is exceeding income: 'consumers have recently not merely spent the whole of their PDI [personal disposable income], but borrowed in order to finance yet further consumption' (Curwen, 1990, p.43). However, the proportion of adults with a building society account rose from 15 per cent in 1968 to 64 per cent in 1986, albeit with a fall in National Savings accounts (Social Trends, 1989), suggesting that many are also saving money. Further, 'there was every sign in the booming house market of 1988 that saving for asset accumulation was as popular as ever' (Curwen, 1990, p.43).

It is unclear how far present levels of consumer debt, with their attendant problems, compare with or exceed levels of indebtedness over the twentieth century as a whole. Most discussions of debt chart its growth over the last decade or so, and comparisons with earlier times are extremely difficult to make, given the changing forms of credit, the widespread practice of informal or unregulated forms of credit, the paucity of records, and the many other social and economic changes which have occurred in the same period.

Certainly, over this century, the forms of consumer debt have altered. A general pattern can be observed in which a particular form of credit becomes available, then widespread, then problematic, and finally it is regulated by governments, who are generally reluctant to intervene, in order to meet public concern over the need to protect both consumers and creditors (who must themselves avoid becoming debtors). Thus, at the turn of the century, most credit was offered by money lenders, who charged high prices and proved difficult to regulate, and by pawnbrokers, a major source of credit for the working class – with licensed pawnbroking for the artisan class and illegal 'pop' shops for the very poor (Parker, 1990). Between the wars, pawnbroking declined as a result of increased prosperity, the slum clearance programmes and the beginnings of state provision and welfare (Parker, 1990). Thus the building society movement grew and local authorities began to advance money for house purchase, as did the Public Works Loan Board (Barty-King, 1991). More 'respectable' forms of credit became available to take the place of pawnbroking. Hire purchase in particular grew rapidly hand in hand with the rise in mass-produced consumer durables (Galbraith, 1970), gradually losing its association with 'buying on tick' (Roebuck, 1973).

After the Second World War, finance houses offered increasing numbers of personal loans, which were more appropriate than hire purchase for the services now demanded (home improvements, central heating, etc., goods which cannot be 'snatched back'). While money lending, pawnbroking and check trading (or trading in shop vouchers) all continued throughout the present century, mail order buying and shop credit at the point of sale grew rapidly after the war (Parker 1990). Home ownership increased in the 1950s as building societies advanced ever larger proportions of the price, encouraged by the then Prime Minister, Macmillan (Barty-King, 1991). Traditional banking attitudes began to change in the mid-1960s, with banks diversifying particularly by making links with or taking over finance houses and credit card companies (Drury and Ferrier, 1984). Bank credit was not regulated until the Consumer Credit Act 1974.

Over the century, there has been a continuing public debate over the responsibilities and obligations of lenders, of the rights of consumers to credit and of the need to protect consumers from themselves, while also maintaining that for 'a free society...people themselves must be the judge of what contributed to their material welfare' (Barty-King, 1991, p.175). The debate culminated in the Crowther Committee Report of 1971, which 'resulted in sweeping criticism of the existing framework of law and suggested a radical recasting of the whole of credit legislation' (Drury and Ferrier, 1984, p.146). As a result, we have seen both increasing government intervention and regulation and the increasing institutionalization of credit organizations themselves, with codes of practice, trade associations, etc. (Barty-King, 1991). In 1974, the Consumer Credit Act reorganized and integrated the regulations regarding many different forms of credit. It focused on three main areas: '(a) The control of credit-granting and hiring institutions. (b) The supply of information to debtors and hirers. (c) Protection of the consumer debtor and hirer' (Drury and Ferrier, 1984, p.148).

Responses to consumer pressures

Today I had a Marks & Spencers account, I don't owe them anything so it was a nil account, but at the bottom it said do you want to start saving with us, and also they offer loans as well. Everyone is trying to make a little bit of money somehow from us, aren't they? It strikes me that it doesn't matter how they do it, I thought that Marks & Spencers sold clothes. They are now offering to lend me money.

I am not saying that there shouldn't be any credit at all, there was credit in our days when a man used to knock on the door every week, you paid him a shilling or something a week for the children's clothes, you know. I am not against credit as such, but when there are full-page newspaper adverts, on the television, everywhere, Dixons, all these shops, £1000 credit, NOW, you know. I think that it is wrong.

A common topic in our discussion groups was the pressure to consume, a pressure which people felt was recent and growing and to which certain groups, for example the young, were especially vulnerable: 'Some young people would say that credit is a normal thing nowadays. They would say that it is a normal part of life nowadays, that you are in debt.'

In our questionnaire, we began to explore people's responses to this perceived pressure by asking respondents how they resist consumer pressures (or how they best manage to respond to those pressures given their means). First, we asked people what stops them borrowing more money than they have already borrowed, if any (Table 3.1). There appear to be four categories of reasons why people constrain their borrowing: some don't borrow because they have moral objections to borrowing, believing that it is better to save up for things; some don't borrow because they are afraid of debt, possibly based on previous experiences of debt; others more pragmatically don't borrow because they think that they can't afford to repay or because they resent the costs of borrowing; and, lastly, some don't borrow because they don't feel strongly enough that they need anything which they cannot afford outright:

Nowadays you are encouraged to borrow money for, say, holidays, borrow for a holiday, which isn't a necessity. In my days you would have saved up

Table 3.1   What stops you borrowing more (or any) money?

	%[a]
Morality	
Dislike/hate being in debt	17
Against borrowing in principle	8
Prefer to save up to get money to buy	4
Foolish to borrow	2
Experience of debt	
Fear of borrowing/repayments could get out of hand	8
Debts are source of worry	5
Too much in debt already	4
Bad past experience of debt	1
Costs of borrowing	
Can't afford to repay	19
High interest rates/high cost of repayments	12
Dislike paying interest/waste of money	9
Need for goods	
Don't need to borrow/have enough money	16
Prefer to live within means/try and do without	10
Don't want to commit to future repayments	10
Goods aren't worth it	1

[a] Percentage of people mentioning each reason (275 respondents in total).

before you went on a holiday. But now you are encouraged to borrow £500 or whatever and pay it back later, but of course you get into debt.

It seems that only one of these groups would borrow more if their economic situations improved, namely those who cite financial reasons against borrowing. Those against borrowing in principle and those who have had their fingers burnt previously are not unmoved by the pressure to have new goods, but would avoid borrowing as the means of obtaining them. Those who want nothing they cannot afford appear to formulate their desires according to their means, rather than allow their means to constrain their preformed desires. These people may be equivalent in incomes and possessions, it is a matter of how they define necessities and luxuries, how they balance the pleasure and costs of acquisition, and of the moral and economic considerations which they consider relevant. People also interpret the similar financial situations differently. For example, one claims that 'while I am training I don't mind being a little in debt, but once I am no longer a student I will no longer allow myself debts', while another does not borrow because of 'being a student and therefore having no chance of paying it back'.

We also asked people how they economize, when necessary, revealing the variable ways in which people respond to an equivalent situation (Table 3.2).

Table 3.2   How do you economize?

	%[a]
Reduce spending	
Stay at home instead of social activities/eating out	22
Cut out luxuries/treats	20
Spend less on food	16
Spend less on clothes	16
Limit spending to essentials/necessities	13
Cut down on bills (phone, heating, hot water, etc.)	9
Spend less on alcohol	6
Cut down on spending generally	6
Save on petrol/travel by cycling or walking	6
Spend less on convenience foods/takeaways	4
Spend less on books/records	3
Spend less on cigarettes/stop smoking	2
Spend less on things for the house	1
Budgeting	
Watch where money goes, keep records of spending	6
Buy cheaper alternatives (e.g. own brand)	5
Stick to planned budget with clear spending limits	3
Make specific food lists	1
Look for waste and cut it out	1
Try to save regularly	1
Refuse requests for money	1
Draw out set amount from bank each week and manage	1
Shopping habits	
Visit shops less/no window shopping/avoid temptation	7
Shop around to compare prices for best buy or bargain	6
Before buying, ask oneself if it is really necessary	1
Cut down on impulse buying	1
Buy food in bulk	1
Strategies	
Postpone spending, defer major purchases	4
Make do and mend	3
Buy second-hand clothes	2
Avoid carrying spare cash	2
Don't carry credit card	2
Plan meals to make cheap food pleasurable	1
Don't carry cheque book	1
Eat at parents'/friends' house	1
Make extra money	
Work harder/do overtime	1
Sell unwanted/extra possessions	1

[a] Percentage of people mentioning each way of economizing (272 respondents in total).

This question reveals people's general priorities, their common and particular concerns, and the intricate linking of psychological values and attitudes with specific economic practices. People would clearly rather cut back on their spending to economize, reducing expenditure on particular, usually luxury or unessential items, rather than calculate a detailed budget and stick to it in a systematic way, as generally advocated by financial advisers. Planning spending is more work and more constraining, although possibly also more successful, than the simpler principle of cutting out certain goods from one's lifestyle.

Many people would reduce spending on their social life first, suggesting that the need to economize reduces participation in social life. This may have many hidden consequences for those who regularly economize in this way: loss of social support, loneliness, a more introverted lifestyle, loss of connection with the world, and so forth. A second form of social participation is also lost when economizing, that of participation in consumption itself – a common and socially shared means of occupying leisure time: people recognize that going shopping is by no means a simple matter of deciding to buy a particular good, selecting an appropriate shop and going there to purchase that good. Rather, they recognize the dangers in going shopping, seeing shopping as a persuasive, pleasurable and tempting situation in which they may lose control.

When people economize, their means of payment changes, as a preference for cash over credit or cheques emerges: this makes clear a popular belief that one has more control over cash, and so it is easier to limit spending by limiting one's means of payment; people are aware that with credit cards and cheques the pressures of the moment of consumption may override previously elaborated budgeting plans, and rather than always battling with themselves at the shop counter they would make it impossible to purchase without building in the time to go away and think it over: 'If one is going to live within one's means, in a situation where one is with friends and family and things all making demands, you have got to be able to say no, sometimes. And with credit cards it is that much more difficult to say no.'

Many principles of economizing – spending less on luxuries, treating only necessities as essential – raise more general issues about how we, as a culture and as individuals, identify needs and wants and the necessary and luxury goods which satisfy them. Strategies of economizing which people do not mention are often as interesting as those they do mention; notably, few people consider the second-hand market, rather doing without altogether than doing without things new and up-to-date. Similarly, few see their general financial situation as flexible, thinking of making extra money or doing more work; rather, they see the financial constraints as fixed, and try to manoeuvre within these. The focus on necessities and luxuries is constructed within an expectation of having the best, having things new, having things when they first appear, and such a focus itself directs attention towards personal needs and wants, an inward assessment, rather than towards examining the parameters of one's financial situation and attempting to alter these.

Finally, we note the variety of strategies which people adopt, many of which are tried and tested for them individually, though often not shared by others. These included the following: hiding or stashing a few pounds away each day or week; more do-it-yourself; think of simple ways to enjoy life; socialize at home; don't spend savings; avoid the sales; buy food in season; look for better interest rate on savings; remind self of financial situation when tempted to spend; use public buildings in winter; dodge fares; discuss finances with partner; don't take children shopping.

Who is in debt and who saves?

Annual income twenty pounds, annual expenditure nineteen nineteen six, result happiness. Annual income twenty pounds, annual expenditure twenty pounds ought and six, result misery (Mr Micawber, *David Copperfield*).

Although personal debt is a widely recognized problem, large numbers of people spend more than their income and so they get into debt. Variability in people's management of their finances is limited, and following Mr Micawber, one might expect three general patterns of income managements: those who live just within their income, with nothing to spare; those who exceed their income, and get into debt; and those who live well within their income, and so can afford to save. Similarly, one might expect those with savings to repay any debts, so that generally only those without debts would have savings. Yet things are not so simple. While any typology has certain problems – masking within-category differences, prioritizing certain distinctions over others – on examining the patterns of savings and debts within our sample, it became clear that several further patterns of income management exist.

From the initial sample of 279 people, we identified six groups of people according to whether or not they had debts, whether or not they saved money regularly and whether or not they had any savings (Table 3.3).[2] The incomes received by each group are also shown in Table 3.3, but were not significantly different across the groups.

Demographic characteristics

While each group contained a similar proportion of men and women, they did differ by age: those with debts but no savings tended to be young, whereas those who saved or had savings but no debts tended to be older (Table 3.4). In general, too, those without debts tended to be older, irrespective of savings. As one would expect from this, those without debts tended also to be either married or cohabiting, while those with debts were more likely to be single. Those with debts and no savings were least likely to be home owners, while those with savings and no debts were most likely to be home owners. There were no significant differences between the groups in their political voting patterns, their patterns of financial management with their partner, or their educational qualifications. The groups differed by family type, although not in the number of dependent

Table 3.3   Sample broken down by savings and debts[a]

	(1) No debt No save No savings	(2) No debt Save Savings	(3) No debt No save Savings	(4) Debt No save No savings	(5) Debt Save Savings	(6) Debt No save Savings
No. in group	20	49	53	17	31	47
% of sample	9	23	24	8	14	22
Income (£)[b]	6,607	7,974	6,759	5,484	8,509	6,588
Own debts (£)[c]	—	—	—	1,565	1,391	720
Joint debts (£)	—	—	—	375	1,613	214
Own save (£pcm)	—	149	—	—	78	—
Joint save (£pcm)	—	59	—	—	12	—
Own savings (£)	—	11,083	12,740	—	2,587	2,016
Joint savings (£)	—	8,060	15,464	—	1,785	2,821

[a] Of the 279 respondents, 217 fitted one of these categories, with 62 thus being excluded from these comparisons.
[b] Income refers to average personal annual disposable income.
[c] All amounts of debts, amounts saved regularly each month and amounts of total savings are averages.

Table 3.4   Demographic characteristics of six groups as defined by debts and savings[a]

	(1) No debt No save No savings	(2) No debt Save Savings	(3) No debt No save Savings	(4) Debt No save No savings	(5) Debt Save Savings	(6) Debt No save Savings
Women	60	59	58	65	65	70
Age 18–34	25	24	17	76	58	53
Age 35–54	40	31	30	24	32	30
Age 55+	35	45	30	0	10	17
Family type						
single	36	23	16	67	46	56
couple	0	9	2	25	21	9
family	18	23	16	8	21	15
empty nest	27	14	18	0	13	0
retired	18	31	48	0	0	9
Home owners	60	65	76	24	52	47

[a] Expressed as percentages.

children: those with debts were most likely to be single, or, to a lesser extent, couples. Families who had debts also tended to have savings. Those with no debts but with savings tended to be older people, either retired or with their children having fled the nest.

Financial situations

The groups did not differ significantly in disposable income, nor in their out-goings, spending similar amounts on accommodation, food and clothes. Of those in debt, people who did not save and had no savings owed the most as an average proportion of their annual disposable income (41 per cent). Those who saved regularly owed only 20 per cent of their disposable income and those with savings only owed 12 per cent of their income on average. This relation between debts and income is seen also in the relative size and number of debts across the groups. A similar pattern is seen with regular saving, where people who save and have no debts save 2 per cent of their annual income each month, compared with those who save and have debts, who save on average just over 1 per cent of their income. Clearly, as a general pattern, saving and borrowing are opposed activities: the more you do of one, the less you do of the other. Of the people in debt, those who save and have savings made higher debt repayments each month (average = £126) compared with both those who don't save and have no savings (average = £65) and those who do save but have no savings (average = £49).

Budgeting

When asked whether there was something they really wanted for £50, £200 and £1000, people with debts and no savings are more likely to say yes, especially compared with those with savings and no debts. This is related to those with debts and no savings having fewer material possessions than other groups on a checklist of 18 durable goods. However, there are no differences across the groups for their estimates of how likely they are to obtain whatever it is that they want, and it seems that those with debts but no savings are more desirous than others (rather than simply less able to satisfy their desires). Hence, when asked how they would pay for whatever it was they really wanted, those with debts and no savings were most likely to choose credit over cash.

These differences may be related to financial planning: those with debts are the most likely to feel their money just disappears each month, especially if they have no savings at all. Those who save regularly and have no debts are the most likely to know where their money goes. Similarly, those who are in debt and do not save are the least likely to plan their budget, feeling that their budget just works out somehow. They are also the least likely to know how they will repay a debt. Those in debt say they rarely have any money left over at the end of the month, except for those who have debts and also save. These people, like those with no debts, generally save any extra income for the future, rarely spending it on a luxury item.

There were no differences between the groups in their definitions of debts (e.g. whether a mortgage or hire purchase counts as a debt), except that those with neither debts nor savings were more certain that owing money to family is a debt. Those with debts are more likely to save up for something specific when they save, especially those who actually do not save at the moment, while those without debts are more likely to save in general, without any particular goal in mind beyond accumulating savings.

What gives rise to feeling in control of one's finances? As one might expect, the more debts one has, the less in control one feels. Interestingly, people feel more in control if they have more credit cards and more savings accounts, though not more bank accounts. However, there is a pattern of positive inter-correlations between numbers of bank accounts, credit cards and savings accounts, suggesting that some people operate a management style involving multiple credit cards, bank accounts and savings accounts, while others use few of each. The dangers involved in multiple accounts are suggested by a positive correlation between number of debts and number of credit cards.

Those with no debts or savings tended to have no credit cards; otherwise, having one or more credit cards seemed evenly distributed across groups.

Explaining personal debt

Little is understood of who gets into debt, why some borrow more heavily than others, or how people get out of debt. While others have examined problem debts among people in financial crisis or poverty (Hartropp et al., 1987), the rise in personal debt among a vast proportion of the general public is also a signi-ficant problem: our focus is on the routine and everyday acceptance or rejec-tion of debt as a means of managing one's budget. Generally, it is people with higher incomes or those from middle and higher socioeconomic groups who borrow more (Katona, 1975; Parker, 1988), although younger people, those with lower incomes and more dependent children face more debt problems and more debts (Hartropp et al., 1987; Berthoud and Kempson, 1990). For the majority, consumer borrowing is associated with optimism, prosperity and confidence in the economy, rather than with personal disaster (Katona, 1975; Leigh-Pemberton, 1989).

Katona (1975) found that most people regarded his hypothetical Mr Smith, who bought a car on instalments despite having the savings to pay for it, as having acted reasonably, maybe as having protected savings which are hard to replace, as having planned ahead, or as having acted intelligently, while few thought him spendthrift or foolish. Parker (1988) suggests that people use credit to safeguard savings, to take advantage of special circumstances, to even out demands on income, as well as to deal with financial crises or adversity.

According to the Protestant work ethic (Furnham, 1990), frugality and in-dustriousness are rewarded, so it seems paradoxical that over the last decade the number of foreign holidays has increased, the proportion of households with a video-recorder more than doubled, and expenditure on clothing, televisions and vehicles has risen sharply (*Social Trends*, 1989), all for those same groups of people who are also suffering the social and psychological consequences of debt, such as marital stress, depression and feelings of failure and helplessness (Hartropp *et al.*, 1987). While some would argue that the gap between rich and poor has also increased over the last decade, it seems to be the majority in the middle, who could not simply fit the stereotype of the feckless and profligate, who both spend more and borrow more.

Credit is not simply a euphemism for debt, though few would wish to borrow routinely on 'debt cards', but reflects a broad change in social attitudes away from the cluster of views in which debt is shameful, saving up is laudable and borrowing is something to be avoided (Hartropp *et al.*, 1987; Parker, 1988). More generally still, lifestyle expectations, perceptions of luxury and need, norms regarding the acceptability and management of debt, and strategies of controlling family finances are all in flux and demand examination. We are concerned to understand what social changes are taking place, how these affect people's daily lives, why people manage their money as they do and what significance this carries for them. Such understanding is itself needed so as better to intervene, advise and support those with problems, and to predict which daily patterns may increase or decrease and with what likely consequences.

What do people owe?

I must point out that if our society did not extend credit, the whole economic system would collapse. Because it depends on persuading more and more people to ask for more and more, whether they need it or not, whether they will get satisfaction or not, the aim is to get people to buy. Once people stop buying, it is like an aeroplane that loses speed in the air, it crashes.

Of the 279 people in the sample, a little over a half owed money to one or more sources, either personally (38 per cent) and/or jointly with their partner (16 per cent). Of those in debt, the average amount owed personally was £1152 in total. This represents 7.7 per cent of personal disposable income overall, or 20 per cent of the personal disposable income of those in debt. For joint debts, the average total amount was £1986 or 14.9 per cent of household disposable income. According to *Social Trends* (1989), the national amount of outstanding debt in Britain was 14 per cent of annual household disposable income in 1987 (excluding borrowing for house purchase).

Of those in debt, some 42 per cent owed money to one source, 23 per cent owed money to two sources, 18 per cent had three debts, 13 per cent had four debts, 4 per cent had five debts, and one person had six debts. These debts were to the following sources: bank overdraft (13 per cent of those in debt), Access card (14 per cent), Barclaycard (13 per cent), friend/relative (13 per cent), mail order catalogue (9 per cent), bank loan (9 per cent), store card (7 per cent), finance company (7 per cent), other credit card (5 per cent), rent/mortgage arrears (3 per cent), fuel (2 per cent), insurance (1 per cent) and other (4 per

Table 3.5   Which of the following counts as being in debt?

	%
Using credit cards and not paying the total each month	97
Having an overdraft	94
Owing money to your family	92
Buying furniture on hire purchase	89
Having a bank loan for a car	83
Having a mortgage	52
Using credit cards and paying the total each month	25

cent). On average, those in debt regularly repay some £47 per month (range £0–1000) from personal debts and £46 (range £0–900) from joint debts.

People agree fairly well over what counts as 'being in debt', although they disagree considerably over whether or not a mortgage is a debt, and all but one-quarter think that using credit cards is not a debt provided you pay off the balance each month:

> I think that there is a difference in buying something that you could save up for, where it is an impossibility to save enough to buy a house, a mortgage. A mortgage really is the only way you can save up and buy a house. Once you have got one, then perhaps you can save up enough to sell your own and put cash to it to buy another, but to start off, there is no other way than to have a mortgage.

Interestingly, credit, overdrafts and family debts, which seem more unplanned and informal, are more consensually judged a debt than specifically negotiated borrowing such as bank loans and mortgages (Table 3.5): 'I think that credit is a planned way of getting into debt, whereas if something unexpected turns up, you might have to have an overdraft or something.'

Who gets into debt?

We compared those who were in debt with those who were not and found that those in debt can be discriminated in a number of ways (Table 3.6).[3] Consistent with the sociological literature on debt, those in debt are significantly younger than those not in debt, possibly reflecting generational differences, particularly in attitudes towards debt rather than different economic demands as a function of one's stage in the life-cycle (see Chapter 6). Unexpectedly, those in debt had fewer rather than more children; maybe those with more children are forced to adopt more conservative and fixed budgeting strategies because the economic demands on them are salient and constant. There were no findings for social class and educational qualifications and, furthermore, those in debt did not differ in amount of disposable income from those not in debt, although personal savings were important.

Table 3.6   Compared with those with no debts, those in debt . . .

- More often reward themselves or bribe others with a purchase, buy on impulse, consider their consumer durables as luxuries, and they buy second-hand less often
- Feel less in control of their finances
- Are younger, with less saved, are more likely to talk and worry about money
- Are less satisfied with their standard of living
- Have pro-credit rather than anti-debt attitudes
- Blame their financial problems on convenience of credit facilities, high credit limits, enjoying shopping, careless budgeting and lack of self-discipline, and find themselves drifting along according to old habits
- Particularly disagree that debt is a failure to manage
- Have fewer children
- Less often blame money problems on demands from children
- More often blame money problems on greed
- Cope with problems by blaming themselves, feeling a victim and becoming frustrated, than by accepting their situation. They are more likely to use flexible rather than fixed budgeting strategies

Attitudes clearly differed across the groups. Those in debt believe that credit is useful, convenient and part of modern life, accepting debt as a means of satisfying needs and wants. Those not in debt see credit as debt, as shameful, to be avoided, a source of problems, and they also believe that one should save up in order ultimately to satisfy needs and wants, and hence are people who build up their savings with their resources rather than servicing their debts with, often, similar resources. Thus the same disposable income may be used for either saving or for borrowing and repaying, resulting in goods being obtained in the present or future, as a result of different attitudes towards credit and debt: those not in debt tend to take a more moralistic position, regarding debt as described by Dickens or Zola, a sordid and dangerous culture of sin and distress. On the other hand, those in what one might term 'manageable debt' – the majority of debtors rather than those facing poverty or disaster – do not feel themselves to be part of such a culture, but rather see debt as 'credit', part of what makes the modern world go round, an everyday, occasionally problematic but generally acceptable way of managing money: 'Far too much credit is given, far far too much credit' and 'I think that there is too much, but I agree that if it is used properly it can be very good.'

Those not in debt more often emphasized the pressure created by children's demands for goods, while those in debt tended to emphasize either internal factors concerning loss of control and greed or external and general factors connected with the credit system, thus blaming the system they also value for its convenience:

I think that when you have children and they are growing and you also want to see them having, I am not saying the same as everybody else, but if a child is different at school in some way, that child perhaps gets picked upon, and it must be very hard to be a parent under those circumstances. That's where the spiral comes on.

These attributional patterns for what we might broadly term manageable debts contrast with the explanations offered by those with considerable problem debts, who focus on unstable, uncontrollable, external disasters (Hartropp *et al.*, 1987). Generally, those in debt feel more out of control of their finances, feeling that they drift along according to old habits, make more impulse purchases and find it easier to get into debt. Those in debt more often report using flexible strategies, varying their budgeting according to the situation, rethinking decisions if the unexpected occurs, while those not in debt are more likely to have a general plan which they try to stick to whatever the circumstances. While at first a flexible strategy sounds more adaptive than a fixed one, it is likely that unexpected or different situations will encourage additional, unplanned expenditure rather than make intended expenditure unnecessary. In other words, the flexibility is likely to work in the direction of borrowing rather than that of saving, and hence masks an actual loss of control over budgeting.

Those in debt tend to experience pleasure in consumption and also express their social worth, social relations and social participation through consumption – wanting an improvement in their standard of living, desiring more consumer durables, regarding purchases as a way of rewarding themselves, seeing their situation as regrettable but inevitable given the demands and facilities of modern consumer culture. That they worry more about money makes sense, given their greater problems, but talking more about money with friends also indicates that social relations partly centre on consumption as a topic of mutual interest and value, and this talk may be both cause and effect of a general dissatisfaction and disappointment with their standard of living experienced by those in debt, as well as providing a forum to establish normative judgements about credit and debt. Finding that people with debts are also more likely to regard their possessions as luxuries, although they do not possess more consumer durables than do other groups, seems counter-intuitive, for one might have expected those who fall into debt to obtain goods to justify their spending to themselves by describing the goods as necessities. Perhaps they are more aware of what their possessions have cost them and have, retrospectively, come to consider such goods as luxuries, as things it might have been better to have done without. Or again, maybe they are more engaged with consumer goods, valuing them for their luxury status, a status which only serves to make them all the more desirable.

The life story of one of our interviewees centred on a recurring pattern of credit and debt. Her account weaves together many of the above themes in living with the maximum manageable debt, showing how her relationship ended when the debt became out of control, and how her explanations for her situation, her economic and budgeting practices, her desires and her identity are all bound together.

Upbringing

Alison was brought up in 'an ordinary working-class family', her father a steelworker, her mother a housewife. Her parents sacrificed many pleasures for their children's education, ballet and music lessons, foreign exchange holidays, etc. They were against credit, believing in saving up and, through their children, investing for the future.

Borrowing for 'survival'

Trained as a nursery nurse, Alison is now a clerical worker of 36 and lives very differently from them, finding that borrowing is 'the only way to survive'.

Budget works out somehow

I now get worried about how I'm going to pay for things, but it's my own fault, I get myself into situations, having work done on the house, committing myself to things, and then thinking, Oh God, where's it going to come from, I'll get the money one way or another, by working hard or putting more onto my mortgage or just tightening my purse-strings for a couple of months.

Impulse buying as pleasure

Depending on my mood about money, sometimes I do the most ridiculous things, sometimes when I'm really upset about how hard up I am, I go out and buy something which I don't really need, this makes me feel better, it makes me feel happy for a while.

Balancing necessities and luxuries

But I can live very very frugally...I don't eat, now that I'm not a couple...it was just a lifestyle, we would have wine with meals, we would have people to supper at weekends, and it would be three-course meals with lavish things, and I don't do that as much, they are special occasions now...now I can live on tuna and baked beans...[Why did things change?]...it was a separation from him, and it meant sorting out the home...I owed so much in solicitor's fees after the break up...I did have to sit down when I got a place of my own, and work out how I was going to pay for the rates, the electricity, the mortgage, and so on, and I found the best way for me was standing orders, to spread it out...there are certain things I am reluctant to give up...I wouldn't part with my car and I wouldn't part with my telephone, they're my two lifelines that I need, they're a link to other people, I'd rather cut down on food and drink.

An extravagant relationship: Working the system

[Did you use credit when you were together?] We would have very lavish trips abroad and everything would go on Visa card, the idea being that we could then pay it off, even with the interest rates it would be cheaper to have it on credit and have it that year than save up for it when the prices have gone up the following year, and we worked out it would probably be about the same. And, occasionally, I would have bank loans, personal bank loans to go abroad, but it was in the days when you could actually ask for a bank loan and say it was for house improvements and you'd get tax relief, which I'm sure everybody does, you'd say it was the damp proof course, this has to be done and that has to be done, but really it was for America . . . Another decision was, we never married because it was cheaper for tax relief on mortgages for two separate people than it was for husband and wife.

'Living beyond my means'

[Earlier, when working with children in Canada] . . . I had financial worries again then, because again I was living beyond my means, but I have always muddled through, I have never got that far behind in payments, I can always juggle my accounts . . . because probably I'm greedy, I want something today, I won't wait for it, I see something, I want a holiday, I'll just think I'll put it on credit.

Comparing oneself with others: Debt as normal

I don't know anybody who hasn't got mortgages or bank loans or overdrafts or incredible amounts they owe on Visa card . . . I think everybody else is doing it, and also you pay the price for it, I mean my goodness, it's not as if we're getting it free, it's legal and we're paying through the nose, on interest rates for it.

Why save?

But sometimes I think it's better to have it today than save up for it and pay for it in 6 months when (a) it may be gone or (b) the opportunity may not be there to do or have whatever it is that's going or it may have gone up in price, so I grab it while I can. Depends how, what mood I'm in, or how desperate I need something. Yes, I know it's ridiculous to pay the interest rates.

Debt as investment

[What determines what you decide you need?] Well, I always try and think of things in terms of investment, the big things that I've done recently have been to the house that I have, and I've had to borrow money and take out an advance on my mortgage, but with the idea that it's an investment, in the long term it'll be worth it, having central heating put in, a conservatory built, having the attic altered into a third bedroom, buying a piece of land, things like that, to me they're things which aren't going to disappear overnight.

Why not borrow more?

I see a silk jacket which is half price, therefore it's a bargain and therefore I'll go out and buy it, you know, it's lovely and I'll never get it that price again, and that's just, that's impulse buying, which gives me a high at that time, but I tend to suffer rather . . . I think, well you're overdrawn already to the tune of x number of pounds, you know, well to hell with it, why not be overdrawn to £200.

Paying for it all

I work very hard, this is one of the reasons, again, since being single again, I've realized how difficult it is to keep up on one salary . . . I will take work home with me, I work weekends, I work evenings, I get to work for 8 o'clock in the morning, I work my lunch hours, and I find it's very healthy, it's a positive attitude, I don't want to cut my standard of living, I had 13 years of very good standard of living [with her partner] and 2 years ago that stopped and I'm reluctant for it to drop any more and so that's why I have to work so hard.

Getting out of control

[Discussing why she split up from her partner . . .] Money did come into it, but again there was a different, yes, um, I'm afraid my partner, he had a different idea about money, I mean I spend beyond my means, but by God he was spending way, way beyond his, and it used to terrify me, I was really afraid that he would get into trouble, and um at one point he did, and that frightens me in a way, to get seriously into trouble over money, to be financially threatened with the courts, because I don't think that's necessary . . . he just didn't care, he would always find the money somewhere . . . and I found there was a difference between me spending my money on my clothes and impulse buying and a difference between him spending our money on his impulse buying . . . we had our own cheque accounts and we had a joint savings account, but the joint savings account either of us could actually withdraw money, and I would become rather cross if money had gone from the joint savings account on, say, an ornate Victorian fireplace when we didn't have a fireplace big enough for it to fit, things like that would make me cross, while as I said, I felt if I wanted to spend anything it would come out of my cheque account, the joint savings account was basically for joint holidays and paying bills.

Regaining control

I do find I have more control over my finances these last 3 years . . . I've trimmed down to just three [credit cards], I've been trying to get my Visa card down for 4 years now, but I needed a holiday, I desperately needed to get away, so I went to Canada, and it was overdrawn to the tune of over

£1000, but I've been trying to get it down for the last 4 years and I never quite seem to manage to do it, and I've got it down at last to £200 and one of my aims for this year is to clear it, I'm determined about that.

A fantasy for the future

One of the agreements when I left my partner was that the house wasn't particularly happy, but I loved my garden, we had about two acres and I was terribly sad and upset to leave that after all those years . . . he wished to buy me out, and I agreed to this, on the understanding, the only reason I'd go, was that on the understanding that within a year, if I had the money, I would purchase back half the garden, he had one acre and I would have the other acre, so this was agreed and I had the solicitor draw up the contract . . . after seeing how expensive it was to move house . . . I hadn't got the money for that year, so I thought I would borrow it from my parents who said, don't be ridiculous, you can borrow it from us, and perhaps if you could pay us back in 5 years, so that's what I've done, I've borrowed from them, to purchase the land back, which I've done, and I've got the deeds to it, and the idea was that I would have a house built there . . . one day I'm determined to have a house there . . . and again, I look on it as an investment, because who knows what's going to happen to an acre of land . . . and it gives me great pleasure as well, I don't have much of a garden, it's lovely to go out there at weekends . . . that's my bit of sanity still, that's why I want it . . . I just get carried away by it.

Getting further into debt: Why do some owe more than others?

We next asked why some people owed more than others, trying to explain the variation in the size of people's debts.[4] We found that demographic position (e.g. age, social class, family size, home ownership and education) had no effect on amounts owed. Two economic variables were important, accounting for half the variation accounted for. First, those with greater disposable income owed more money, showing that while disposable income does not determine whether or not one gets into debt, it does affect the amounts owed. Secondly, those with greater numbers of debts also owed more. Although it could have been that some acquire a single, major debt, while others frequently borrow rather small amounts, instead it seems that the number of debts is not a way of spreading a debt, but rather of increasing the amount owed.

The more one owes, the more one believes that events in one's life depend on external circumstances and luck rather than on individual efforts and abilities. Those more in debt disagree that people tend to get the respect they deserve in life, possibly reflecting a sense of unfairness in others' judgements of their own position. Those more in debt were also less cool, calm and reassuring in their coping strategies when faced with problems, lacking confidence in their ability to manage their affairs. Those with more debt are less likely to attribute their financial problems to peer pressure (trying to keep up with the Joneses), in contrast to the social comparison hypothesis which holds that people are motivated to keep in step with their peers and to differentiate themselves from those who belong to different groups (Cameron and Golby, 1990).

Attitudes towards credit and debt of those more in debt differ from those who owe less, showing an ambivalent acceptance of credit facilities, realizing that they bring problems but still thinking that it is better to borrow than to wait for desired or needed goods. Thus while those who get into debt more often have pro-credit attitudes, those who get further into debt more often recognize the problems with credit, and yet they still prioritize its advantages.

A variety of economic practices were predictive of how far people were in debt: the more debt people have, the more likely they are to think about money, and the less likely they are to buy themselves something as a reward, and the fewer bank accounts they have. Possibly, they are using credit cards as an alternative though risky form of budgeting, for those who owe more are also more willing to use credit cards, and the less often they enjoy shopping for clothes or shop in a few favourite shops. Presumably, as one's debts increase, pleasure in consumption is outweighed by problems and worries, and thus economic practices change.

Who is more willing to use credit cards?

Have it now, have it now, pay later. Of course it comes apart. They don't advertise that it affects you.

I am surprised that they get away with this, 'your flexible friend', I mean, they are insulting your intelligence, as if they are giving you the money. I think that it is shocking.

We asked why some people were more willing to use credit cards than others, and found that those who are more willing to use credit cards tend to be women and to be older, although these demographic variables accounted for little of the variance.[5] More important are economic factors: people who have more disposable income, more debts and who save less on a regular basis are more willing to use credit cards, with disposable income accounting for much of this variance. A range of attitudes towards credit and debt are important: those more willing to use credit accept the redefinition of debt as credit, rejecting the view of debt as shameful, wrong and to be avoided, instead seeing credit as useful, a means of allowing one to have now what one wants or needs:

You can make a credit card work in your favour, can't you, if you work it properly. If you have money invested and you don't want to put it in the building society, you don't want to draw it out, you can borrow the money, and leave it in there until you have to pay it, so you are still getting the interest and paying at the end of the month.

They reject the view that credit has its disadvantages as well as advantages, bringing problems as well as solutions, although they are inclined to see the use of credit as reflecting a failure to manage one's finances properly rather than as a normal part of everyday life.

Those who are more willing to use credit cards have suffered fewer recent major life events, and so can feel more secure, although they do have larger debts. They more often attribute their financial problems to the convenience of using credit cards. In terms of economic practices, those who are more willing to use credit cards are also more likely to pay off the total owed each month. They tend to enjoy window shopping and the process of consumption, and are not so economical as those less willing to use credit, less often shopping around for the best buy or a bargain.

Getting out of debt: Why do some repay more than others?

Next we asked why some people with debts repaid more of their debts each month than did others.[6] As with amounts of debt, debt repayments were not significantly predicted by sociodemographic variables such as social class, age or number of dependent children. However, not surprisingly, the more income people have, the more they repay of their debts. Indeed, the amount of disposable income proved more important for repayments than for size of debts. Disposable income does not discriminate those with and those without debts; however, it is a moderate predictor of how far one gets into debt, and an important predictor of how much one repays. Repayments are also predicted by the amount owed: the more one owes, the more one repays, provided one has the resources to do so.

Enduring psychological characteristics also affect repayments: those who repay more place greater value on achievement and self-direction and make a positive interpretation of borrowing as an appropriate use of credit. Those who repay more are more likely to blame external disasters for their financial problems rather than examine the factors surrounding the consumption of goods, and they would be less disappointed if their standard of living did not improve in the next 5 years. This is consistent with the other predictors of debt repayments, suggesting a general picture of those who repay more as people who feel relatively in control of their debt repayment, while their debts are seen as neither a source of shame nor as caused by themselves.

The attitudes and behaviour of the high repayers are less in conflict than for those who repay lesser amounts. This supports the earlier suggestion that for those whose attitudes are pro-credit, borrowing plus repaying is an acceptable form of budgeting, and one which allows one to have goods immediately. While those in debt generally tend to make stable attributions for their financial problems, those who repay more are more likely to see their debts as temporary, caused by external, unstable and uncontrollable disasters, rather than by stable causes like greed or the convenience of credit, which presumably motivates them to tackle their problems (Weiner, 1986). That debt repayments are, for them, part of a budgeting strategy, is supported by their being more likely to pay off their credit card bill each month, to take less pleasure in shopping with their family, and they spend more time thinking about, but not worrying about, money.

Explaining saving

You'll find watching your money grow almost as rewarding as watching your baby grow (advertisement for Halifax Building Society, *Observer*, 21 April 1991).

I think that the older generation generally speaking, they want things that they can't really afford at times but they usually save for it, or go without.

Theories of saving argue that saving allows people to distribute their income over the life course, providing themselves with financial security for possible hard times ahead and for their retirement (Modigliani, 1970). Saving is also of importance to the economy, because personal savings are a significant source of investment funds (Katona, 1975). Many theories have attempted to explain saving (Wärneryd, 1989), from the early economists who emphasized social-psychological factors such as thrift, self-control and patience, to Keynes (1936), who argued against the trait approach, claiming that consumption was a rational response to macroeconomic factors in society and predictable from income. Although Duesenberry (1949) introduced a social comparison process in the explanation of saving, suggesting that people consumed at the level set by their reference group and saving the remainder, modern economic theories attempt to model consumption as a function of income without any recourse to psychology.

Generally, savings are treated simply as residual unspent income, consumption postponed, an approach criticized by Douglas and Isherwood (1978) for neglecting the distinct cultural and moral meanings of saving. These accrued cultural meanings – whether we see someone as thrifty or mean, generous or profligate – also result in practical definitional problems, for economists include instalment payments or money left in the current account at the end of the month as savings, while ordinarily they are considered debts or lax budgeting respectively: saving is usually thought of as money specifically put into a bank or building society account for known purposes or for a rainy day.

Economic models are attempts to model amounts of consumption and saving using income. As Lea *et al.* (1987) point out, one problem with this is that income theories do not adequately provide remedies for economic problems such as that of stimulating saving among the public, or predicting the growth of alternative culture (green, organic or second-hand goods, or resistance to consumer goods). One resolution was offered by Katona's (1975) emphasis on willingness to save as a result of felt optimism or pessimism about the economy (termed consumer sentiment), for he argued that it is psychological factors such as economic beliefs that lead people to react to macroeconomic changes in predictable ways (see also Lindqvist, 1981). Understanding an economic behaviour such as saving demands an understanding of the everyday socioeconomic practices, the stresses, the social networks, the coping strategies, the moral judgements and the everyday understandings and attributions of the people involved.

What do people save?

On average, our respondents have £5120 (range £0–300,000) in personal savings, which they add to at an average rate of £38 (£0–1500) per month. Jointly, people have an average of £6689 in savings (range £0–100,000) which they jointly add to at an average rate of £64 per month (£0–3000). Investments average £6807 (£0–300,000) personally and £3435 (£0–100,000) jointly. There were no gender differences in amounts saved each month, either personally or jointly. However, men had significantly greater savings than women in total. Men's savings averaged £8751, compared to the average for women of £3060.

Who saves and who does not save?

We compared those who save regularly with those who do not save to see which factors differentiate these groups (Table 3.7).[7] Demographic variables were of little importance except that savers tended to have had more education than non-savers. Income theories were supported by the finding that people who save

Table 3.7   Compared with those who do not save, those who save regularly . . .

- Feel better off financially compared to 1 year previously
- Feel more in control of their finances
- Do not blame high credit limits for their money problems
- Do not feel fatalistic about their lives
- Let more people know of their financial situation
- Think they manage better than their parents and are better off
- Know how much money is in their bank account
- Tend not to accept a financially problematic situation
- Tend not to cope with financial problems through expressive and negative strategies
- Have more disposable income
- Disagree that credit is necessary despite its problems
- Believe that people get the respect they deserve
- Disagree that people's problems are due to bad luck
- Expect to be better off financially in 1 year's time
- Would be satisfied if their living standards didn't improve
- Think about decisions before taking action
- Believe that usually they can carry out their plans
- Have spent more years in education
- Use fixed rather than flexible budgeting strategies
- Less often blame money problems on fluctuating income
- Tend to blame money problems on a lack of self-discipline
- Tend to shop in a few favourite shops, not buying on impulse, and feel satisfied with their abilities and the economy

regularly tend to have higher incomes than those who do not save. Saving is related to optimism and satisfaction about personal economic circumstances and the economy as a whole (Katona, 1975). Locus of control also discriminated between savers and non-savers: those who do not save are more fatalistic, whereas savers believe more in personal factors such as hard work being rewarded and people getting the respect they deserve (Wärneryd, 1989). Those who do not save regularly also feel less in control of their finances and do not monitor their finances so well. In terms of attitudes, non-savers think that credit makes life complicated and is both useful and problematic, while savers tend not to endorse these attitudes: 'I can remember the day when you, if you got into debt it was just too horrible for words. I think that although I personally find credit cards very useful, I think that they are awfully dangerous.'

Savers and non-savers can also be discriminated in terms of their explanations for any money problems they have, savers emphasizing lack of self-discipline, bad luck and high credit limits, whereas non-savers point to fluctuating income. Non-savers prefer flexible strategies in financial management, which may mean that they tend to spend whenever they feel like it, or that they feel they have to spend whenever a desire is provoked by external stimulation. In contrast, savers use more fixed financial management: maybe people only save by making themselves regularly put a certain amount away each month according to a fixed plan. When coping with problems, non-savers tend towards acceptance, expressed emotion, self-blame, victimization and reliance on others. Non-savers tend not to tell friends or relatives of their financial position, keeping their finances private. It seems that savers, through talking to friends and relatives, receive social support for their approach to finances and information about ways of coping with finances, whereas non-savers feel themselves victims of external circumstances, coping by blaming themselves and getting upset, and availing themselves of social support. Savers tend to shop in a few favourite shops, using a fixed strategy in contrast to non-savers who shop around. Generally, non-savers seem to give up control over their finances, making things complicated, thinking themselves victims of external events but then chastising themselves when things go wrong. In contrast, the saver believes in personal control over finances, in fixed rather than flexible budgeting, in keeping things simple.

The life story of one interviewee centred on a lifetime's habit of careful budgeting and saving up. Sandra, now a clerk in her 30s, sees her life as continuous with her parents', and as distinct from that of many of her generation. She feels out of tune with the consumer society and lives a quiet life centred on work, saving, parents and friends.

Family background

My parents were always very careful with money. My mother never worked once she got married. My father drew a wage and then gave her so much housekeeping each week, which she tended to put away, so much into funds for housekeeping, so much for coal – in those days, so much for gas, and so forth. And that was instilled into me from quite an early age. She used to talk about it. I knew what the consequences of not doing it were, so I must have got that from her. I mean, they were never ever overdrawn. And as I've gone through life I've never been either. When I was a child, if I wanted something, my parents would say, well, we can't afford it, or wait till Christmas, or wait for a birthday, and I think I appreciated things more and accepted the fact, although they said I hardly ever asked for anything.

Early savings habit

I had pocket money which went up as I got older, and I was encouraged to save from that. I tended to buy National Savings stamps, one a week, and build them up, I think you had ten, and then got a certificate, so that's how I was encouraged to do that and I always did religiously every week.

Continuing the pattern

As soon as I got my first wage I opened a building society account and saved regularly. I was 16 when I left school. I started as a cleric [sic] in a stationers. I gave so much a week to my mother for housekeeping, put so much by for saving in two different building society accounts, some was not to be touched and some I looked on as current funds. I earned five pounds and five shillings. I saved about half. I spent mainly on everyday household things and toiletries that you needed, sweets if you felt like treating yourself, not for going out, because I drew that out of one of the funds. I didn't go out that often at that age, I was never one to go out very much. [How long did that continue for?] It's still going now. I stayed there for about 10 years. Obviously I had rises as I went along, and I stayed living at home. Obviously, I put by more and more as my income went up.

Comparisons with others: Being distinctive

I don't really know what my friends were doing, it was never something that I discussed with them. Probably not to the extent of putting money by for particular things. I think they all saved, well, I know they all saved, probably not as much as I did.

Keeping finances private

I've never discussed finances, personal finances with other people. [Would you know if any of your friends were in debt?] I don't know whether my friends would admit it, I certainly wouldn't.

Never, never use credit

If there's something I want, I go out and buy it. [Would you use credit?] Never, never. I've always been brought up with the belief that if you can't afford it you don't have it. No, never, not for a car or anything. A mortgage is different, I suppose that's credit. I just wouldn't consider it. My mother and I shared buying a car. I pay cash and that's it. There's odd occasions when I've carried a Barclaycard and there's odd occasions when I've used it, but I'd rather pay by cash. I rarely use mine.

Other people

From talking to people, people would, particularly for bigger items, pay hire purchase or credit facilities. I think there's more people that would pay weekly, monthly or whatever, than would pay outright. Because they can juggle their finances that way. It's the common attitude of keep up with the Joneses, next door's got a new car, so we'd better have one, we can't really afford it, so that's the only way they can go about it. Because of the society we live in, the pressure is on, and it's so easy to get credit facilities, they think it's what's expected of them, almost, to have all of these things, whereas in the old days, I'm going back to my parents' time, you saved until you could afford it.

Other values

As far as I'm concerned, life doesn't revolve around material possessions. To build up good friendships and good relationships with people I think is more important than having a good stereo system and a fantastic car.

Why do some save more than others?

We asked why some people regularly save more than others.[8] It turned out that none of the demographic variables were significant predictors, but both economic and psychological variables were important. Disposable income, expenditure and resource variables were all important: the more disposable income people have, the more they save; the more they spend on clothes and the less they spend on food, the more they save; and the more money people have saved already, the more they save each month. The relation between income, savings and amounts saved regularly is not surprising. Why should those who save more spend more on clothes and less on food? Are higher savers more concerned with their social image, buying clothes for self-presentation and comparison with others? Interestingly, the more people save, the less they argue about money with their partners or discuss money with their friends. Alternatively, clothing may be valued as a commodity just as saving is valued: compared to purchasing non-durable goods, spending on clothes may be seen as a way of investing in long-lasting objects which, like money in the bank, one keeps in the wardrobe for future occasions (Friedman, 1957):

> For women I think that buying clothes is much more in terms of our personality, so you are buying something to save something. I suspect that that is not so true of men. But of course the amount of time that you keep clothes has changed an awful lot, I mean there were only, when I was young, every man had to own at least one suit and you would expect that to last him most

of his life. So you spent an awful long time choosing that. It did cost a lot. It was a thing you saved up for. It was a costly thing to save up for.

This is consistent with the findings for both spending on food and for valuing enjoyment, for the regression also showed that the more importance people assign to enjoyment as a value in their lives, the less they save. It seems that the person who saves more, spends more on durable goods, less on goods which are immediately consumed, and values enjoyment less, while, conversely, the person who saves less, spends on food rather than on clothes, and values enjoyment more. The more one saves, the less one tends to shop around for the best buy or bargain and the more one uses the second-hand market, maybe again being more concerned with obtaining high-quality, long-lasting goods that have already proven their durability: the saver does not spend to enjoy but rather to possess goods of value at home as well as in the bank, although they may enjoy the process of saving up itself:

> It is sad in a way because there must be a certain amount of pleasure in actu-ally you know, saving up for six months for a particular item, and then saying, right, there is the cash in my hand, and go out and buy it. Whereas now it is so easy to sign the thing and it is bought. There is nothing to look forward to, quite the same. It is a different attitude altogether.

Regarding attitudes, the more people save, the more inclined they are to disagree with the notion that being in debt means people do not manage their money properly; possibly those who save the least are making the most moralistic judgements in criticizing others, in order to maximize the difference between themselves, on the margin between saving and borrowing, and the 'outgroup' who are in debt (Tajfel, 1982).

Why do some have more savings than others?

Why do some people have more total savings than others?[9] We found that the demographic variables of age, sex and number of children were significant pre-dictors of amount of savings. The older people are, the more they have saved: presumably, as people get older they gradually add to their stock of savings and people are less able to save when they are younger, when their income is least and expenses most. Men have more savings than women: this may be a result of the tax system which, until recently, taxed men on their wives' savings, or it may be due to inequalities in income or it may reflect patterns of financial manage-ment between husbands and wives within the household (Pahl, 1989). The more children people have, the less they have saved: clearly, children drain people's resources considerably.

Disposable income predicts amounts saved (the effect of age has already been taken out, so these income differences are not due to life-cycle differences). The amount of money invested was a major predictor of total savings: those who have greater savings also have greater investments – presumably those who save more spread their savings in more complex ways, using investment plans as well as building society or bank accounts. Further, those who regularly spend more on insurance also have greater savings, indicating a similar concern for the future (indeed, many people save through life insurance schemes which provide tax advantages over building society savings).

Important psychological variables concerned general values and specific explanations for one's own financial problems. Thus, the more importance people placed on achievement as a value in their lives, the less their total savings (on this view, the decision to spend more on insurance reflects a less individualistic, competitive and more conservative, family-oriented strategy). Secondly, the more people saved, the more they attributed their financial problems to bad luck and the less they attributed them to the occurrence of unexpected repairs. It makes sense that, for those who have savings, unexpected repairs are not seen to be the problem that they are for those without resources (Hartropp et al., 1987). Interestingly, those with greater savings are more likely to make attributions to bad luck, the external and uncontrollable factor typically identified by attribution theory (Weiner, 1986). Those who have the resources to deal with certain problems may feel more vulnerable to those problems for which financial resources are inappropriate.

While for recurrent saving the demographic variables were irrelevant and psychological variables were important, when predicting total savings, the converse was true. Psychological variables play a greater role in predicting how much people save on a regular basis, while the amount of total savings people have reflects not only cumulative recurrent savings but also demographic factors. For example, older people may have greater savings because these include redundancy, retirement or lump-sum insurance or retirement payments. They are also more likely to have inherited money from their parents or other relatives. Similarly, those with more (not necessarily dependent) children may have less savings because they have helped with setting up a home, a deposit on their child's house, costs of a wedding, purchased a car for a 21st birthday, helped with costs of training or further education, and so forth, in addition to the costs of dependent children.

Is saving the opposite of borrowing?

Saving and borrowing are popularly seen as opposites. The meaning of saving and borrowing hinges on the deeper moral debate about the power of the individual to work the system rather than succumbing to social and commercial pressures, and was much contested in many of the discussion groups. For example:

I think that it is fair to say that if you have made up your mind to buy object x, y and z, whatever it may be, you are going to be spending your money on that object anyway, so a clever person gets the object now and pays for it later. Rather than saving for weeks and months and years, and finally getting their hands on the object. That is the clever and appropriate use of credit. Debt is what happens when it gets out of control.

My generation would say you know, you have to save up and pay for it. We see it the other way around.

I think that you are actually speaking about fashion, because I don't think that one is better than the other, in the old way of thinking it was fashionable to save, and now it is fashionable to be clever.

But this is now why there are so many people in debt, because of your new fashionable idea. It's because of a lack of understanding about that idea, because of lack of control, I don't think that the ideas themselves are unworthy.

Well it also reflects what life is like. Youngsters can't save up, because by the time they have done that the thing has gone. There is this feeling amongst young people, now, now. And I think that often this is a reflection on life. Going very fast.

Traditional stereotypes describe the debtor as self-indulgent, reckless and impatient, whereas the saver is thrifty, controlled and patient. Recent theories, and the present findings, move away from such individualistic trait theories towards an appreciation of the complex of demographic, economic, psychological and practical or local factors which affect different kinds of saving and borrowing, showing often that demographic factors are less important than some theories propose, while the operation of economic factors must be analysed in the context of a range of sociopsychological factors such as attitudes, locus of control, coping, satisfaction, attributions, social networks, discourse, consumer activities, and so forth.

However, the traditional opposition between saving and borrowing is often assumed. There are three problems with this. First, saving and borrowing are not themselves homogeneous categories; for example, recurrent saving must be explained differently from total savings, being in debt is explained differently from getting further into debt, and repaying debts is not simply the reversal of this process.

Secondly, in many ways, saving and borrowing are similar. For example, as both are positively correlated with income, both may be used to even out varying incomes or varying needs over the life course (Modigliani, 1970), with savings providing present resources drawn from past income and borrowing providing present resources drawn from future income. Both saving and borrowing involve participation in consumer society, making choices as a modern citizen, acting on beliefs, contributing to economic trends.

Thirdly, our six groups of different patterns of income management discussed earlier show that while some spend more than their income permits and others spend less, further patterns exist, particularly those who neither borrow nor save, but live exactly within their income, those who both borrow and save, presumably balancing their income and outgoings according to a more complex

Table 3.8   Compared with debtors without savings, debtors with savings . . .

- More often buy themselves something as a reward
- Finished their education at an earlier age
- Spend more on food each week
- More often blame money problems on losing a job
- Think they manage their finances better than their friends
- Are more likely to enjoy shopping for presents
- Would be disappointed if their living standard didn't improve

formula, and those who maintain both debts and savings – even though they do not actually save money on a regular basis, nor do they use their savings to repay their debts. As these different groups of people do not differ greatly in their disposable income level, we cannot simply say that the more one's income the more likely one is to save money, while the less one's income the less likely one is to get into debt. What then determines the way people spend or borrow money? Do these different groups of people vary according to their family circumstances, their attitudes or personality, their shopping patterns, and so forth?[10]

Debtors with and without savings

Why would some people retain their debts when they have some savings? (Table 3.8). It seems that those with debts without the cushion of savings are somewhat resigned to their situation, expecting little improvement, managing worse than their friends, yet not particularly keen on spending money on food, rewards or presents. They also tend to be more educated. Those in debt who also have savings more often identify losing a job as a cause of their problems: their savings could represent redundancy payments, or money saved from a previous period of higher earning. This group, who have retained their savings, are none the less more likely to be living at their previous standard of living, spending more money on food, rewards and presents, and hoping for an improvement in their finances in the next few years.

Debtors who do and do not save regularly

Those who have debts and do not save regularly, like those with no savings, tend to be more educated than those in debt who save regularly (Table 3.9). People in debt who also save regularly feel more in control of their finances than those who do not save, knowing their bills and being less accepting of their problems. Rather than being dissatisfied with the economy, they not only save but also repay more of their debts regularly, so it is not that those in debt who do not save are instead repaying their debts but rather that saving and repaying go together (for economists, repayment of debts constitutes a form of saving). If this

Table 3.9   Compared with debtors who do not save, debtors who save regularly . . .

- Are more satisfied with the state of the economy
- Repay more of their debts
- Think getting a good job depends on luck
- Blame demands from children for their financial problems
- Do not blame enjoying shopping for their financial problems
- Disagree that they accept whatever financial problems arise
- Think they manage their finances worse than their friends
- Think they manage their finances better than their mother
- Would be more satisfied if their living standards didn't improve
- Give less value to concern for others
- Possess more consumer durables
- Are more likely to know what their bills will be
- Finished their education at an earlier age
- Think their friends don't know their financial situation
- Less often buy themselves a reward
- Disagree that credit facilities bring their own problems
- Feel more in control of their finances

group felt they had got into debt as a result of financial mismanagement, they would surely use the income which they presently save to repay even more of their debts, so as to pay them off as soon as possible. That they do not do this, maintaining both savings and repayments concurrently, indicates that for this group, as for debtors in general, being in debt may be a particular financial management decision, not simply an unpleasant situation to be escaped if at all possible. Living with debts for those who also save, appears to be a choice based on a particular vision of how to live in modern society, where one saves for particular things, in addition to managing one's debts.

Those in debt who do not save regularly also seem aware of their actions, rejecting a fatalism or external attributions for their problems, although they are dissatisfied with the economy. Rather, they accept their problems, still buying themselves presents as rewards, still enjoying shopping, valuing a concern for others, and while feeling out of control, they hope for an improvement in their circumstances. Ironically, this optimism is expressed less by people who are both in debt and saving, although they seem to have regained more control over their finances, doing more to bring about improved finances in the future.

People who neither save nor borrow

Who is it who lives just within their income, neither borrowing nor saving? (Table 3.10). These people seem to be locked into a rigid strategy of financial management. They operate fixed, inflexible styles of budgeting, not thinking especially about each decision, avoiding credit facilities and the flexibility – and

Table 3.10   Compared with other groups, those who neither save nor borrow . . .

- Less often think about decisions before taking action
- Tend to think that success depends more on luck
- More often discuss money with friends
- Use a more fixed, less flexible financial management style
- Would be disappointed if their living standard didn't improve
- Think that their peers possess fewer consumer durables
- Less often blame demands from children for money problems
- Are less willing to use credit cards
- Can think of more things they want to buy for themselves
- Less often blame advertising for their money problems
- Less often blame the development of new products for their money problems
- Are less satisfied with the state of the economy

the dangers – which they offer. They seem unimpressed by the demands of the consumer society – advertising, new products – and although they do desire consumer objects, they do not seem to have discovered any ways of obtaining them, beyond a general fatalistic belief in luck and a hope for improvements in the future. Both saving and getting into debt depend on an engagement with the consumer society, a formulation of financial strategies tailored to one's needs and desires, whether these are to be realized in the present or the future. Those who neither save nor borrow seem rather to have made a fixed plan based on income and outgoings and to stick to it, regardless of their desires or developments in the consumer society. They do not express distinctive attitudes or values; rather, they have adopted a different financial strategy which works well enough to ensure its continuation.

Conclusions

We have seen that saving and being in debt are related but not opposite activities – people can be characterized in terms of both savings and debts, with some people having neither and some having both. What discriminates these people, aside from income and social class, are a variety of psychological variables including enjoyment, involvement in consumption, satisfaction, the way they explain and cope with financial difficulties, and so on. We were also able to predict the amounts of savings and debt people had, using a combination of economic, demographic and psychological variables. Variables such as social relations, self-control and coping were related to amount of saving. A variety of economic behaviours such as spending on clothes and food were also related to the amounts people saved. In general, psychological variables were more associated with the regular savings habit rather than with total savings, which was more related to demographic and income variables.

The amount of debts was partly a function of disposable income but also of self-control, coping and budgeting as well as shopping practices. People's willingness to use credit cards was related to perceived convenience, whether people could pay off the monthly bill and how economical people were. In terms of repaying debts, those with higher incomes, who valued achievement and who were fatalistic about disasters, paid back a larger proportion of their debts each month.

The main psychological variables which helped to explain savings and debt were a cluster of variables to do with self-control, budgeting and coping strategies, and well-being. It is clear that social psychological variables in combination with economic and demographic variables considerably enhance our ability to predict and explain who will save and get into debt.

THE MEANING
FOUR | OF POSSESSIONS

The possessions people have in their homes are changing rapidly, as people respond to technological developments in the market. The domestic environment and the range of domestic objects within it have changed dramatically (McDowell, 1983; Forty, 1986; Madigan and Munro, 1990) over the last few decades. The reasons why people want things, the relations they experience with goods, enter into everyday calculations about what they can afford, what is worth waiting for, what they want next and where they can economize. The goods people possess affect their social reputation, their image of themselves and their self-esteem, their desires for future purchases, and their assessments of their relative standard of living and status in relation to others, both present peers and past upbringing.

> I like buying clothes. If the children are dressed nice, I get the pleasure out of that. You get sort of pride from other people looking and thinking that your children are smart. I think the way you dress your child can have a psychological effect on them. My boys like modern clothes, and I do my best to keep them in fashion, even if I go without myself. If they want a pair of bell-bottoms because they're in fashion, I like to buy them. I feel if they go round looking dirty and scruffy, people look down on me (quoted in Oakley, 1974, p.147).

In this chapter, we begin by examining which goods people possess, whether they regard them as necessities or luxuries, how they pay for them and what goods they desire. We follow Douglas and Isherwood (1978), among others, when they challenge the economist's notion that people value goods solely for their role in social comparison, emulation and competition processes, arguing that 'instead of supposing that goods are primarily needed for subsistence plus competitive display, let us assume that they are needed for making visible and stable the categories of culture' (Douglas and Isherwood, 1978, p.59). Goods do not simply reveal social relations; they are also participants in social relations. Indeed, commodities have their own biographies and social lives (Appadurai, 1986). For example, while the computer means only what we, as a society, give it to mean, from the point of view of people's response to or use of the computer, it arrives as a given, with a specific history, 'personality', even a masculine gender, and it is by accepting or negotiating with this given meaning that people appropriate such an object into their everyday lives.

We construct a theoretical framework through which the significance of possessions may be understood by first exploring the different ways in which personal and social identities are bound up with objects. We then analyse these relations between people and objects on several levels – intrapsychic, biographical, family dynamics and gender relations.

Ownership of domestic and personal goods

You very quickly take what used to be a luxury as something people now consider to be a necessity. There is an upgrading in standards all the time.

We identified 18 household consumer durables, varying from the commonplace to recent developments, and asked people which they possessed, how they regarded them and how they paid for them (Table 4.1). On average, our respondents possessed 7.15 of these goods, although the number of goods owned is positively correlated with disposable income. This number is also positively correlated with various measures of economic satisfaction, although not necessarily with satisfaction with one's health or abilities.

People were also asked to estimate how many of these goods were owned by their peers or friends in a similar situation to them. Interestingly, while men considered their peers to have a similar number of goods to themselves, women consistently credited their peers with, on average, 1.4 more goods. This difference may reflect the fact that women tend to have less control over how household money is spent (Pahl, 1989) and so they may feel the lack of one particular object they desire and know their friends to have, while men are more able to acquire whatever they want and presumably assume that their friends do the same. From her interviews, Pahl (1989, p.169) notes that 'in general, husbands were likely to perceive a greater degree of sharing [of economic resources] in marriage than wives, who were more aware of conflicts of opinion and interest'.

I'd like a compact disc player but that's a bone of contention... well she thinks of it as being a bit of a luxury, but eventually, when I'm ready to buy one I will get one and that will be the end of the matter. So I will get one (Frank Irving)[1].

Table 4.1   Which of the following do you have in your household?

	Owned by sample (%)	Judged a necessity[a] (%)	Bought with credit[b] (%)	Owned by population[c] (%)
Colour TV 1	86	41	16	91
Colour TV 2	28	20	4	
Colour TV 3	7	6	1	
Black-and-white TV 1	38	17	4	
Black-and-white TV 2	4	11	0	
Video-recorder 1	51	14	11	53
Video-recorder 2	4	50	0	
Washing machine	79	90	18	84
Dishwasher	20	31	5	10
Tumble dryer	32	50	7	42
Car 1	70	82	24	
Car 2	25	65	7	
Microwave	35	31	5	39
Compact disc player	17	4	4	
Stereo/hi-fi	69	29	13	
Telephone 1	89	93	6	85
Telephone 2	33	42	3	
Computer	30	39	3	18

[a] Judged to be a necessity for oneself rather than a luxury. These judgements were only made by those who possessed the good.
[b] Bought with credit or a loan rather than with cash.
[c] As reported in *Social Trends* (1991), where figures were available, for the general population in 1989.

I would like to get one [washing machine] but my husband said it's not really necessary . . . [use the launderette?] . . . they just ruin them [clothes], it crumples them, too difficult to iron and some of them you won't be able to use it again . . . so I prefer to wash it by hand (Linda Bell).

Certain goods which people possess are clearly considered to be necessities, most notably the telephone, the washing machine and the car. Such goods play two key roles, allowing for the daily management of a modern household and providing connections with dispersed social networks. Everyone has their own, overlapping version of this list:

I couldn't live without it [washing machine] . . . I couldn't live without that either [freezer] . . . washing machine – I've got no option. It's got to be used whether I like it or not (Lynn Irving).

Other goods are clearly considered to be luxuries, such as the compact disc player and the additional television sets. These goods also play key roles, for which it is significant that they are defined as luxuries: the compact disc player represents the latest music technology, one not yet naturalized into a necessity like radio or television, but therefore one which signifies status and material comfort; the additional televisions may in fact play important roles within a family (e.g. allowing for the separation of teenagers in conflict with parents), but significantly families feel they could reasonably be expected to return to the single set scenario of some years ago, though not to being without a set at all, and so the flexibility of family dispersal around the house allowed by several televisions is still valued as a luxury (Livingstone, in press).

Table 4.1 shows an association between judgements of necessity and use of credit in purchasing an object which seems counter-intuitive. The social representation of credit is of a facility which encourages unnecessary or indulgent consumption, while cash/saving up reflects careful budgeting for necessities. In fact, the converse seems to be true, with credit associated with necessities rather than extras: respondents report using credit more often to buy their first television, video, car or telephone, more often judged as necessities, and less often to buy multiples of these goods, these being more often judged to be luxuries. Presumably, while more people are buying their single television, video, etc., on credit, because they lack the savings or income, it is those with more money in the first place who can afford the multiple goods, thereby not needing credit. While a second video is also less likely to be bought with credit, it differs in being judged more a necessity: it seems people have a special reason for buying a second video-recorder.

If we ask the question the other way around, not focusing on how people assess what they actually possess, but asking in general what people think are necessities and luxuries for modern living, rather different answers emerge (Table 4.2). Many 'necessities' were uncontentious, partly because people mentioned basic survival needs and psychological or spiritual needs first, thus altering the conceptual frame to one in which it becomes more problematic to see a television set as necessary. Again, consumer durables which have developed more recently are more often seen as luxuries, while older goods are more contested, seeming to be part necessity, part luxury, depending on one's perspective. Generally, few consumer durables were seen as consensual necessities. Luxury items seemed to be those which were considered desirable for the status they conferred rather than for their usefulness. All who mentioned them agreed that alcohol and cigarettes were luxuries. Interestingly, little attention was paid to goods or facilities provided by society rather than possessed by the individual.

As norms of affluence and possessions change, so do social definitions of poverty and wealth: once a television was a symbol of affluence, now its near saturation makes its absence a sign of poverty. The relative poverty thesis states that the definition of necessities is socially determined, depending on each generation or even decade (Mack and Lansley, 1985). An acceptable standard of living thus includes not only physical health, but also the activities of social participation, which have no meaning outside the society people are living in, but are of enormous importance for members of that society. Following Townsend (1979), it is generally agreed that people must be able to participate in the living

Table 4.2 Items defined as necessities and luxuries[a]

Category	Number of mentions
Uncontentious necessities	
Basic needs (e.g. shelter, food, clothing, warmth)	61
Psychological needs (e.g. companionship, security)	29
Social provision (e.g. transport, employment, nurseries)	8
Consumer goods (e.g. furniture, cooking utensils)	3
Miscellaneous (e.g. garden, bicycle, deodorant)	16
Uncontentious luxuries	
Status objects (e.g. expensive clothes, helicopter, boat)	13
Disposables (e.g. luxury foods, alcohol, cigarettes)	12
Consumer durables (e.g. microwave, tumble drier, dishwasher)	7
Multiple objects (e.g. second car, holiday home, several televisions)	5
Miscellaneous (e.g. swimming pool, pets, hairdresser, no worries)	12
Contested goods (mentioned as both necessity and luxury)	
Consumer durables	
car	17
washing machine	11
television	12
radio	6
record player	6
video-recorder	6
fridge freezer	4
telephone	4
Leisure	
entertainment	11
holidays	14

[a] Items listed by 30 people when asked freely to describe the difference between necessities and luxuries (see Livingstone and Lunt, in press a).

conditions and amenities customary to the society to which they belong. Desai (1986, p.3) argues that the 'economic entitlement to an adequate living standard should be such that citizens can take full part in the political community'. Both of these principles depend on a consensus about these basic living conditions and amenities (Mack and Lansley, 1985), a consensus which rests on lay theories of needs and wants, necessities and luxuries, or, more broadly, on a lay theory about the relation between human nature and material consumption (see Chapter 7). Below this socially determined standard of living, however defined, people in poverty suffer many hardships – physical, psychological, social and political, such as loss of social contacts, family connections, leisure activities, social obligations, privacy, dignity (Brown and Harris, 1978).

We also asked people about the goods they would like to buy in the future. Many people, between one-third and one-half of the sample, appeared to have

Table 4.3 Is there something under £50 that you really want to have?[a]

Object	%
Clothes	23
Books (often specified, mainly reference works)	11
Electrical kitchen goods (toaster, teasmade, etc.)	9
Shoes	8
Electronic equipment (radio, walkman, cassette, etc.)	8
Furnishings (chair cover, curtains, rug, lamp, etc.)	7
Hobbies (tripod, chess set, etc.)	7
Bicycle/bicycle parts	6
Kitchen goods (carving knife, teapot, etc.)	4
Telephone (usually extra phone)	3
Garden plants	2
Handbag	2
Food	2
Luxuries (Belgian chocolates, vintage port)	2

[a] Goods listed by the 35 per cent of respondents who answered 'yes'.

an agenda of desired goods, while others did not particularly conceive of desires much in advance of satisfying them. Baxter (1988) suggests that such 'unsatisfied wants' may provide a better explanation of the decision to work or to work longer hours than explanations based on changes in real wages. Tables 4.3, 4.4 and 4.5 reveal a considerable variety of desires held by different people. There are many similarities between the lists of desired goods in Tables 4.3, 4.4, and 4.5 and the lists of items on which people would cut back if they had to economize. Industries and retailers for clothing, holidays and cars/petrol would seem to be the most vulnerable to variations in personal finances, being goods people both commonly desire and see as areas for economizing; thus they should do especially well in a boom and badly in recession. Kamptner (1989) notes also that clothing is the preferred gift most frequently mentioned by men and women, because, she suggests, it is both a luxury one cannot always buy oneself and also because it is so individual – or individuating – a gift, fitting the receiver in age, sex, appearance and style.

Interestingly, desires for relatively cheap goods concern personal possessions (clothing, books, hobbies), while more expensive goods are more household-oriented (car, home improvements, hi-fi), though holidays come top of the list here.

The meanings of personal and domestic objects

Lists of goods such as those presented in Tables 4.3–4.5 do not tell us much about why people possess, value, desire or judge necessary different kinds of consumer goods. Cultural and historical comparisons make it clear that there is no necessary relation between objects and meanings, rather this is an area for

Table 4.4   Is there something between £50 and £200 that you really want to have?[a]

Object	%
Clothes	19
White goods (microwave, tumble drier, etc.)	8
Camera/camera equipment	6
Home improvements	6
Colour TV	6
Holiday	6
Furniture	6
Electronic goods (cassette, walkman, etc.)	6
Video-recorder	4
Hobbies	4
Garden plants/equipment	4
Compact disc player	3
Typewriter	3
Shoes	2
Guitar	2
Bicycle	2
Carpet	2
Hi-fi equipment	2
Furnishings	2

[a] Goods listed by the 43 per cent of respondents who answered 'yes'.

empirical research and cultural analysis. Hitherto, very little research has explored the meanings of objects. For all the social sciences, the relations between people have been considered paramount and research has been slow to recognize the social nature of people's relations with objects. People's relations with other people are conditioned by the material context in which they are inevitably located, just as relations between people and objects are inevitably socially located. Following Marx (1976), Baudrillard (1988, p.29) makes a stronger claim, that people are 'no longer surrounded by other human beings, as they have been in the past, but by *objects*'. The forces of fashion, technological development and market pressures ensure, moreover, that these objects are forever changing (Davidson, 1982).

How then do material objects come to acquire social meanings and how are they incorporated into everyday experiences? Certainly we are all skilled readers of object meanings in everyday life. We can make fine discriminations about the social class connotations of a living room carpet or three-piece suite. We readily draw conclusions about people from the number of books or televisions in their houses. We accept that a house is not 'modernized' unless it has fitted kitchen cabinets or central heating. We guess people's politics from their dress and their income from their car. We hoard significant mementos in our attics, display

Table 4.5   Is there something between £200 and £1,000 that you really want to have?[a]

Object	%
Holiday (mainly abroad, 1/3 specified places)	22
Car (often replacement car or second car)	14
Home improvements (new kitchen, shower, porch, etc.)	10
Hi-fi equipment	8
Video-recorder	5
Word processor/computer	4
Carpet	4
Furniture	4
Kitchen white goods	4
Bicycle	4
Compact disc player	4
Music equipment (piano, organ, amp, etc.)	3
Cooker	3
Boat	3
Dishwasher	2
Television	2
Three-piece suite	2

[a] Goods listed by the 52 per cent of respondents who answered 'yes'.

family photos on top of the television and hang onto our children's drawings and our teddy bears. We also recognize as inhuman and devastating the 'deselfing' (Goffman, 1961) which results from an imposed loss of possessions, as in mental hospitals or old people's homes or concentration camps. As Kamptner (1989) found, asking what people would rescue in a fire reveals the powerful attachment we feel to our possessions, not just as things we own but as part of ourselves.

Based partly on her research on elderly people's feelings about their possessions and partly on Csikszentmihalyi and Rochberg-Halton's (1981) research, Kamptner (1989) discusses a range of categories of object meanings. Objects may convey memories or recollections of important past events and they may remind one of specific or special relatives or friends (symbols which maintain self-identity). Objects may form part of one's personal history, marking a significant moment, or always having been there (symbols of the life-review). They may represent a personal accomplishment or symbolize freedom or independence (symbols of the ideal or future self). An object may be itself personified, providing someone to talk to or care for (symbols of significant others, rather like parasocial interaction with television personalities: Horton and Wohl, 1956). Further, one may identify with an object, it somehow expressing oneself (symbols that express qualities of the self or which mediate conflicts within the self). Objects may carry cultural or religious associations (symbols of the generalized other, reflecting back a social self: Mead, 1956). They may affect one's mood, providing pleasure, escape or security. They may simply be useful, providing convenience or learning or some other form of help. Objects may be valued for their intrinsic qualities, such as being irreplaceable, part of a collection, or handmade, though appreciating such qualities itself reflects cultural value judgements (objects as signs of status).

The same object, e.g. a teddy bear, may be personally meaningful for many of these reasons: it may remind you of your childhood, seen as a time of security and innocence; it may remind you of the grandmother, now dead, who gave it to you. You take it to your new home because it has gone everywhere with you in your life. You may confess your fears to no one but your teddy. You may feel it to resemble yourself, being short and dumpy and rather battered. Certainly, some objects lend themselves more readily to certain meanings – photographs bring back memories and mark personal history, a watch may signify an accomplishment, a walkman may represent pleasure, freedom and a sense of being oneself. But generally, objects are open to different meanings and to different categories of meanings, for the relationship between people and objects is not given.

Relations between people and objects

The everyday relations between people and personal or domestic objects are fluid and negotiable because they are determined by a multiplicity of processes ranging from the intrapsychic to the cultural. In the remainder of this chapter, we consider the different levels – intrapsychic, biographical, family and gender – on which people and objects interrelate, as this helps us both to build up a picture of the complexity of this often invisible or unnoticed relationship and to integrate a growing body of research on this relationship which otherwise appears rather disorganized or contradictory.

Intrapsychic object relations and the social self

It is clear that between what a man calls *me* and what he simply calls *mine*, the line is difficult to draw (James, 1890, p.291).

Household objects constitute an ecology of signs that reflects as well as *shapes* the pattern of the owner's self (Csikszentmihalyi and Rochberg-Halton, 1981, p.17).

In his ethnographic study of imaginary social worlds, Caughey (1984, p.241) shows how 'we do not live only in the objective world of external objects and activities . . . [when we spend] much of our lives in imaginary worlds, we are engaging not in private but in *social* experiences', experiences which are 'subjectively compelling' and which involve imagined relations with others, imagined other selves, lifelong fantasies, and the enactment of cultural myths. Segal (1985, p.22) argues similarly that 'our heads are full of phantasies. Not just *fantasies* – by which I mean stories we make up to amuse ourselves – but "stories" we are deeply involved in and convinced by and which go on independently of our conscious awareness or intention', and these phantasies involve people and objects in which we have invested meaning and emotion.

Turkle (1984) draws on Kleinian psychoanalysis to explore the object-relations, literally, through which people experience the personal computer. While object-relations usually refer to human objects, the point that instincts or motivations are not so much determining of our relations with objects but rather are constructed through those relations can also be applied to relations with inanimate objects. For example, Turkle shows how an object like the computer is symbolically powerful because of the interaction of cultural myths in which it is embedded with the psychic anxieties, emotions or dilemmas faced by particular individuals. Turkle (1984) describes how, for one of her interviewees, his relationship with the computer changed his self-conception. Having dropped out of his engineering course, Barry worked at repairing electronic equipment and felt himself a failure for not being 'analytical or theoretical', characteristics he both admired and desired. When one day he bought a programmable calculator and started to play with it, he found that numbers could be concrete and fun instead of theoretical and difficult, and so mathematics became manageable – 'they [the computer and calculator] put mathematics in my hand and I'm good with my hands' (Turkle, 1984, p.169). While his job is unchanged, privately Barry became confident and optimistic, no longer failing on his own terms. He became a person who knows what he'll be doing in 6 months' time, for him a sign of being in control, and now feels he can learn more generally – from a failure and a drop-out, he has become a learner.

Of course, objects can also be instrumental in achieving everyday necessary functions – keeping warm, cutting the grass, storing food, providing entertainment. Prentice (1987) distinguishes instrumental and symbolic functions of possessions, where instrumental functions allow people to manipulate or control the environment to meet a need. Hitherto we have been discussing the symbolic as the key mode in which people relate to objects, just as symbolic communication dominates our interactions with others, particularly significant others, although we also use interpersonal communication to pass the salt and ask which is the right train. Even the notion of control or instrumentality, much discussed by Furby (1978) as an undoubtedly indispensable aspect of our relation with objects, has its symbolic dimensions. In relation to the need for control or the value given to instrumentality, we may question the definition of necessity (do we need vases to contain flowers?), the personal gratification obtained from controlling the environment (don't we feel better people for keeping our lawns trim?), and the social signification of controlling/technical discourses (as we see below, men in particular use this discourse to deny emotional investments in objects and to fit the masculine stereotype).

Forty (1986) discusses how the design of an object changes not only the object but also the social perception of that commodity, i.e. design gives it an image: the TV in the cabinet is furniture, stable, reliable and taken-for-granted; the flat screen hi-tech TV on a pedestal is trendy, sophisticated and attention-seeking. He attacks the popular belief that form follows function by demonstrating the range of forms which over time have been considered adaptive for the same function. However, the emphasis on function mystifies the identity and pleasure roles of commodities: 'its [design's] disguising, concealing and transforming powers have been essential to the progress of modern industrial societies' (Forty, 1986, p.13). We could extend this mystification from images of products to all images of economic life, for social practices involving debt, credit, saving, etc., all depend on how they are designed and packaged, and so are all subject to the myth of form following function as they are popularly and commercially represented in terms of function rather than symbolic meanings.

From their ethnographic study of Chicago families and their possessions, Csikszentmihalyi and Rochberg-Halton (1981) analyse the symbolic meanings of objects as a balancing of two dynamic forces: *differentiation*, 'separating the owner from the social context, emphasizing his or her individuality' (p.38), and *similarity*, where 'the object symbolically expresses the integration of the owner with his or her social context' (p.39). Within an individualistic culture, the force for differentiation tends to be popularly valued (as idiosyncratic or creative), while that for similarity is devalued as keeping up with the Joneses, emulation, conformity. Of course, such evaluations can be turned around, contrasting the deviant and destructive with the connected and neighbourly.

The value placed on these two forces, the emotional investment in each, and cultural factors such as gender and generation all affect the balance struck within each person. Csikszentmihalyi and Rochberg-Halton describe two dimensions of orientation to objects which represent cultural factors: the dimensions from action to contemplation and that from self to other. They found, for example, that men and younger people expressed a more differentiated and action-oriented sense of self in relation to possessions while women and older people tended more towards contemplation and similarity or other-orientation. Dittmar (1989) and Kamptner (1989) also showed how, for men, the meaning of possessions was more self-oriented and instrumental, whereas for women possessions were used to express more symbolic, other-oriented functions.

The role of objects in individual biography over the life-cycle

To ask someone to tell their life history is to ask for a story, a story with a narrative structure (beginning, middle, end), with a cast (central and peripheral characters, a hero or heroine), a plot (problems to be solved, order to be regained), and, whether explicit or not, the story will be a moral one, with conclusions reached, lessons learned and judgements made. Life stories function to orient people to their lives, generating a perspective, finding or imposing continuity and purpose, identifying a meaning by sifting out what seems to matter and making sense of it (Perring, 1991). They describe a moral career, with 'the regular sequence of changes that career entails in the person's self and in his framework of imagery for judging himself and others' (Goffman, 1961, p.119).

As part of the research, we asked a diverse group of people to tell us their life stories. While their brief was to focus on money, possessions and financial decisions, what came out was their hopes, disappointments, worries, children, divorces and satisfactions. This merely reinforces the point which came home to us many times during this and other research (Livingstone, in press), that people cannot but reveal themselves when talking about the objects in their lives.

As Kamptner (1989) and Csikszentmihalyi and Rochberg-Halton (1981) have noted, relations between people and objects are contexted within individual biographies – objects enter and disappear at significant moments, remain present through life events and are transported to new situations – and part of their meaning derives from this embedding in a biography. For example, Mary, now 52, was brought up during the war, when money was tight, so she wore second-hand clothes and learned to save. With four brothers to be educated, she received little training but was ambitious, working her way up as a photographer for the local paper, to buy her own house and become comfortably off. After marriage and her first baby, for which her independent life – job, car, income – was put aside, she reveals the threat to her identity which this transition occasioned through her talk and fantasy about her bicycle:

> We lived fairly simply, I don't keep up with the Joneses, so we managed all right, and as soon as I did start earning money again, my first money went on a bicycle, and it was sort of like a symbol of freedom in a way because although I had myself settled for not earning money, the first money that I did actually earn properly, I bought a bicycle with, which was marvellous, I could actually cycle around, and one of my recurring dreams is losing my bicycle still, it must be a symbol of freedom, very odd isn't it?

A longer story shows the intricate process whereby the object environment both reflects and constructs an adult identity. Ralph, now in his 60s, describes his life thus:

A working class childhood as lack

I was one of nine children, of a definite working-class home in London. As a child I *never* had any new clothes. I never had any birthday presents, Christmas presents, any presents of any sort, and I was never taken on holiday, not even for a day. I did feel it at Christmas times when everybody would take their Christmas presents out into the street to show everybody – nothing big they had, because we were virtually all the same, but I never had *anything*.

Compensatory practices

And, I decided, right from when I remember, about 9 years old, I would have Christmas presents, and I joined the Christmas Club. Where you would go into one of these bookshops that sells toys. It was called Bell's Bazaar and you paid a ha'penny or whatever you could afford, and he'd write it on a card for you, and you'd save it up for Christmas, and the thing is, I never got pocket money, so what I had to do was do other things, such as knocking on doors asking for their jam jars. You used to get returns on jam jars, a farthing for a one-pound jar, a ha'penny for a two-pound jar. And also I collected horse manure for people, and I put it onto this card and come Christmas time I had about five or six shillings.

Social comparison

That was enough to buy me a Mickey Mouse Annual and/or a Teddy Bear Annual. I'd buy meself two annuals so that on Christmas Day I could go out into the street, 'Look what I got for Christmas' you see. But anyway, that went on, you know . . . I did go to school in rags, there's no doubt about it, the bottom was out of the trousers literally, not just at the gut, hardly any slippers on my feet, and anyway, I got by, and then, as soon as I was 14 I left school.

Becoming different, defining oneself against

My father and mother would go drinking over the working men's club every Friday, Saturday, Sunday, and me father would go virtually every night as well, and most of my brothers and sisters were older than myself and they'd go over to the club or they'd, if they were at work they'd go to the cinema or whatever, and I would have to stay to look after the smaller ones, which I did. And when I did get invited to go to the club one night, I didn't enjoy it a lot because the smoke got in me eyes, the smell of the beer, and it turned me into a complete, at that very young age, a non-smoker and teetotal. I've been like that ever since.

The saving habit

The end of 1938, December, beginning of 1939. I eventually got a job, at Barking, in Barking Creek, and I walked all the way there, six or seven miles, morning and night. My pay was 10s 4d per week. I gave my mum nine shillings and I had 1s 4d and I never knew what to do with all this money, so I decided to go to the Post Office, and got from them a white form that you could put penny stamps on. When you had filled up those twelve boxes, that was a shilling, or five pence nowadays, they gave you a proper savings book. Whenever you filled up one of those they transferred it. And that's what put me on the road to saving. I saved tuppence a week.

Finding a way through the system

And I saw that there was some houses being built private. And £1856, superb. And when I went and asked about it he said, 'Oh no, you've got to have a building licence'. And so I said, 'What's that?' And he said, 'Well nobody can sell a house unless you've got a building licence. Go and see the council.' So I saw the council and I got Pooh poohed, so, my wife said, 'Go and see Mrs. Jones', whom I think she worked with, big woman, and we'd had a baby by now, lost him, he had a heart attack at 5 months old. And she knew of the case because there was lots in the paper and she said, 'You in the army?' I said, 'Vauxhall Regiment'. She said, 'Oh well, we'd better do something about that.' And she said, 'I've got one licence left', she said, 'I'm not going to make you any promises, but I'll do me best for you.' Blow me down, I got it. So I went on to the builder, and I said, 'I've got me licence'. He said, 'Right, I'll give you £200 for it.' Cor . . . £200 in those days, you know, and I said, 'No . . . In any case I'll have to ask me wife, but no, I don't think so.' So I went over to me wife, and me father and mother said, 'Go on, take the money! You don't want to have this hanging over you.' And her father said, 'Yeah! I know someone at work who is buying a house, forty years of jam sandwiches', he said. He didn't say that everybody else was having jam sandwiches. But, anyway, to cut a long story short, I said, 'No, let's go ahead!' So I said, 'OK, we'll have the house.' £1856 and ten shillings, freehold. Built properly, no cardboard walls, or anything like that, you know. Brickwork everywhere, bedrooms, the lot. It was absolutely marvellous, it was. And I was then working for Fords, and my money jumped right up then to £12 something a week, and I was in the money.

Domestic relations

Oh no, she wasn't working no. I was very, very lucky. I had definitely got a wife in ten million. She was absolutely fantastic at budgeting. And a lot of our money went on the mortgage repayments. We had no furniture, you see, when we bought a house we had no furniture. Well, we had a bed, three-piece suite, a small dining table, half the size of your desk, two wooden upright chairs, that was it. So we got the house, and she said, 'No, what we've got to do is to pay the mortgage.' So I said, 'Well I don't want it to go to twenty years.' I said, 'What I'll do, I think, I'll pay a bit more.' So I started off paying ten pounds a month, and put it up to twelve pounds ten, and what I used to do, we saved money every week.

A defiant consumer

We'd go out and see what we wanted. Go to the shop, Times Furnishing, and tell them we wanted a bedroom suite. They said 'Payments?' I said, 'Oh no, I want to pay cash.' They said, 'Have you got the cash?' I said, 'No, but I'm going to save for it.' They said, 'Oh well, you can have it.' I said, 'No, I want to save for it and I want to pay for it in cash.' They said, 'Well what are you going to do?' I said, 'Well, I've got a bed, I can sleep on a bed.' Anyway, that's how we got all our home. We saved for it, and when we had the money we paid cash. And see, that hire purchase, nowadays it's all credit cards, isn't it? You know . . . I think credit cards are terrible, terrible. I'm against it meself, I've got a one track mind I suppose.

Ralph tells a coherent story which, for him, is about progress: his early experiences fit his later attitudes, everything is leading somewhere, to their present state of comfort and security. This story is also a way of differentiating himself from others, first from his family when a child, as he sets out determinedly on a different path, then from modern consumer culture, with its emphasis on credit and having things now, while he saves, single-mindedly. His story is peopled with those who try to deter him from his chosen path, and each time he overcomes them. His connected self is experienced only in relation to his wife, as a cohesive unit they face the world and get what they want from it. Emotional and financial investment in objects go hand in hand to construct an identity.

Ellen, also in her 60s, tells a very different story, although the consistencies, from upbringing to adulthood, from one problem solved to the next, from the tight linkage between consumption and identity, desires and practice, are also present.

A background of financial stress

From the time I can remember, there were always rows about money, because father had been brought up in a very poor and disciplined way, so there was this clash with my mother who was extravagant . . . in the thirties he only allowed her three pounds a week housekeeping money, so frequently things disappeared from the house to the pawn shop round the corner, I remember going down there . . . there was a kind of tension about the whole set-up.

Domestic relations

Ellen worked variously as a maid, waitress and shop assistant. She started living with a man who drank, while working as a charlady in exchange for their room:

I then got involved with um, I hadn't been married, so really he was my first partner and we moved down to England to the Channel Islands, where he drank all the time and I used to work in fields picking up potatoes and also I worked as a charlady there in exchange for a room. There'd be quite a long time, nearly 7 years, that we were together in various places, frequently homeless, and living I don't quite know how.

Living on goodwill

It was desperate, I know what it's like to be in poverty, scratching around for food, by then I had three children, it was a bit of a juggle . . . I didn't work at all during that time, it was a kind of um I think it was getting into debt, living on the goodwill of the people, borrowing money, not paying back, and moving on and this continuing. And for a time he did have a job, he had two jobs in the end over the time I knew him, but unfortunately they paid him monthly, so um, there was a lost weekend, and then another month of scratching . . . they were always fed somehow, they're probably healthier for it, I know there were problems like with the NSPCC, I mean they would get on the trail when they saw children walking about without shoes on, so that was something I'd have to fend off.

The costs of independence regained

When I left, I couldn't cope any more so I left, they [the children] would go to a kind of morning thing run by nuns, then they went to school.

Ellen got the children into a Catholic boarding school where she paid what she could by working in a shop in London.

We'd be ever so brave, living by day . . . it was awful [the children being in school], I felt torn in half, anyway I could get them back, then I did have a chance to get them back.

A way of life

She took them to stay with a friend in Devon, where she worked in the dairy making butter and worked as a cinema usherette in the evening, this way making enough money:

Eventually that fell through, so had to find somewhere else, so then we found a house in [another town] . . . we went there with our usual carrier bags, everything in carrier bags, and I got a factory job there . . . I gradually got into debt there . . . gradually the debts were mounting up and I was sinking under it, so um I had a job in [another town] while the eldest girl had a scholarship and the others went back temporarily to the convent, and then I moved to where I had friends on a caravan site and my father said he would help out and I got a job locally in a factory.

The story continues with another child, another man, another job, a council house.

A way of managing

I was just always in debt, years of being in debt . . . [budgeting] I worked it out on paper, but then I suddenly blew what I'd got, I'm not very good at keeping a steady budget . . . when you're living next to the knuckle, it's much better to go and blow the money while you've got it, it is . . . I'd buy a dress I couldn't afford, I remember once I bought a hat, I don't wear hats, it was like a chamberpot, and they cost the earth, but I felt OK, you know, a hat, something useless, totally useless . . . it would give me a thrill.

A life of hoping

I look back on my life as one long fear of somebody coming knocking on the door, forever hiding . . . you go somewhere new, thinking you're going to start again, took me a long time to begin to grow up, I always thought things would turn out all right, I think if you don't think that you either change your life or collapse . . . what bit of credit I got I wasn't very good with, because that wasn't the only one I ran up, I ran up another bill somewhere else, several bills would lie around unpaid, it was a bit rough . . . if you could get the credit, it was great.

Ellen's moral is that you have to carry on hoping, doing your best, while Ralph's is that life is what you make it. For Ralph, an unstable and stressful background was the reason for differentiating himself, establishing alternative motives, while for Ellen, a not dissimilar background set a theme for her life, for like her mother, she found ways to get what she wanted, though credit had replaced the pawn shop. Ralph seems to carry from his childhood a sense of life being against him, so he must battle to carve out his life, while for Ellen, life is slippery, her desires always slipping away from her while she battles, with lapses, to stand still.

Finally, we consider the life story of Ann, who is in her early 30s, and is from a working-class background with few qualifications. During and after her brief marriage, her major ambition, and her major achievement, has been to buy and own her own home. For the sake of this possession, she has dedicated much energy and ingenuity, for she has managed to buy a pleasant three-bedroomed house while unemployed, and with little or no income except that obtained through letting rooms to between two and six people at a time. She exemplifies the motivating force of the desire to own, defying the normative expectations and economic constraints which usually apply to people in her social position. She bought her first house when she was not working and was living with her partner, an overseas student.

A difficult start

I couldn't sign on, I stupidly told them I was married, so they wouldn't let me sign on, which was a shame, because he couldn't get a grant. That was quite difficult then, we had to borrow off my friends. He borrowed mostly off his family. We decided it's cheaper to get our own house than rent, so we borrowed off my family as well. And then I was working again, and then I couldn't continue working because I hurt my feet.

A solution

I was about to sell the house and then suddenly hit on the idea of letting some rooms and sleeping in the scullery. So that's what we did. A three-bedroomed house, let the bedrooms, lounge, and we slept in the scullery, and we could pay the mortgage, so it was OK. We lived in the scullery, it was a bit small, there was a one foot gap round the side of the bed, it was OK, we managed, I mean, I don't care, I've got a house now, a few years of roughing it. It was quite scary, but I was just determined that I would keep the house. There were different lodgers at different times, that was essential that they stayed, because obviously signing on doesn't pay the mortgage.

On her own: Getting ambitious

When we split up, I figured the house was more mine than his, and he agreed. Then I moved house, and had to extend the mortgage to move here, because it's quite big, and I've had an extension put on there, it's only just finished. I couldn't stand the fact that the kitchen was the only place you could see the garden from, and I refused to be a housewife who stayed in the kitchen, so I needed, psychologically I needed the space where I could see the garden. It was 1979 when I first had a mortgage, and my first house was £14,500 . . . No it's [the present mortgage] is not that big, I think it's in the region of £25,000, which isn't that big, by some people's standards, I had to get an extra £10,000 when I moved here.

Relaxing into a pattern

I thought that in order to keep my mortgage I would have to have a job, and so I tried every single thing that was going, one day I walked into every single shop in the High Street seeing if they had vacancies . . . and I didn't get a job. I didn't lose the mortgage, and as time went on, I thought, well, that seem's alright then, so the pressure is off. I don't ask too many questions, I never defaulted on the payments, so it's OK, and then I got a loan for the extension as well, I got another £10,000 to do that. I sort of said there were people staying here, and rather enlarged the number there were and the amount they paid, and they didn't ask any more questions. They said they didn't really want to know that I was paying it just through people being here . . .

Certainly, many other conclusions can be drawn from all these biographies. But it is also important to frame these within the context of family, gender and culture, as we now discuss.

The domestic environment and the dynamics of the family

Home ownership and state suburbanization have opened up a new lifestyle based on family possession of consumer durables (McDowell, 1983, p.157).

The family is more than the sum of its individual members, for dynamic properties emerge from the interaction between members. Family dynamics are expressed and managed through shared goals, family myths, rules and routines, conflicts and tensions, and each family develops frameworks for explaining and understanding the events which impinge on it or occur within it (Byng-Hall, 1978; Reiss, 1981; Olson et al., 1983). The family, then, provides a powerful context for the consumption desires, decisions and practices of its members as well as being itself a consumer, in the form of 'the household' or 'a joint decision' and, most particularly, as the site of 'home'.

Families cannot talk of their domestic goods without revealing their family dynamics, personal identities and gender relations. Talking about the television or telephone, for example, is imbued with notions of who lets who use what, of moral judgements of the other's activities, of needs and desires, of justification and conflict, separateness or mutuality. Similarly, families cannot talk of their lives together without talking about their ideas of home, their material origins and aspirations, and the possessions they own. Cohler and Grunebaum (1981) identify eight dimensions of family organization, each of which may undergo negotiation or contestation by its members. Each relates to the relations experienced between people and personal or domestic objects as well as the relations between people, as exemplified below.

1 *The definition of family boundaries.* How far a family extends itself beyond or differs from the nuclear unit will be marked by the patterns of gift-giving among relatives and friends. Which areas of the house are public (the parlour, the kitchen) and which private spaces – what can be seen by whom? Goods may be public (borrowed from libraries or friends or community centres) or uniquely owned.

2 *The establishment of role boundaries within the family.* Are goods owned in common or specific to one (group of) individual(s)? Use of new technologies (e.g. personal computer) may be used to mark generational differences (e.g. used by children) or gender differences (e.g. used by men/boys). Are children's toys all over the house or put away in bedrooms, is everything done in the kitchen or are tools in the garage, sewing in the bedroom and homework put away?

3 *Locus of family operations.* Key objects may be the telephone and the car, facilitating connection with social networks or community events, or they may be the television and video, symbolizing closing the door on outside hassles and relaxing in private.

4 *Closeness and separation.* Does everyone have their own radio or even television, or do family members cluster together in the living room? Are personal stereos an expression of autonomy and difference or withdrawal and rejection? Cohesion and dispersal, with their more extreme forms – enmeshing and disengagement – represent the key family dynamic (although see discussion of gender, below) identified by many researchers (Reiss, 1981; Olson *et al.*, 1983) which parallels on an interpersonal level the intrapsychic dynamic between similarity and differentiation when construing the self in relation to others (Csikszentmihalyi and Rochberg-Halton, 1981).

5 *Definition of unacceptable behaviour and basis for sanctions.* Is cleanliness next to godliness, with no feet on the white sofa, or are goods chosen for comfort and ease? If the toddler throws food on the floor, is she desecrating the home or expressing independence or just playing? Do 'we' keep things tidy and nice because 'the neighbours might see', because 'I said so' or because 'it's the right thing to do'?

6 *Expression and control of affect and impulses.* Are objects used to express affection or aggression? Do clothes express sexuality? Are possessions freely lent or kept apart?

7 *Establishment of family identity and goals.* Is the house kept just like the parents' parents kept theirs? Do Christmas gifts and meals perpetuate family traditions? Who has a secret drawer or locked cupboard for private mementos?

8 *Family problem-solving techniques.* Are presents used as bribes or rewards for good behaviour? Are goods withheld or withdrawn for bad behaviour? Does the family have a council around the kitchen table, or bang doors and retreat to bedrooms during conflict? Are children allowed to grow up and spend their own money, wear make-up and ride a motorbike, or do parents want to keep things like they used to be?

From interviewing families about their domestic use of information and communication technologies (Livingstone, 1988, in press), one of the authors contrasted two families in terms of family dynamics, one cohesive or enmeshed and one dispersed or disengaged. So brief a summary can inevitably offer only a crude characterization of a relationship, but none the less can illustrate how family dynamics provide a powerful context for the use of objects in the home.

The cohesive family (Dole) have three of their own children, one adopted, several fostered and, in addition, Christine is a child minder. The children provide the central focus for the family. Daniel wishes he could give up his job to stay at home and join her to look after the foster children, their 'real work'. He enthuses about the children, their needs and progress, the rules and resources they have developed to cope, to maintain boundaries, to escape chaos. Christine and Daniel share many concerns, they are deeply involved in the fostering, they talk of each technology in similar rather than contrasting ways, their talk is of 'we' not 'I'. Unlike many women, Christine is not especially fond of the telephone, for her orientation is inwards, towards the close relations within the home, rather than outwards towards a social or kin network (an other-orientation often motivated by isolation and loneliness). Furthermore, the fostering provides a dominant meaning for the telephone – as work, as child-oriented, as problem-raising/solving – for most calls are to social workers/support groups, etc. Christine says: 'I don't actually use it [telephone] to chat on but I use it to arrange things on. You know, if I want to talk to somebody, I'll phone them up and ask when we can get together.' Daniel explains how bedrooms, playrooms, toys and televisions are assigned to different categories of children (own, fostered, child-minded): 'How she and I look at it . . . all kids need to have their boundaries . . . regimented, sounds boring, but it works, for adults too . . . makes existence a lot easier.'

Their use of the television symbolizes the sharing, cohesive nature of family relations, as they see and value it, to the extent that Daniel happily watches traditionally 'female' genres such as soaps:

Normally we'd either be all in the front room, together as a family, at the end of the day, the one time when certainly the two older ones [their own children] would be with Mum and Dad, tidying up the loose ends as to what had happened at school and what was going to happen tomorrow . . . On the telly we'd be more likely to watch a documentary type factual piece of information . . . particularly if about children, the social side of things, which for the last 8 years as foster parents we have obviously been very involved in. So all that sort of thing is of great interest to both of us, great interest, it's no hard work listening to at all . . . she goes for the soaps more, that's not to say I'll walk out of the room when *Coronation Street* is on. If they're on, and I'm in the room, then I'm just as likely to sit down and see what's going on (Christine confirms this view).

Shirley and Mark live very different lives, as a relatively disengaged couple (Lyon; Livingstone, in press). She describes them as being 'like ships in the night', for they rarely see each other. Mark regularly works late and even when he returns, he goes out to jog many miles each evening. Shirley works full-time and manages the house and children. Their views of their technologies are quite different, they talk of 'I' not 'we', the children joke about hardly ever seeing their father. As for many working women, within the family her money is not her own (Pahl, 1989), for her great desire, for the music which allows her peace of mind, is unnoticed by him:

Everyone else has one [walkman] except me. I want one . . . As I can afford it, that's what I'm going to buy [cassette player] . . . if I had my own, I'd be using it all the time . . . I like music, I need it . . . a relief . . . very relaxing, keeps me sane . . . can't afford it, low on the list of priorities.

Mark sees things differently, planning to buy a better stereo, though feeling generally, unlike Shirley, that television is better, 'more real', than music tech-nologies. The cassette player thus symbolizes both Mark's ignorance of Shirley's desires and also her isolation which creates the desire, an isolation which itself results not only from their difficult work schedules but also from the dispersal of the family, each with their own personal stereo. Partly as a consequence, Shirley locates her pleasures, self-worth and identity outside the home altogether, talking enthusiastically about her work, their appreciation of her, and her promotion prospects.

Objects as symbols of power in gender relations

The theme of gender has surfaced several times already in this chapter, for it pervades discussion of the intrapsychic, biographical and familial relations between people and objects. Bem (1991) argues that gender is the most funda-mental and ubiquitous theme organizing everyday understanding and practice. Many would agree with Pahl (1989, p.170) that 'inequality in the wider society meshes with inequality within the household'. Studies of the family introduce a focus on dynamic processes and emergent properties often lacking from studies of the household, but they frequently neglect the impact and reproduction of social inequalities within the family (Williams and Watson, 1988). Talking to men and women about the goods they own continually throws up issues of gender, in terms of gender identity, masculine and feminine ideals, role expectations and conflicts, power inequality and ideology. Much is revealed by different patterns of construing the world (Table 4.6), for as Bem (1991) argues, ideology, culture and practical experiences of inequality combine to produce different 'lenses' through which men and women view the world. This is also

Table 4.6 Constructs for representing domestic objects, by gender[a]

General construct	Exemplars	Opposites	Typically used by women/men
Necessity	Lifeline, would miss it, important, use a lot, essential	Luxury, manage without, rarely use	Women
Control	Control over, in control	Not in control, chaos	Women
	Stimulating, achievement, challenging	Passive, unrewarding	Men
Functionality	Functional, utilitarian, a tool, technical	No point, no role	Men
	Convenience, makes things easier	Hassle, tension	Women
Sociality	Company, when on my own	Social contact	Men
	Sociable, lifeline, connectedness	Privacy, isolation, loneliness	Women

[a] Based on personal construct interviews with 16 families talking about their domestic information and communication technologies (see Livingstone, in press).

true of social class, as Bourdieu argued in *Distinction* (1984). For Bourdieu, meanings of goods, popularly claimed to be aesthetic, functional or a matter of taste, are instead constructed by different class positions, each with a taste culture reflecting and reproducing the social class of those who belong to it. Dittmar (1991) shows how working-class people more often talk of the pragmatic and instrumental functions of objects, while middle-class people talk in more symbolic terms about objects as self-extension.

In interviews conducted by Livingstone (in press), women were more often concerned about things being necessities or luxuries, where necessities were required either for domestic tasks or for retaining a sense of self, while luxuries were often unobtainable desires. As women are generally responsible for housework (Oakley, 1974; Henwood *et al.*, 1987), their home is full of necessities, while for men, for whom the work/leisure distinction is clearer and maps onto that of work/home (Morley, 1986), home contains entertainment and relaxation.

> Lifesaving, dear, lifesaving, particularly that [washing machine] comes first, followed by that [tumble drier], followed by the telephone. Stereo record player comes next. Without them I couldn't survive. They are my lifelines (Shirley Lyon).

Women and men both talked of control, but while women were more concerned in using goods to impose control on the potential chaos, thus focusing on the washing machine or tumble drier, men talked in terms of the potential rewards and challenges offered by using objects to exercise control or power or skill, talking of the stimulation and achievement experienced when using the home computer or electric drill:

> I like the video because it gives you control over when you watch things (Gloria De Guy).

> [I use the computer] when I want to be a bit more active than just sitting down and watching, but actually want to do something a bit more... stimulating (Daniel Dole).

Domestic technologies may facilitate interaction between people or they may provide a substitute, a social interaction between person and object. In general, men talked of using technologies as a substitute for social contact, their key technologies being the radio, personal stereo and television. For women, technologies were valued for facilitating actual social contact (Moyal, 1990), and so the telephone and the car were vital, though in so far as they created spare time, the microwave and dishwasher were similarly valued.

> It's [telephone] a connection to other people, other worlds, prevents me from being isolated. And if you can't get to see people, you can chat to them. So I enjoy the fact that it's there, to be in contact with people (Lynn Irving).

Men emphasized the 'purely functional' meaning of objects, focusing less on the role of the object in their lives and more on its inherent properties:

That's functional [the telephone] . . . for example, I ring my brother if I want to ask him if I can borrow his sledgehammer . . . I don't really want to know what he did yesterday and I don't tell him what I did yesterday . . . as I say, it's purely functional (Paul De Guy).

In contrast, women were concerned with the utility of objects in relation to how they allowed them to function in their everyday lives. This more contextual meaning meant they tended to refer outwards to domestic practices when justifying object use rather than identifying its technical, economic or aesthetic features.

Such patterns of accounting – whether meanings of goods are seen as located within one's life or within the object itself – have consequences for the negotiation of the value of goods in the household, with implications for purchase and use. Men gain a sense of inevitability or naturalness for their valued goods which coincides with the dominant marketing strategy of advertisers (it's the latest, greatest and most comprehensive), whereas women have to justify why their particular circumstances warrant a new purchase (it would stop the rows between the girls if each had a television, or, given that you come home later than the children, a microwave would warm up your dinner).

Such accounting differences also allow men to more easily disguise, or not recognize, psychological reasons for product use – does one man really prefer television to radio because the combination of audio and visual channels is 'obviously' more relaxing or is it that it allows him to take the dominant role in the living room and not cook dinner with the radio in the kitchen? It can't be so obvious that audio and visual channels are better, because another man finds the absence of a visual channel on his stereo more relaxing. Or is it rather that he cannot hear the telephone or the demands of his children when he puts on the headphones?

The expression of gender relations is far from homogeneous; rather, it depends on factors as varied as family tradition, occupational status and personal desires. We end by considering two women talking about the objects in their homes (taken from Livingstone, 1988). The interviews with each are summarized below.

Gina

Social circumstances

Gina is around 30 years old, as is her husband. She runs a small dress hire business from her home and cares for her four children. Bob is a car sales executive for a prestigious company, and the family is rising in social status and income very fast, bringing them from working class to fairly well-off home owners in a comfortable London suburb. They own three televisions (two colour), three radios (two walkmans), a video-recorder, an Amstrad computer, hi-fi unit, compact disc player, two telephones and answering machine, a range of white goods in the kitchen and computerized toys.

A sense of powerlessness

Gina habitually uses a discourse of powerlessness – she dislikes the radio which she feels she cannot turn down in volume (it later emerges that she sees this as her husband's technology), she 'suffers' in the living room as others decide what to see on TV, she regards the telephone as 'a lifeline' to retain her sanity, she uses the microwave 'in desperation', she claims to subordinate her needs to those of her husband.

Regaining control

While she feels she cannot turn the technologies on and off (this is the domain of other people's power), she talks of turning herself off or on to the technologies (and, implicitly, to associated members of the family), thereby regaining control. Further, observations of her daily life suggest she is something of a matriarchal figure, surrounded by supportive female relatives and friends who create an environment in which the children are firmly controlled, Bob is ordered about and treated as a spare part, and Gina talks extensively on the phone thus drowning the TV programmes she had not chosen, etc. Her discourse of powerlessness, far from describing her role in the family, serves instead to mystify the nature and extent of her control (and to preserve her feminine self-image).

Gender and status

Possession was a key construct for Gina, and she assigned people to goods thus: home computer (Gina), colour TV in main room (Gina and children), colour TV in second room (Gina), black and white TV (son), radio (Bob). This shows a clear alignment of the status of the technologies with gender: she appropriates the high-status technologies. Although Bob is associated with certain status technologies (hi-fi, video), he is prevented from the opportunities to use them or uses them outside the home (portable phone, compact disc player).

Brenda

Social circumstances

Brenda's family is also working class made good. They have moved to a prosperous part of Surrey where they feel awkward and out of place. In their early 40s with four children, they are firm supporters of Margaret Thatcher, and committed to private ownership, spending money mainly on their house, proud that the children have never needed to use a train, distanced from the neighbourhood around them. She runs a part-time clothes-selling business, he is an electrician. They own four televisions, two videos, one computer, five radios, a stereo and a telephone.

Past and present self

Brenda's life is centrally organized around the contrast between her ideal, now past self, dating from before her four children and her mundane, frustrated present self. Her ideals are low-tech (her romantic novels, her Elvis Presley records) and she enjoys them as enveloping sensations, cocooning her in a private world. Life before technology maps onto life before children. Her present is ironing, cooking, caring for children and, far from providing concentrated escapist activities, goods function simply to make her present more tolerable, providing a secondary, though frustratingly interrupted, activity. For her the video is not masculine (Gray, 1987), she was the first to learn to work it as an essential for entertaining her hyperactive son, although unlike Gina, who is learning the computer for her work, Brenda experiences the computer as masculine, external, a reason to regret her mindless, domestic life (blamed on the children).

Waiting to be authentic again

She longs for time alone with her husband, for them to talk, yet feels him to be 'welded to the TV', she feels tied by her children, especially as the two younger ones were a mistake. She is waiting: 'How old will I be before I can be a person again?' The family is disparate, for her children do not get on together and they use technologies to allow them to avoid each other: for example, all six of them watch *Neighbours*, but none watches together, using either different televisions, the video, or watching different broadcasts. Further, they do not discuss what they have seen.

Material goods and cultural meanings

> Practical mastery of classification [concerns] the sense of social realities that is . . . what makes it possible to act *as if* one knew the structure of the social world, one's place within it and the distances that need to be kept (Bourdieu, 1984, p.472).

Processes of appropriation and negotiation are themselves constitutive of everyday culture: 'consumption is the very arena in which culture is fought over and licked into shape' (Douglas and Isherwood, 1978, p.57). This process of negotiation is one in which the consumer transforms or appropriates the mass-produced object. They do not necessarily take on the meanings which are publicly associated with the object but work symbolically on the object meaning, bringing objects into the home and under control, giving them local meanings, translating 'the object from an alienable to an inalienable condition' (Miller, 1987, p.190).

This process of translation is constitutive of the culture, and, in a circular fashion, it is this 'more general construction of cultural milieux which gives such objects their social meaning' (Miller, 1987, p.191). Miller (1990) argues that through such processes we also construct the domestic, the home, the private realm, and ourselves as private, domesticated individuals. Kamptner's various categories of object meanings or of ways in which self and object are related capture these processes of meaning construction, showing the ways in which people can work on objects to create social and personal meanings, for consumption work 'may signify the time of possession, a particular context of presentation as ritual gift or memorabilia, or the incorporation of the single object into a stylistic array which is used to express the creator's place in relation to peers engaged in similar activities' (Miller, 1987, p.191). As a consequence of consumption work, consumption cannot simply be reduced to the nature of the commodity and the consumer is more than simply the process by which the commodity is obtained (Miller, 1987). Rather, through the combination of intrapsychic, biographical, family, gender and cultural forces, a person-object relation is negotiated which in turn gives rise to identities, understandings and everyday practices.

FIVE | SHOPPING, SPENDING AND PLEASURE

The meaning of shopping

> Shopping is no longer just the mundane act of going out and buying a product
> ... retailing has been imbued with a whole new ethos, a new significance,
> a new cultural meaning – and commodities themselves seem to have taken
> on a new central role in people's lives (Gardner and Sheppard, 1989, p.43).

Going out to shop is a conspicuous moment in consumption. People leave the
privacy of their homes to enter the public domain of retail. Shopping is a social
activity which links the world of production and marketing to the world of
ownership and possession. It is a highly public moment in the circulation of
goods. When people express their preferences at the point of sale, this is a
moment of public expression of consumption. The shop is the site where the
personal forces of need and desire meet the social forces of provision and
display. The person comes to the shop with acquisitive desire tempered by
notions of personal control and economy and the marketer aims to persuade, to
seduce the person to become involved in the world of buying.

Shopping can be understood through a series of oppositions: from decision
making to pleasure, from utility to involvement and desire, from individual
resource to social environment. Shopping is not just about the provision of
goods and information for the consumer, involving marketing goods in terms of
qualities which satisfy particular needs, for the shopper is seduced, also through
marketing, into an activity which involves a loss of individual control and the
construction of a cultural experience. In this chapter we begin by looking at the
tradition of consumer research, based on the decision-making approach, and,

through an analysis of people's approach to and experiences of shopping, move on to a more social and cultural understanding of shopping.

Consumer research: The shopper as decision maker

We used to keep a stock cupboard or shelf of a few extra necessities in case we have unexpected visitors or something, so we always have something to fall back upon. I think that people tend to do that, although they put things in the fridge now and keep them for a few weeks rather than on the back shelf with the dryer. But it is the same sort of principle.

But you don't need to do it so much now, because the local shops open longer.

Not if you live in a village. There are less shopping facilities in the village. We used to have two general stores, a butcher and a shoe shop, when we moved there 20 years ago. There is now one general store and that doesn't stay open for long hours, either.

The quantity and variety of research on consumer behaviour is enormous. It 'deals largely with the processes that underlie the decision to purchase or use economic goods and services' (Fishbein and Ajzen, 1975, p.149). Consumer research focuses primarily on consumer perceptions, assuming that objective assessments of price and quality are mediated by the consumer's perceptions of goods and services, and that it is these perceptions which provide the grounds for purchasing decisions (Friedman and Zimmer, 1988). People make different decisions and there are different kinds of decisions to be made. Consumer research regards the shopper as a problem solver: the individual has various needs which can be satisfied by material possessions and shopping is the means by which the goods which will satisfy these needs are obtained. The problem to be solved is represented as a series of decisions – what to buy, where to buy it and how much to spend on it, and the solution is a particular purchase.[1]

One of the first problems the shopper has to answer is which shop? The rational model suggests that the predictive factors will be prices and travel costs plus some index of time involved in purchase. Shoppers are seen as primarily interested in getting value for money, based on their understanding of the relation between price and quality. In accordance with the rational model, people with higher incomes invest less time in shopping, while those with less resources invest more time in bargain hunting (which would cost more in time costs for the wealthier consumer). Goldman (1977) termed this trade-off the 'economy of information'. Under this formulation, by offering services and added value to relatively wealthy customers, retailers can mark up the price of their products.

What information do people need about products? The retailer can add to the cost of finding out about relative prices by moving special offers around the product range, keeping prices of staple goods low and increasing product uniqueness (often through own brands), so that direct comparisons are difficult.

There are a number of cultural influences on purchasing decisions, mediated through the judgement of value. For example, there are sociocultural variations in 'good value' in furniture (buying furniture depends not only on subjective calculations of price and effort but also on cultural judgements of taste: Bourdieu 1984), and those on lower incomes are more knowledgeable about the prices of meat (reflecting rational decision making and allocation of resources: Goldman, 1977).

How do consumers estimate distances when shopping? People decide where to shop on the basis of their perceptions of the distance to be travelled, creating a problem for retailers, who use objective measures of distance to choose locations for shops. Generally, people overestimate the distances involved, although this depends on direction, familiarity and point of origin of the journey (Coshall, 1985). Unfortunately, consumer research rarely considers the consumer as a member of a particular social group, class or cultural background, and so such factors are not used to improve our understanding of the relation between actual and perceived distance.

Once the person has made the decision of where to shop, what decisions do they then have to make? Research in supermarkets shows that more goods are bought if they are displayed at eye level, that heavy goods are bought more if displayed at floor level, and that the recall of location of goods is best for peripheral aisles. Moles (1972) suggests that an ideal layout of goods would be according to categories in semantic memory. Again, this assumes that consumers can be treated as making the same, cognitively based, consumption decisions. Even research on the ways in which attitudes influence shopping decisions is very much in the tradition of decision-making research (Fishbein and Ajzen, 1975), suggesting that people are likely to buy something if they decide that on balance it will have value for them and that their peers will approve of them buying it.

Criticisms of consumer research

Consumer research focuses on the here and now of shopping, neglecting, for example, whether people are satisfied when they return home and whether they complain (Lea et al., 1987). Framed within an information-processing paradigm, it presumes that people are in control of their choices, neglecting impulse buying and treating shopping as a 'cold' rather than a 'hot', involved activity. The focus on the point of sale distinguishes between repeat purchases of everyday produce – seen as habits rather than choices and as concerning necessities rather than luxuries, and the more novel buying of consumer durables – which depends on decision making, problem solving, choice and luxury (Katona, 1975; Lea et al., 1987). There are many methodological problems in assessing quality, value and price on the one hand, and in characterizing ordinary people's perceptions of quality, value and price on the other (Zeithami, 1988). The predominant use of focus groups in consumer research tends to result in a celebration of the right of the individual to see things his or her way and act accordingly. Changes in the marketing and technology of retailing in recent years have brought many distinctions employed by market researchers into question, for the emphasis on individual differences misses out the implications of changing social and cultural conditions of what is essentially a social activity, and construes needs as individual rather than social, influenced by advertising, social norms and peer activities. We must address not just the cognitive issues of people making choices over which environment to shop in and for what, but also the issue of involvement in different environments (in terms of emotions, self-presentation, management of interactions) and, indeed, whether the consumer can gain a form of social participation through being a consumer, exercising consumer rights, participating in a valued leisure culture.

Shoppers' involvement, motivation and consumption style

Shopper profiles

Can we characterize consumers in terms of shopping styles? (Oumlil, 1983). Certainly, shoppers vary in how involved they get in shopping (Martineau, 1952). This involvement is affected by various personal and social motives (Tauber, 1972).[2] Personal motives include diversion from daily routine, self-gratification (expected utility of purchase), keeping up-to-date with new products, shopping as physical exercise, shopping as sensory stimulation (looking, touching, smelling). Social motives include social encounters, communicating with like-minded people, and pleasure in bargaining. Such work on individual differences in shopping treats shopping within the problem-solving tradition as a motivated behaviour under a variety of personal and social influences. Shoppers can then be characterized according to these various motivations to shop.

For example, Stone (1954) segmented shoppers into the following types: the economic consumer, who regards shopping as buying and is oriented to efficiency, making judgements according to objective standards of price, quality and assortment of goods rather than service; the personalizing consumer, who was most concerned with social interaction in shops; the ethical consumer, who was motivated by duty, shopping in small shops to help out the local trader; and the apathetic consumer, who dislikes shopping, finds no satisfaction in relations with staff and only shops out of necessity, being primarily concerned with convenience and minimum effort.[3]

Classifying people into shopper types

Part of our questionnaire was concerned with the experience of shopping. We asked people whether they enjoyed shopping for food, clothes, presents or furniture, whether they enjoyed shopping with other people, whether they hunted for bargains, whether they shopped in a few favourite shops, whether they waited for the sales to buy expensive consumer durables, whether they reward or bribe themselves or others by buying something, how they feel on buying something expensive, whether they tend to buy on impulse, and whether they use the second-hand market. The questions covered four main areas of shopping experience: pleasure in shopping, use of economy strategies in shopping, use of shopping to reward/bribe self or others, and use of the alternative/second-hand market. We then grouped respondents into subgroups according to their answers.[4] The resultant five shopping groups can be described as follows:

1 *Alternative shoppers (12 per cent of sample).* These people are not especially economical when shopping, neither shopping around nor waiting for the sales, although they do not often buy on impulse. They use the alternative market, buying second-hand books, clothes, and attending jumble sales. Generally, they find little or no pleasure in shopping, and do not buy presents to reward themselves or others. They seem to stand outside the pressures and pleasures of modern consumerism, not seeing shopping as leisure, not expecting things to be new, nor playing the game of bargain-hunting.

2 *Routine shoppers (31 per cent of sample).* These people are not particularly economical when shopping, neither shopping around nor waiting for the sales. They rarely buy on impulse and do not use the alternative market, except occasionally the 'for sale' columns of the newspapers. They find little or no pleasure in shopping and do not use goods for rewards, promises or bribes. They appear to shop on the high street whenever they need something, but seem disengaged from modern consumerism.

3 *Leisure shoppers (24 per cent of sample).* These people find shopping pleasurable. They are very likely to buy goods to reward themselves or others. They are neutral about the alternative market or else avoid it. Regarding economy, they are not especially economical, for they often buy things on impulse, not especially shopping in favourite shops, sometimes but not always shopping around for a bargain, sometimes waiting for the sales for expensive items. They come closest to the stereotype of modern consumerism ('I shop therefore I am'), enjoying a range of shopping experiences, enjoying window shopping and happy to spend time shopping, using objects for social functions, wanting things to be new, and not trying to spend particularly economically.

4 *Careful shoppers (15 per cent of sample).* These people find shopping fairly pleasurable, enjoying shopping for clothes, presents and furniture a little less than shopping for food, window shopping and shopping with their family. They do not buy goods for social functions. They avoid the alternative market but are moderately economical in their shopping habits, tending both to shop around for the best buy or bargain and to shop in a few favourite shops, and generally avoiding impulse buys and sometimes waiting for the sales. They seem to be careful shoppers, enjoying the activity of consumption more than the selection of products, liking things to be new, but not becoming involved to the extent of buying goods as a reward or bribe.

5 *Thrifty shoppers (18 per cent of sample).* These people find some pleasure in shopping, especially enjoying shopping for clothes, food, presents and shopping with the family, compared to window shopping or shopping for furniture. They tend not to buy goods for rewards, although sometimes they do

Table 5.1 Demographic information on shopper types

	Alternative	Routine	Leisure	Careful	Thrifty
Sex (% female)	62	49	75	44	82
Age (years)[a]	44	49	38	47	43
Social class					
(% class I and II)	65	56	62	63	52
Home owner (%)	53	69	59	66	69
Personal disposable					
income (£)[a]	4,566	9,101	6,313	9,120	5,220
Household disposable					
income (£)[a]	7,333	14,930	12,068	12,604	9,578
In debt (%)	42	44	51	39	40
Political vote					
(% Conservative)	18	44	29	18	22
No. of credit					
cards[a]	0.8	1.3	1.3	1.3	0.9

[a] Significantly different across groups.

buy goods to persuade themselves or others. They are economical, shopping around for the best buy, waiting for the sales for expensive purchases, not especially shopping in favourite shops or buying on impulse. They use all forms of the alternative market to buy goods. These are thrifty shoppers who are only moderately engaged in consumerism, finding some pleasure in shopping, but economical, not needing things to be new, and not using goods for social functions.

The shopper types above show how everyday economic decisions are bound up with variables traditionally neglected by market research, such as pleasure, social relations, involvement with material goods, engagement in the alternative economy. To use goods as a reward or bribe indicates an engagement in relationships as social exchange. To use the second-hand market often reveals alternative conceptions of clean/dirty, old/new, spending/preserving, indicating an alternative ethic not always dictated by poverty, or, indeed, not always endorsed by those who use the second-hand market for economic reasons. Finally, to enjoy shopping indicates the experience of consumption as leisure, a way of satisfying social as well as material desires, as connected with other leisure activities such as do-it-yourself, a celebration of the domestic space.

Who, then, are these different shoppers? Having found a classification of shoppers in terms of their involvement in shopping, we then related the classification to the other things we knew about the subjects from the questionnaire as a whole.[5] The different types of shoppers must be understood in the context of a range of economic, social and psychological factors (Table 5.1). We found that they differed in their amounts of disposable income, but not in their amount of personal debt, the amounts they save regularly each month or the amount of savings they have.

1 *Alternative shoppers.* This group tends to contain people of higher social class and more education, with lower disposable incomes and average to low savings. They are often single and are less likely to be home owners. They experience more major life events than others and identify stress as the main cause of their financial problems. They tend to be private about money, not telling relatives of their financial situation, rarely even thinking about money. They believe that credit brings problems rather than resolutions and that it is better to save up than have things now. However, they also see credit as useful, a normal part of everyday life, although they themselves are less likely to have credit cards.

They are fatalistic in their beliefs about events in people's lives, feeling that fate or unexpected circumstances often intervene, that people's worth may well go unrecognized and that they don't get the respect they deserve, that they drift along according to old habits and that they do not manage better than their fathers did. They use a variety of coping strategies to deal with these life events and financial problems, saying that they become emotional, rely on others, feel a victim, feel threatened, and try to minimize the problem and to keep calm.

In general, however, they are satisfied with their lives, feeling that the economy and the government are doing well, though they are likely to vote Labour or Green. They would not be disappointed if their standard of living did not improve in the next 5 years.

2 *Routine shoppers.* This group tends to be older than others, with a higher proportion of men, more married, with more children, more education, higher income and savings, and lower expenditure on rent/mortgage payments. They tend to be satisfied with their standard of living and with the state of the economy, and are most likely to vote Conservative. They are private about money, not telling their relatives of their financial situation, rarely arguing about money with friends, rarely even thinking about money. They do not particularly want to buy many things, seeing what they have as necessities rather than luxuries.

Their attitudes are anti-debt, regarding debt as shameful and to be avoided, believing that credit brings problems rather than resolutions and that it is better to save up than have things now. However, in their own lives they have and use credit cards, feeling them to be useful. Attitudes in general and one's own behaviour are opposed here, just as for the alternative shoppers, who were not against credit for others, but used it little themselves. They resist the redefinition of debt as an acceptable and normal part of everyday life, and repay any debts they have at a higher rate. They are fatalistic in their beliefs about events in people's lives, feeling that fate or unexpected circumstances often intervene, that people's worth may well go unrecognized, that they do not get the respect they deserve, and that they do not manage better than their fathers did, although they feel better off than their fathers were at their age, blaming their financial problems on maintaining higher living standards and the demands of children.

3 *Leisure shoppers.* Leisure shoppers tend to be younger and to have fewer or no children. They are more likely to be women, and tend to have lower disposable income than other groups, although, together with their partners', their incomes are average. They spend more on accommodation, have slightly more debts and lesser savings than other groups. However, their being younger and yet having a similar income to older groups, while having fewer children, suggests that they may have relatively more income to spend on leisure and pleasure, although this extra may be taken up by higher mortgage payments than the older groups pay.

Leisure shoppers have an internal locus of control: they generally feel that events in people's lives, including financial events, are under their own control, they think about decisions before taking action, they are confident of carrying out their plans, they feel they manage their finances better than their father, and they know what is in their bank account. However, their attitudes, as is common in younger people, are pro-credit rather than anti-debt. Consistent with their attitudes, they own at least one credit card, want to buy more things, see their possessions as luxuries, and consider it easy for them to get into debt. Any financial problems which result they attribute to enjoying shopping and to maintaining a high standard of living. They do not see money as private or embarrassing, but think about money, argue with friends about money, and tell their relatives of their finances more commonly than do others.

Leisure shoppers have relatively few family demands upon them, although they are disadvantaged by high mortgages. They feel in control in organizing their lives and are fairly satisfied with their standard of living and with the economy, although they run risks regarding debts. They do not feel fatalistic or consider debt shameful, but embrace modern credit and consumer culture – both its pleasures and its costs – with confidence.

4 *Careful shoppers.* This group contains people who are older, more often men, with higher disposable incomes and more savings. If they have debts, they repay more of them than do other groups, reflecting their higher incomes. They do not regard credit as a source of problems, and willingly and frequently use credit cards. In general, however, they are against debt and try to avoid it, seeing it as wrong and shameful. They tend to feel in control of their lives, believing that events in people's lives are under their own control, not drifting along, believing that people get the respect they deserve. However, regarding the lives of others, they also think that things go wrong in people's lives, causing problems, and that there will always be wars no matter what people do.

They are satisfied with their lives, suffering few major life events, feeling themselves better off than their parents were at their age, feeling satisfied with the workings of the government, although they are often Labour voters. They think more about money, and attribute any financial problems they have to maintaining high living standards and to the demands made on them by their children: that which makes them satisfied thus also causes them problems. They also feel the pressures of consumer society, feeling victims of the development of new products and of advertising, and instead placing more value on spiritual matters like love, beauty and wisdom.

5 *Thrifty shoppers.* This group contains many more women, tends to be younger, of a lower social class, lesser education, lower disposable incomes and lower savings. They experience more major life events than others and identify stress as the main cause of their financial problems, more often arguing with friends about money, and often thinking about money.

They feel fatalistic regarding control over events in people's lives, feeling that they drift along, that people's misfortunes result from mistakes, that people's worth often goes unrecognized, that getting the right job depends on being in the right place at the right time, and that there will always be wars no matter what people do. They use a variety of coping strategies to deal with these life events and financial problems, saying that they become emotional, rely on others, feel a victim and feel threatened, although they also try to accept the situation, to seek information and to keep calm.

They regard credit as useful and they want to buy more things, but they also regard it as a source of financial problems and are less likely to have a credit card so as to avoid the attendant problems. Their attitudes are generally hostile to debt, regarding it as wrong and shameful, to be avoided. They value spiritual concerns like wisdom, love and beauty. They identify a range of external causes for their problems – development of new products, advertising, children's demands, fluctuating income, stress, unexpected repairs, lack of savings, high living standards – as well as a few internal causes, namely a lack of understanding of finances, lack of self-discipline, enjoying shopping and greed.

This group is less privileged than the others, with more problems and less satisfaction. They have apparently responded to their financial problems by placing more value on spiritual matters, blaming their problems on external disasters and consumer pressures. They feel fatalistic about their lives, but try to cope, not always successfully, and they are against debt.

Shopping as a gendered activity

On the whole they [men] are the ones responsible for the choices over the whole range of things, like with a car, the husband will say let's have a look under the bonnet, and you say, I want a green or blue one. And I must confess that I am much more interested in my car being blue or green than what is under the bonnet. Though I have to choose my own car, so I hope it will be all right under the bonnet.

I start getting fed up with shopping before my wife does. I just get fed up with the whole procedure of being in a shop, I am thinking of supermarket shopping really. The main weekly shopping where we both go along and we choose things together, things that we have every week, but after a while I get fed up and say, have we got much more to get, I want to get out.

Having developed within a culture which differentiates among men and women, masculine and feminine in relation to almost every conceivable issue (French, 1985; Bem, 1991), mass consumption has always been gendered. Indeed, consumption depends upon desire, which is also socially constructed in different ways for women and men (Coward, 1984). The household manuals popular among the Victorian middle classes contained examples of 'typical' budgets and advice on a range of consumption issues in order to counter the incompetence and extravagance of wives (Pahl, 1989). The wife acted as the husband's agent with responsibility for the administration of his money. Mrs Beeton set out the duties of the mistress, which included keeping accounts and budgeting so as to achieve the prudent management of household income. Such duties were clearly understood within a moral framework based on gender and on the Protestant work ethic, a framework which is still influential today (Pahl, 1989).

Patterns of spending are highly gendered even in families where the woman is a wage earner (Piachaud, 1982; Pahl, 1989; Moore, in press). Wives are more likely to pay for food, clothing for themselves and their children, presents and school expenses. Husbands are more likely to buy their own clothing, and to pay for the rent or mortgage, the car, repairs, decorating, meals out and alcohol. Both parties buy consumer durables, buy Christmas presents and make charity donations. The various allocative systems adopted by couples to distribute their income and spending between husband and wife are based on their moral views about responsibility and gender roles (Pahl, 1989). Where wives manage the money, they are usually responsible for almost all spending, with some sharing of consumer goods, meals out, holiday expenses and expenditure on children. In housekeeping allowance systems, the husband buys most things, leaving the food, clothes and children's needs to his wife. When Pahl examined spending on leisure, she found that men and women have different definitions of leisure, which allow husbands typically to have more spending money than wives. More-over, husbands tend to overestimate the amount of money their wives spend on leisure and to define housework as part of the woman's leisure activities:

> I detest shopping – I never know what to get. I don't mind if I'm going out shopping for clothes or for something for the house, which isn't very often, but I don't like shopping for food, because I never know what to get each day. I don't like the price of the bill at the end of it. I hate Thursdays, the day I do most of my shopping, because the bill goes up every week (quoted in Oakley, 1974, p.146).

Women are often responsible for shopping because men see shopping as an activity which demeans their masculine self-image: there are husbands who will not go in shops, husbands who will go in shops but who will not carry the shopping bag for fear of being labelled 'effeminate' (Oakley, 1974, p.93). However, routine, day-to-day shopping is undoubtedly a chore for housewives. None the less, it is commonly accepted as part of the housewife's role: women use the activity of shopping as, say, an opportunity to get out as a break when caring for a young baby, or as a way of helping an elderly neighbour by taking her shopping (Oakley, 1974). Shopping also provides a way of structuring time:

> I must shop every day for something, even if it isn't every day for food. I can usually think of something I want, and I think this is partly brought about by having the car. It's also because I like to think each day what I want to eat, and not buy for two or three days at a time. [Do you like shopping?] I quite enjoy going round a supermarket if I've got time, and lots of money, and I know I can choose all these lovely foods. I hate being rushed over shopping. If I've got someone coming to lunch and I haven't thought what to eat I go out and I buy foolishly and in that way I don't like shopping. If I know what I want and I go down and I can buy it and I don't have to keep hunting around, that's alright (quoted in Oakley, 1974, p.131).

The supermarket

> No matter how much the gastronome accustomed to the most refined cookery may deplore modern mass food, taking the long-term perspective there is no doubt that – in Western countries but not yet in the world as a whole – more varied cookery as well as more plentiful food is more widely available than ever before (Mennell, 1985, p.321).

Most research on shopping, from consumer behaviour to cultural studies, emphasizes 'high-status' shopping – purchasing consumer durables, the shopping mall, conspicuous consumption, shopping for luxuries – and neglects the more everyday experience of shopping. This is partly driven by economic analyses of preferences which indicate that as disposable income rises necessities take up a smaller proportion of income, and so the purchase of luxuries becomes a more interesting issue for the growth of retail culture while the purchase of necessities is somehow linked with mundanity. But in everyday experience, the purchase of relatively cheap, non-durable goods is what most of us mean by going shopping, and in social science, analysis of the mundane is generally revealing of a culture. Let us now consider the supermarket. The supermarket has not merely replaced a number of local shops, making shopping for non-durables cheaper and more convenient. The supermarket has grown dramatically in the last 20 years, using the technology of the post-industrial revolution, and the impact on local areas through the decline of the small trader has been considerable (Gardner and Sheppard, 1989). The impact on the domestic sphere is equally important.

One image of the supermarket is that it is the place where basic needs are satisfied through the acquisition of necessities, where basic household expenditure takes place and where women are mainly responsible as routine shopping is part of housework rather than leisure. The oppositions building up here are precisely the challenge for those marketing the supermarket. Through various marketing techniques, the supermarket is deconstructing these oppositions by bringing in elements of what is assumed to be absent in the consumption of necessities into the everyday – desires, luxuries, extra spending, shared activities, leisure. In this way, the supermarket aims to celebrate the everyday, lifting it into the realm of luxury.

The traditional oppositions are closely tied to gender. The realm of the necessary links to basic needs (the natural), which are the domestic responsibility of women, and to economic restraint. In contrast, the realm of luxury is linked to permanence (as in consumer durables), to rational decision making rather than routine habit, to conspicuous consumption and, through its greater costs and greater desirability, to economic and cultural power: hence to masculinity. Before the supermarket, these distinctions were encoded in shops with the local shop providing the necessary provisions and the town centre the durables. Thus the woman was also coded as local (Ortner, 1974).

This traditional view poses problems for the retailer wishing to expand the market for non-durable goods such as food and other domestic products, for to expand the market and increase profits, people must be persuaded to move away from an economic and routine orientation. The supermarket works to overcome its coding by bringing into the realm of the necessary elements which represent luxury, and yet the link to necessity and normality must not be lost: people must also see the supermarket as a normal, regular activity where they can buy those things needed for everyday existence. The provision of luxuries has to work both in the interstices of the mundane, like day-dreaming, and it has to transform the notion of the everyday. The supermarket adopts some of the characteristics of the game show – easy questions, material rewards, prizes for all, celebrating the ordinary, being part of mass culture.

The opposition of routine vs choice is subverted by offering a wider range of products and by introducing new products. The provision of foreign products, representing other cultures, aids in this by encouraging 'culture grazing', although only snapshots of each culture are represented, providing little real choice of goods within, say, Chinese cuisine. This slide show of snapshots of foreign culture is pleasurable – walking around a supermarket is like leafing through the pages of a travel magazine or watching a travel programme on the television. The exotic is overlaid on the everyday and conveniently available, offering the opportunity to experiment with new identities. This is not a matter of offering different products to different ethnic or social groups, but creates a place where traditionally separate categories of food are mixed which encourages experimentation and the mixing of styles. The supermarket with its diversity of products appeals to a broad range of shoppers with quite different orientations.

Following Mennell's analysis of a spectrum of eaters, there are a variety of supermarket shoppers. Unlike previous shops which catered for particular, localized segments of the market, the supermarket simultaneously supplies people from all walks of life and from all localities. Traditional British products such as suet, gravy powder, jelly, joints of meat are available for those who are conservative in their eating. Shoppers can buy foods which are high in quality and reproduce bourgeois taste. People can buy convenience foods. There are always new, experimental goods in the supermarket for those who want to indulge in the latest eating fads. Shopping baskets can buy into one of these approaches or mix and match them reflecting the taste and individuality of the consumer. On a cultural level, as Mennell argues, this diversity and openness in the range of goods available brings about a 'culinary pluralism [which] is the counterpart of something which is more familiar in the arts: the loss of a single dominant style'. The distinction between shoppers now reflects more their interest and involvement in food and in consumer culture generally rather than traditional class positions.

The provision of exotic products also collapses the distinction between local and global, as does positioning supermarkets out of town to necessitate travelling in the car to get there. In fact, given the quantity of goods now involved in 'doing a shop', a car journey seems essential even if the supermarket is round the corner: the time spent in the car, however short, encodes distance from the local. The contrast between supermarkets participating in this new retail culture (e.g. Sainsbury's) and those which simply offer cheap necessary goods (e.g. Kwik Save) demonstrates this, for the latter rarely provide car parks.

At the same time, the pleasure must not be allowed to interfere with the serious business of filling the shopping basket, and there are strong elements of control in the supermarket. Some of the controls are physical – barriers around entrances and tills which direct the consumer towards the goods and prevent a rapid escape, aisles which distribute foods strategically around the shop so as to ensure maximum exposure to goods (especially those with high profit margins). Others are psychological – the music which creates a certain atmosphere, the smell of freshly baking bread, the convenience of a free town-centre car park or of the out-of-town car park with cheap petrol pumps. The goods convey pleasure while the environment conveys pragmatism – both are encoded in the supermarket.

Shopping in cultural context

Shopping as leisure

Shopping is encouraged to be almost an activity in itself to be enjoyed. I don't know how many people do, but it is sold like that, come to the mall, and the pretty fountains and the plastic palm trees.

It's an emotional thing. They go out and have a good shop, and I do that sometimes, and some people I know do it as well. It's a social contact too, isn't it?

Has shopping become a form of leisure? In the 1980s, there was much talk about the growth of leisure activities with people retiring earlier, working shorter hours and having more disposable income. The retail sector has tried to make shopping part of this leisure culture. While early attempts to classify shoppers assumed that shopping was a purely practical affair, involving decisions about what to purchase where and how often, our classification of respondents into shopper types, as well as arguments about the gendered and cultural nature of shopping, show that the practical and symbolic, useful and pleasurable, are intertwined in shopping. However, the conception of shopping as leisure is problematic for women when men assume that going shopping is time off (Deem, 1982).

We have thus far implied that shopping is a unitary activity, although the above discussion claims different things for food shopping, clothes shopping, local or supermarket shopping, and so on. Clearly, nipping out for a pint of milk differs in many ways from wandering around town in one's lunch hour or from going out to buy a new dress for an interview. Among other aspects, shopping can be broken down into purposive shopping, window shopping, comparing goods, exposing oneself to new ideas and cruising (Jansen-Verbeke, 1987), and each aspect of shopping bears a different relation to pleasure and leisure.

The future of shopping

Benetton exemplifies post-Fordist manufacture (Gardner and Sheppard, 1989). The tills of the 3200 shops are linked to a central computer which analyses market trends in styles and colours. This information is relayed to the design department and the ordering department so that changes in manufacture can be made rapidly. In contrast to Benetton, the fashion industry in Britain is an example of the failure of Fordism which involves the denial of innovation and the creation of a mass market through mass production. A consumer-driven economy depends on consumers buying, and so retailers have to find ways of enticing consumers and making them able to pay. One way has been to give the consumer credit facilities. Another is the dramatic change in the shopping environment and the more sophisticated use of advertising and market segmentation techniques. Such changes certainly contributed to retail companies' success in the mid- to late 1980s, aided by the fact that household disposable income rose 3 per cent per year in real terms in the 1980s and, as people spend more when they feel better off, retail spending grew at 8 per cent per year (Gardner and Sheppard, 1989). Changes in mass consumption now pose a number of challenges to the retail industry. How can they increase consumption motive in the context of the Protestant work ethic? How can they bring men further into the marketplace? How can they change perceptions of shopping from that of a chore to that of a valued and pleasant activity?

The politics of shopping

Galbraith (1970) has emphasized the importance of the consumer for the continuance of capitalism, arguing that consumption is neglected in neo-classical economics. If consumers have significance, what power do they have? The consumer movement plays a monitoring and protectionist role, pressing for more regulation, information and consumer rights, but has no overt political purpose.

More specific consumer groups exercise some political power at the point of consumption (rather than focusing on production for political activism), using consumer boycotts (as for South African products) and selective buying (as for green or organic products). These attempt to counter the political apathy and feelings of powerlessness among ordinary people. Nava (1991) discusses uncertainty over whether consumers have any real power: although consumers can choose among a greater variety of goods, exercising more choice in mass consumption, and gaining a sense of identity through consumption, critics argue that such choices reflect no real freedom or power. For example, Hebdige (1979) sees youth culture, with its specific styles of consumption of clothing and popular music, as a form of protest and of political consciousness raising, yet Tajfel (1982) questions whether disengaging from mass culture represents active political protest. The valorization of the consumer clearly raises as many issues as it resolves.

GENERATIONAL AND LIFE COURSE INFLUENCES ON ECONOMIC BELIEFS

SIX

In my day we were encouraged to save a bit more. I think that today's children ask for something and they get it. I mean, when I was a child, you jolly well had to save up for it if you wanted it.

My parents don't live on credit at all, unlike me. They have always saved for whatever they've wanted, but I'm afraid that I don't go along with some of their views. I generally live on credit, it's the only way to survive.

Of course, this to a large extent I suppose, psychologically comes down to force of habit. Now my children, they don't do what I do, they don't think the way I do, you know, the younger generation, they are clued up a lot more than we are, aren't they, and they are not afraid to be experimental and involved with new things.

I don't see why they should be a different species because they are the young these days. I don't think that they are a different species. I think that it is much harder for them.

Understanding social change

Not enough has been written on how different periods or generations affect the actions and world views of those growing up in them (although see Schneiderman, 1988). In interviews and discussions, people continually referred to some notion of how things are these days, how they were when they were young, how different times affect parents and children differently, and so forth. In this chapter, we attempt to address three issues. One concerns the relation between people's understanding of historical change, which informs their life stories and accounts of their actions and beliefs, and historical accounts of social change over the present century. The second concerns the relation between explanations for differences between age groups which refer to membership of different generations and those which refer to being at different stages of the life-cycle. Finally, we consider how far our respondents of different ages differ from one another and why.

Social change in the twentieth century

The sense of change, for both social scientists and ordinary people, depends on an often implicit comparison point. When people comment on the development of consumer culture and its implications, are they making a comparison with medieval times, with the period before the industrial revolution, with Victorian times, with the inter-war period, or with the 1960s before the pre-housing boom? Historians date the development of consumer culture at different points, and the emergence of consumer culture is much debated. Lay people tend to talk loosely of 'before', 'in the old days', and so the historical claims of their accounts can be confusing, often serving purposes of justification rather than explication. Indeed, many researchers also imply a stable past and talk as if the major changes have happened only recently. None the less, times have changed in Britain since people now retired were young, separating the daily experiences of the different generations (Halsey, 1986).

> Between the mid-nineteenth century and the mid-twentieth the population grew and became more urban, more mobile both socially and geograph- ically, more rapidly and fully informed about what was going on in the nation and across the world, while more people were educated to higher levels. The majority of the people became more prosperous, owned more possessions, enjoyed a greater variety of foods, better health and health care, more lei- sure and more security (Roebuck, 1973, p.10).

In relation to mass consumption, the following changes are especially signifi- cant:

- *Consumer changes:* greater range of consumer goods available (fuelled by a technological revolution in processes of mass production); reduced durability of goods, in terms both of serviceability and desirability, replaced by increased expectation of having the newest and most fashionable version of the same product.
- *Marketing changes:* explosion in the mass communication technologies which advertise, propagandize and persuade us to buy – in terms of exposure, target- ing, expense and technique; development of shopping centres and malls at the expense of town centre and local shops.
- *Economic changes:* increased availability of financial services for credit, changes in the forms of credit available, more flexible mortgage lending, debt

facilities, and investment schemes; increased complexity and diversity of finances.

- *Social changes:* introduction of the welfare state, increased home ownership, improved pension plans, increased leisure time, escalating divorce, cheaper travel, available contraception, more liberal sexual attitudes, more female employment and gender equality, greater importance of childhood and more defined consumer/fashion subgroups, increasing elderly population, and so forth.

Some would argue, however, that in essentials, little has really changed over the last 60 years. Social mobility is fairly constant (Goldthorpe *et al.*, 1969), with relations between social classes little changed and the majority of the population still with little power or wealth. Halsey (1986, p.103) writes of 'the historically marching column of social ranks', each moving forward, but keeping the differentials constant. Similarly, feminist scholars have commented on the lack of changed relations between men and women, whether one looks at the division of domestic labour, waged labour or income (Pahl, 1989). This social stability can be traced both to the operation of socioeconomic structures and to the family, 'the reproductive social cell of class, of status, and of culture' (Halsey, 1986, p.97). Yet, many of these stable structures are under stress, with the reduction in unskilled labour, the growth of new technologies, the rising rates of divorce and single parents, and so forth. We must therefore ask about the profundity and the degree of social change which may have occurred. Yet this is often unknown; for example, we can trace the changes in forms of credit, from the pawn shop to the credit card, but it is less easy to discover whether the amount of personal debt, or the consequences of debt, are greater today than they were 70 years ago.

Moral panics and 'the times'

I think that there is a dividing line in a certain extent, in that when you are born and brought up, I am in my late 40s, and I can remember taking money to school for my national savings certificate stamps, just the stamps, every Monday. And it would worry me a great deal if I was borrowing money that I could not pay back, whereas my children laugh and say, well I have three plastic cards, I don't care, the credit limit is so and so. And I say, well look, say you lost your job next month, what are you going to do about it? I think it is a bit sad that for some reason the younger generation seem to think that it is the right way to go about their finances.

My feeling is that it [the problem of credit and debt] has accelerated in this last 20 years. I think that first it was gradual, and then in this last 10, 15 years, from the '60s.

I feel that sometime, I am not quite sure when, but something happened to encourage the younger generation to take on this heavy debt commitment.

Attitudes towards money and family consumption patterns are historical phenomena. Even confining ourselves to the present century, different decades have received widely different popular characterizations in relation to mass consumption. Indeed, they are characterized significantly in terms of consumption, as in the years of depression in the early 1930s, when money was tight and you made do with hand-me-downs, in the austerity of the 1950s, with continued post-war rationing, in the post-war generation who in the 1960s had 'never had it so good' and furnished their houses with the newest domestic technologies, and in the materialistic 1980s, when goods were no longer made to last, and you could have the most fashionable goods now because debt had become credit, nothing to be ashamed of. And so on.

We are all familiar with these images in our own lives and in the lives of our children, our parents and our grandparents. Certainly, the mass media have contributed to these images, codifying and stereotyping them, reinforcing and perpetuating them. Roebuck (1973, p.129) notes how 'poor conditions and unemployment attracted official and national interest during the twenties and thirties, while prosperous contentment went largely unnoticed and unrecorded'. Certainly, this bias is evident in many of our respondents' stories. These images have a life beyond that of media stereotypes (Oskamp, 1988) or advertising/ marketing images (Forty, 1986), functioning as social representations of the times which are actively constructed and reproduced by each generation in its thinking about itself and its parent generation and child generation (Moscovici, 1984). By social representations, we refer to 'the equivalent, in our society, of the myths and beliefs systems in traditional societies . . . the contemporary version of common sense' (Moscovici, 1981, p.181).

These generational representations become part of people's constructions of their own identity and of their relationships within or across generations, providing metaphors, frameworks, explanations or dimensions for social comparisons between self and others. They may affect the ways in which people respond to present changes by affecting their perceptions of those changes as well as their understanding of their own place in relation to change. Undoubtedly, these representations serve to simplify the complexities of our social history, often tending to exaggerate the hardships of earlier years (after all, the Second World War made opportunities, even fortunes, for some, while the suburbs expanded dramatically in the 'depressed' 1930s) and to underestimate the hardships of present times (for the poor, the 1980s increased their relative deprivation, while for the young, the housing boom of the late 1980s created hardship rather than wealth).

> Even the clichés of the 'roaring twenties' and the 'grim thirties' are inadequate and inaccurate indicators of the extremes of feeling and rapid shifts in mood [in the interwar years]. For some people, especially the workers in long-established industries such as shipbuilding and textiles, the twenties were simply a dress rehearsal for the Depression, while for many people, such as those employed in new industries like car-making and electronics,

the thirties were good years of rising material standards (Roebuck, 1973, p.110).

However, people feel themselves to be living, as indeed, they always have, in a social environment which is dramatically changing, to which they feel they should or cannot adapt, for which they feel great welcome or regret. There is a sense of moral concern around perceptions that spending has become our preferred form of leisure, personal debt is out of control, children do nothing but watch television, everyone lives for themselves alone, children are all being spoilt, life too complex, debt too easy, participation dependent on consumption, and values based on having rather than doing. We suggest later that this sense of change has accompanied all periods to a greater or lesser extent, and that it plays a role in providing a contrast (through a golden age representation or an apocalyptic vision) for motivating debates on issues of public interest. For example, it is clear that materialism was rife in the times of the present older generation as well as in present times. In the 1940s and 1950s:

> The newly housed and re-housed workers wanted the best household equipment they could possibly afford, more fashionable decorations, neater and more ambitious gardens . . . As well as adding new elements of social competition and distinction to the lives of the masses, changing housing conditions altered old patterns of life (Roebuck, 1973, p.172).

However, this materialism was construed then by many in terms of the grounding and solidifying of family life and domesticity, whereas now similar developments are discussed in the discourse of disruption and decline.

Generations and the life course

Life course and generation: Competing and complementary explanations

The different social sciences all draw on some notion of life-cycle, life course or life stages through which people pass. Consumption patterns, attitudes and identities must affect and be affected by the ways in which people pass through these stages and the different paths they take. The construction of a lifestyle depends on how one negotiates these basic life stages, and hence on how one deals with cultural and family expectations of achievements at each stage. In economics, the life-cycle refers to the changing position of the individual or household over the life course in terms of financial resources and commitments (Modigliani, 1970). The social psychological and sociological notion of life course is broader, including also identity needs and desires and social and work commitments (Levinson, 1978; Hepworth, 1987).

Life course differences concern personal, biographical, financial and leisure resources and commitments. Life course explanations tend to assume social stability. Generational differences concern the historical and cultural climate regarding consumption, focusing on often-neglected sociohistorical influences on attitudes and values (Gergen, 1973). They thus tend to assume social change.

The concepts of life course and generation overlap, and so represent competing and complementary explanations which need to be disentangled, for comparisons across people over the life course inevitably involve comparisons of people from different generations.

The life course approach tends to assume that, for example, young people now live under similar conditions to those of earlier generations, irrespective of differences in sociohistorical context. For example, although Csikszentmihalyi and Rochberg-Halton (1981) describe differences in the significance of objects for grandparents, parents and children as generational, their explanations refer to the different life course commitments and resources of people at each of these stages, not to the different conditions under which each was socialized. We would argue that the opinions and experiences of a 60-year-old, for example, reflect both his or her stage in the life course and the views and generational opinions of his or her youth. On the other hand, the generational approach tends to assume that everyone now lives according to contemporary ideas, participating equivalently in modern consumerism, irrespective of the different resources and commitments of their stage in the life course. Clearly, both kinds of explanation are needed to account for differences of opinion between, for example, parents and children, otherwise generational differences may be wrongly attributed to life course factors and *vice versa*.

Generation gaps and conflict

A 'generation' (as defined by *Longman's Dictionary of the English Language*) is 'a group of individuals born and living during the same period of time' and also as 'the average span of time between the birth of parents and that of their offspring'. It is the contradiction between these two definitions, for the lives of parents and their children overlap considerably, which gives rise to the narrower, commonsense definition of a generation as a group of people who reached early adulthood during the same period of time. Hence the notion that each individual has their time, 'in my day', which refers not to the span of their life, for indeed they are still alive when they say it, but to that time when they were in late adolescence/early adulthood. *Longman's* defines a generation gap as 'a wide difference in character or attitude'. Generation gaps in experiences of consumption may reflect differences in morality, values, expectations and responsibilities, yet little has been written on the problem – or the myth – of the generation gap, although it is frequently invoked as the cause of societal conflict in popular discourse.

The concept of generation or generation gap has a mythic potency, permeating many popular discussions about, among other things, the family, social conflict and changing consumption patterns over the present century. Researchers also tend to give emphasis to their accounts of present unease by imputing it to social change, arguing that such unease is new:

> No age has ever been more child-centred ... yet parental anxiety, exacerbated by marital uncertainty, is endemic ... most parents have lived through

a dramatic shift in the standards expected of them. It is not enough, as it once was, to look after bodily health and physical security. Parents must also answer for the mental and moral character of their sons and daughters, despite influences from the street, the so-called peer group, the mass media and youth culture which children cannot escape, and with which parents cannot contend. They are increasingly made to feel amateurs in a difficult professional world . . . Such circumstances . . . may add up to intense frustration. Relations between the generations in all classes are prone to anxiety and conflict, and the family is hard-pressed (Halsey, 1986, p.112).

As Hepworth (1987) notes, the concept of generation draws on several domains of meaning, and yet is very difficult to define. Its key assertion is that of the discontinuity of age groups, and it centres primarily on the basic opposition between young and old, with a range of associated oppositions attached which predominantly valorize the young:

young	old
modern	traditional
progressive	regressive
change	stability
innovation	convention
foolishness	wisdom
innocence	experience
strong	weak
now	then

The notion of generation also involves 'an appeal to the shared experiences of a particular generation of men and women who are urged to discover a common identity and a common cause' (Hepworth, 1987, p.143), so that within a generation, generational representations are used to construct identities by minimizing within-group differences in contradistinction to representations of neighbouring generations (Tajfel, 1982). Hepworth emphasizes the considerable anxieties which surround discussions of generational differences, for the younger generation are popularly identified with great hopes for the future and regarded with great disappointment for rejection, failure or apathy in their response to these weighty expectations. Much of this talk has the ring of nostalgia about it, invoking a 'golden age' view of history. Commenting on what he sees as 'the secular materialism of the post-war world' (p.113), Halsey (1986) describes a similar anxiety:

A traditional culture weakened by multiple forces of change falters in its transmission to the next generation and the lonely crowd of adolescent age-mates look to each other for guidance. They too, like their parents, are essentially powerless, even those who enjoy relative material prosperity. Their powerlessness is reflected in their collective amnesia, their lack of knowledge of the history of their conditions, and even more in their uncertainty as to their future. No wonder that fashionability, hedonism, and a

desperate individualism serve as substitutes for a securely held morality . . .
In short, a weakening of the bond between parent and child, and exacerbation of conflict between them, are a fundamental and paradoxical part of the so-called century of the child (Halsey, 1986, pp.113–14).

Our interviews with people were peppered with references to 'the older generation' and 'the younger generation'. This opposition between young and old becomes increasingly problematic as lifespans increase, for the 'older generation' may contain generation gaps within itself, as between parents of 80 something and their children of 60 or so. This is true also for the 'younger generation', which may include teenagers of 15 and their parents of 35. It is unlikely that the social representation of the older or younger generation is sufficiently powerful to minimize these differences. Certainly, the social representation makes it difficult to find public expression of these within-group differences, for the dominant comparison is between the younger generation, those whose 'time is now', and the older generation, those whose 'time has passed', however these generations are themselves composed.

Listening to the pre-war generation talking of their youth, one senses their great concern to voice earlier, but still living experiences, experiences which the present world seems to deny, to make unreal. They retell their stories of pre-war poverty almost in amazement, for present social representations make it all seem so implausible. The enthusiasm, humour, nostalgia and solidarity expressed during these discussions hints at the confusion underlying so rapid a change in people's lifestyles. They tell their stories with an implicit plea for recognition, and the consequences for understanding between generations – or misunderstanding and rejection – should not be underestimated:

I lived in the North East, well the Midlands, and times were very hard, pre-war, I was born in 1924, and in the '30s particularly it was very hard, and when I was 11 years of age we used to stop school at 1.30 on a Friday, which was traditional in Grimsby, and I used to go straight from school onto the market and I used to look after a stall on the market, 11 years of age, mind you, until 10 o'clock at night, and then on Saturday, at 8 o'clock in the morning I was on the market until 10 o'clock at night. Looking after a stall at 11 years of age. I got 1s 6d for that which I gave to my mother to help keep the family going. That was, we didn't have the money to spend, but it was drummed into us by my parents, that if you wanted anything, you saved your money. My mother used to give me something back, a few coppers, and the same as you, I bought a pair of roller skates. It took me 12 months to buy a pair. But when we used to have the penny savings bank, taking pennies to school, we were taught that you do not buy anything unless you had the money to do it. When you grow up, always have some money in reserve, you must always have some for insurance.

Many other such tales were told in the course of our interviews. People want to tell of their own lives, but also of what they perceived as a different moral

world, with its different codes of responsibility and judgement, family relationships, personal expectations, and so forth. If underlying similarities exist
between past and present, this is in one sense beside the point – perceived
differences are real in their consequences. The different world of consumption is
portrayed as reflecting a different moral code, and the accounts are heartfelt –
these differences matter to people:

We kids in the slums of Birmingham used to have various ways of earning
money whenever we could.

We used to go around with buckets collecting horse manure that we would
sell to people that had gardens in the allotments.

I've known lads come to school without boots, in the winter, and the police
used to collect money amongst themselves and buy boots for the children
who needed them. And that's how it was.

You certainly never hear the term 'orange boxes' any longer, and yet many
of my friends expected to start with them.

In my area if you owned a bike, a bike was, you know, how did you manage
to buy that, sort of thing. Now two hundred yards down the road you will
see hundreds of them lying around.

I mean when the young get married today they start off with everything,
washing machine, fridge, everything. Whereas we used to have to save up
for it, you didn't start off with it all.

My first holiday was after I had got married. A week at Blackpool, and that
was the highlight of my life then, and now they are talking about sending
people to Florida.

I used a tea chest for about 4 years as a bedside unit.

You were happy to start with your bed and cooker, but I don't think that a
lot of young people are happy to start with that.

My mother-in-law used to put everything in teapots. Everything.

These are not just accounts of a (supposedly) different way of life, they are
also moral, implying a contrast between the good old days and a disapproved
present. It was clearly judged better to have a tea chest and save up than to
borrow for a bedside unit. Such accounts tend to construct a dubious continuity
between 'in our day' and their own parents' times, implying for example, that
they too value their mother-in-law's budgeting with tea pots, but that their children would not. Similarly, these accounts do not recognize that their parents
could have claimed a similar gulf between themselves and their children who,
unlike them, expected in the end, after saving up, to get their own fridge and
washing machine rather than doing without. The implication is that the younger
generation are responsible for the changes and problems, which they, the parent
generation, see all around them. Nor, in our discussion groups, did people tend
to recognize their own participation in present consumer culture, for although

the culture of their youth was influential, they have not been entirely unaffected by developments during their adult years and have participated in both the advantages and problems of consumer culture in its present form.

The discussion groups and interviews produced far less talk from younger people about the differences between themselves and their parents. Many claimed continuity across the generations in attitudes, values and habits. Some felt they were less profligate, more hard working and stable than their parents. For others, the comparison was irrelevant, they simply saw themselves as doing what everyone else was doing when they discussed their use of credit or their pleasure in shopping and furnishing their homes with the latest goods. Maybe feeling in tune with the times makes for little to say.

Certainly, there were a number of accounts which contradicted the dominant representations of younger and older generations, recognizing the existence of debt among past generations and of careful budgeting or saving among the present generation:

> I know a young couple who have traded up and are now going to have a baby, and they are a most conscientious couple, they will not get into debt, although their jobs are very stressful.

> I think that old people keep up with the Joneses as well. Some of them are pretty awful.

> It is a long time ago since there was a credit system, what did we call it, the never-never, that was a name for it, the hire purchase. That was a long time now, wasn't it?

> Mail order actually has quite a long history. I don't think that it is one of the present things that is being thrown up, it has been going on since the 30s and 40s.

> My parents were living largely on credit or in debt. They had a mortgage, a company car, salaried rather than waged job, fairly good spread of the latest consumer durables bought often on credit. They were not in debt or suffering but they were certainly stretched. But it was common for people of that kind to live in that way. Live now, pay later. I would say thoroughly average.

In diverse and significant ways, the popular belief in the generation gap is influential in itself, regardless of the validity of the historical claims implicit in such beliefs. For example, the power of a social representation is to mystify or deny alternative or contradictory images. Thus we found relatively little talk in our discussions of money-lenders and pawnbrokers of the past or of greater financial and employment stability of the present. In general, despite the focus groups being composed of people of mixed ages, most talk was consistent with this dominant representation, asserting again and again the differences between generations, the folly and greed of youth, even from quite young people, and the wisdom of age. Thus the valorizing of youth seen continually in marketing and advertising materials was contradicted here. Interestingly, the exceptions arose when people talked of their own children, for here an alternative social representation, that of 'progress', structured the discourse.

Assigning people to generations and stages in the life course

Our respondents varied widely in age and were at different stages in their own lives. We divided them into five groups according to their stage in the life course, separating families from single people, people with dependent children from those with independent children, and so forth. We assume that the retired people in the sample are generally from the generation who are parents to the families in the sample, while those with independent children, but not yet retired, are likely to be the parent generation to the single people and the young couples. In this way, the present analysis can address issues of both generation and life course, capturing the different concerns of generational difference, position in historical time, and household or family constraints and pressures.[1]

How do consumption and finance enter into the perceptions and expectations of people at different stages in the life course? Do material considerations bind groups together or push them apart? How are generation, family and individuality interlinked through the cultural aspects of consumption?

Identifying the life course stages and generations

Respondents were divided into five groups according to their stage in the life course (Hepworth, 1987) as follows:[2]

- *Single:* people not living as part of a couple or family, and people not cohabiting, divorced, widowed or parents. This category was restricted to the 'young', namely under 35 years of age.
- *Couple:* people either married or cohabiting, with no children. To include only those who may yet have children, this category was restricted to those under 40 years of age.
- *Family:* people who, as part of a married or cohabiting couple, have one or more dependent children living with them.

Table 6.1   Demographic differences between the stages in the life course[a]

	No. in stage	% of sample	Average age	Average no. of children	% Home owners
Single	58	27	23	0	16
Couple	25	11	28	0	44
Family	58	27	42	2.14[b]	90
Empty nest	30	14	51	2.17	93
Retired	48	22	69	2.25	83

[a] Based on 219 respondents (60 people did not fit these categories).
[b] 1.81 dependent children.

- *Empty nest:* people who, whether married, divorced or widowed, have been or still are part of a couple who are not yet retired but whose children have left home.
- *Retired:* people who are either retired or living with a retired partner and who are or have been part of a couple whose children have left home.

The notion of generation can be superimposed on this classification: singles and couples form part of the 'younger generation', while empty nests and retired people form the 'older generation'. Families fall in between. Demographic information for each of the groups is shown in Table 6.1.

Credit, borrowing and debt

Across the stages in the life course people did not differ significantly in their amounts of disposable income. They also saved roughly the same amounts. For both income and savings, there was considerable variability within each stage in the life course. However, the groups differed in their debts: more young people were in debt and, for those in each stage who were in debt, younger people owed a larger proportion of their disposable income than did older people (Table 6.2). This supports the consensual representation that younger people borrow more than older people.

The sources of debts also varied across the stages in the life course. Single people owed most of their money to friends or relatives (49 per cent of those in debt), to the bank in the form of an overdraft (46 per cent of those in debt) and to credit card companies (mainly Access and Visa). Couples borrowed mainly in the form of a bank loan (45 per cent of those in debt), though debts from credit cards, friends or relatives and overdrafts were also common. Families tended to owe money to finance companies (31 per cent of families in debt), credit cards and mail order companies, and to a lesser extent overdrafts. The borrowings of empty nests were primarily in the form of bank loans (38 per cent of those in debt), credit cards and mail order accounts. Finally, the retired owed mainly to credit companies or for fuel bills (although very few of the retired people were in much debt at all).

There are two trends apparent here. First, there is a move over the life course from private sources of debt such as friends and relatives to public, or contrac-

Table 6.2 Percentage in debt and amounts owed, by stage in the life course

	In debt (%)	Average amount (excluding mortgage) owed by those in debt (£)
Single	67	1,090
Couple	80	735
Family	50	662
Empty nest	43	316
Retired	21	158

Table 6.3 Percentage who agree that the use of a credit card is a debt even if you pay off the total each month, by stage in the life course

Single	22
Couple	20
Family	12
Empty nest	67
Retired	33

tual, debt such as bank loans and credit cards. Secondly, there is a move from unplanned to planned borrowing. Single people particularly tend not to take up bank loans or finance company borrowing, but rather run up debts on credit cards or their overdrafts. Later, people begin to combine planned and unplanned borrowing. These differences in sources of borrowing may reflect both the culture of socialization – what counts as the normal source of borrowing when one is young – and differences in the resources available to each stage in the life course, as well as different preferences regarding planning, control, privacy, and so on.

When it comes to purchasing consumer durables, who is most likely to pay cash rather than borrow? According to the older generation, it is the young who borrow most. Our findings about how actual purchases had been paid for confirmed this, although families act similarly. Singles, couples and families more often borrowed to buy a colour TV, video-recorder or tumble drier, though not because they felt more strongly that these goods are necessities rather than luxuries (see below). Rather, they seemed less willing to restrict themselves to those agreed necessities: 'I've always hated the idea of having to adapt my behaviour, what I liked, to necessities.'

Families were also more likely to take out loans, especially to buy goods like a washing machine. Buying a car with credit was spread across the groups except for the retired, who still paid cash. However, loans and credit cards differ, for younger people use credit cards the least, especially compared to families, but also compared to empty nests and retired people, and they are also significantly less likely to possess a credit card. Some 49 per cent of singles did not own a credit card, compared to between 12 and 27 per cent in the other groups.

Despite some disagreements within groups over the definition of debt, there were no overall differences between groups in their definitions of debt: it is not that younger people do not consider certain types of borrowing as debts, but rather that they find borrowing more acceptable as a means of acquiring goods. Singles and couples reported finding it easier to get into debt than did the families, while the retired considered it not at all easy to get into debt.

An exception related to the use of credit. The age groups disagreed about whether use of a credit card counted as a debt even assuming you do pay off the total at the end of the month (Table 6.3), although there were no differences in whether groups actually did pay off the total credit card bill each month. There

Table 6.4   Reported frequency of use of credit cards, by stage in the life course

Single	3.9
Couple	3.2
Family	2.8
Empty nest	3.3
Retired	3.4

Note: 1 = for most purchases . . . 5 = never.

is an interpretative issue here: is using a credit card and paying off the total each month a clever and convenient budgeting practice so as to obtain a short-term interest-free loan or is it a risky borrowing practice which may lead to further debts? Interestingly, the young are not so different here from the retired in their judgements. The families are notable in favouring the use of credit cards in this way, while the empty nests are particularly emphatic that even this use of credit cards constitutes a debt. Maybe the empty nests are the most judgemental for they are undergoing the new experience of watching their adult children's financial practices with little power to intervene. They, being themselves in transition, express the generation gap the most clearly.

We can account for the families' tolerance of this use of credit cards if we examine people's reported frequency of use of credit cards. When asked 'how often do you use credit cards', the groups differed significantly (Table 6.4). Contrary to popular belief, the younger people reported least use of credit cards and it was the families who used them the most, which was consistent with their definition of credit card use as being different from debt. Also contrary to popular belief, retired people seem to use them as often as others, revealing a gap between their attitudes and behaviour.

Possessions

I never had a pair of shoes until I joined the army, I just had a sixpenny pair of plimsolls from Woolworths, and that was a big thing for me. But nowadays, younger people, they want everything. A car isn't a luxury to them, a coloured television isn't a luxury. That is the society today.

I live on a big estate. One of the big ones. And the young people that are there, I look at them and think, I am old enough to be their mother, it is not nice, but they buy a starter home and then they trade that one. They are not there a couple of years. They have no community. As soon as they have a baby, they want a four bedroom house, I am not saying all of them, but there are people like that, and these are the people who are in debt up to their ears.

Most people in each group own a colour TV, hi-fi, washing machine, telephone and car, and half own a video-cassette recorder (Table 6.5). Other goods are owned by a minority. Apart from the compact disc player and the tumble

Table 6.5   Which of the following do you have in your household? Percentage who answered 'yes', by stage in the life course[a]

	S	C	F	EN	R	P[b]
Colour TV	74	80	97	87	96	**
Video-recorder	47	60	72	57	40	**
Hi-fi stereo system	78	92	78	63	50	***
Compact disc player	28	28	12	17	13	
Washing machine	57	60	97	93	90	***
Dishwasher	19	0	33	27	19	*
Tumble drier	33	32	43	37	31	
Microwave oven	31	36	53	47	27	*
Telephone	76	80	95	97	96	**
Car	55	64	88	90	65	***
Home computer	33	28	62	17	15	***

[a] S, single; C, couple; F, family; EN, empty nest; R, retired.
[b] Chi-square test on frequencies (*$P < 0.05$, **$P < 0.01$, ***$P < 0.001$).

drier, the groups differ significantly in possessions. However, people do not simply accumulate more goods as they get older, for there is no general correlation between stages in the life course and number of properties owned. If we classify goods by the stage in the life course at which they are typically first acquired, three patterns of goods or ownership can be identified.

1 *Staple goods* (colour TV, washing machine and telephone) are owned by most groups. If not acquired earlier, most people purchase these goods on beginning a family and they retain or replace them through subsequent stages of the life course. For these goods there is a significant positive relationship between stage in the life course and number of properties.
2 *Hi-tech goods* (hi-fi and compact disc player) are owned primarily by young people and are owned in decreasing proportions by older groups.
3 *Family goods* (video-cassette recorder, dishwasher, microwave, tumble drier, car and computer) are acquired by families and are less often owned by both younger and older people (although they may yet become staples for subsequent generations if retained by contemporary families through later stages). For these goods, there is no overall association between stage in the life course and number of properties, because the stage of acquisition is in the middle of the life course.

It seems that different goods are acquired according to people's stage in the life course and hence according to their specific personal and social requirements. Similarly, whether they are retained and upgraded or not depends on the type of good – staple, family or hi-tech.

If goods once defined as luxuries are now considered necessities, this would make the desire to possess these goods, and the hardship of doing without them,

Table 6.6 For each of the goods you possess, is it a luxury or a necessity?
Percentage who answered 'luxury',[a] by stage in the life course[b]

	S	C	F	EN	R	P[c]
Colour TV	52	75	62	68	61	
Video-recorder	81	93	90	82	82	
Hi-fi stereo system	53	78	89	72	85	**
Compact disc player	94	100	100	100	100	
Washing machine	25	27	4	8	3	**
Dishwasher	67	—	68	75	86	
Tumble drier	65	88	44	57	50	
Microwave oven	78	78	73	92	46	
Telephone	12	5	2	14	10	
Car	28	20	4	15	19	*
Home computer	100	57	72	25	17	

[a] Judgements of luxury were made only by those who possessed the good (hence sample sizes vary).
[b] S, single; C, couple; F, family; EN, empty nest; R, retired.
[c] Chi-square test on frequencies (*$P < 0.05$, **$P < 0.01$).

seem the greater. Table 6.6 shows whether people who possess various goods
see them as necessities or luxuries. For example, 52 per cent of singles who had
a colour TV judged it a luxury and 48 per cent judged it a necessity. There is a
notable consensus across life course groups in these judgements: most agree that
the video-cassette recorder, hi-fi, compact disc, dishwasher and microwave are
luxuries and that the telephone, car and washing machine are necessities. People
disagree about the colour TV, computer and tumble drier, although this disagreement is not related to life course. The life course groups disagree systematically only about the hi-fi (seen as more necessary by singles), the washing
machine (seen as most necessary by families and later stages) and the car (most
necessary for families and least for singles).

It seems that staple goods are seen as necessities (with some dispute over the
colour TV), especially from the stage of family onwards, and these goods are
retained in the household from this stage. The hi-tech goods are seen as luxuries
(with some dispute over the computer) and the family goods are a mixture of
luxuries and necessities. Establishing a family involves increased acquisition of
both necessary staples and, importantly, also of luxuries, which may or may not
become a long-term part of the household. For example, before people have
children they are more likely to consider that a washing machine is a luxury.
Later, even once the children have left home, a washing machine is still judged
necessary to everyday life. Similarly, after children arrive, a car becomes more of
a necessity, and again this judgement is maintained after the children have left
home. Clearly, key objects change their significance for people after they have
children, and these new meanings do not revert back in later life when the
original conditions for their change in meaning no longer apply. These new

Table 6.7   Control over budgeting, by stage in the life course

	'Lose track' (%)	'Works out somehow' (%)	'Money disappears' (%)
Single	69	60	42
Couple	43	50	17
Family	47	51	31
Empty nest	35	50	10
Retired	30	29	13

'necessities' may later gain new justifications, as washing machines save an elderly person an exhausting trip to the launderette or a telephone keeps the infirm in contact with family.

The representation of the younger generation as more acquisitive and greedy, seeing more goods as necessary to their way of life, seems more myth than reality. Only in relation to the hi-fi do single people consider something a necessity which others judge to be a luxury. In all other disagreements, the young seem less likely to judge something a necessity, rather than more likely. It seems that everyday demands and commitments serve to change the meanings of these goods, rather than the consumer culture of one's generation.

Budgeting and control

They, especially my father, avoid getting into debt at any cost. His mother had been a bad manager and there'd been rows about it when he was a kid.

If younger people are borrowing more, budgeting and being in control of one's finances becomes a key issue (Furby, 1978; Kamptner, 1989). When asked 'do you feel in control of your finances?', singles and couples reported feeling least in control, the families and empty nests fell in the middle, and the retired felt most in control of their finances. Single people felt that they could not predict the amounts of their bills. Those without dependent children but in work (the couples and empty nests) were more confident of knowing the contents of their bank account while the singles were the least confident. When they borrow money, some 15 per cent of the singles, compared to few or none of the others, report having little or no idea how they will pay back the debt. Singles more often feel they lose track of their spending when they use credit and that 'my budget seems to work out somehow' rather than 'I plan my budget to make the money coming in meet the expenses'; this is especially noticeable when they are compared with retired people (Table 6.7). Again, when asked whether 'my money just seems to disappear each month' or whether 'I know just where my money goes each month', singles and families were more likely to say that their money just disappears (Table 6.7).

Furby (1978) argues that possessions are important to adults because they increase control over the environment. The loss of financial control experienced through the acquisition process, especially for younger people, must undermine this advantage of goods, though possessions may instead satisfy other needs, particularly symbolic or identity needs and pleasure.

Comparing personal financial management with one's perceptions of both parents, certain differences between the life stages emerged. The single people often considered that they managed their finances worse than their mother (40 per cent) and father (56 per cent), while the retired especially thought that they managed much better than their mother (38 per cent) and father (36 per cent) with very few thinking that they managed worse than either parent. The findings reflect not so much a general age trend as a discontinuity between single people and those of any age with a partner or family. Whether they have yet to dispel a mystique about parental superiority or whether they simply feel the weight of challenges ahead, single people do not feel very positive about themselves or the future. They are also the target of considerable disapproval and incomprehension from people older than they are.

The general sense of managing better than one's parents may be explained in several ways. People may be referencing the sense of general improvement in living standards, with life becoming easier. In this case, the perception of personal progress would explain people's judgements of improved financial management in comparison with their parents, rather than the other way around. However, these judgements are not carried forward to their children: 53 per cent of those with children think that they manage their finances better than their children, and only 9 per cent think that their children manage better than they do. Remembering that these children are, of course, the generation from whom our sample of single people is drawn, it would seem that the middle and older generations attribute their own successes to their good management, while the younger people feel pessimistic for the future partly because they feel inferior in their abilities to manage their finances. Both generations are making internal, or personal, attributions, and on this basis making predictions about the future. Of course, the justification for these attributions remains open. Are the older generations really managing better? Or do things look better with the benefit of hindsight? Or, further, are their reference points different, with the older people remembering external problems of the pre-war and war periods, while the younger people judge themselves by expectations of mass media images of success?

Spending, identity and pleasure

It seems that younger people find a pleasure in acquiring objects, seeing this process of acquisition as relevant not only to their material lives but to other aspects of their lives also. The material and the immaterial – spiritual, intellectual, emotional – have become interlinked. When asked whether they would buy themselves something as a reward or bribe, singles and couples said yes, while empty nests would only sometimes, and families and the retired would only rarely reward themselves thus. As there were no differences between groups for promising other people a present as a reward or bribe, it may be that while buying things for oneself is still culturally a relatively private matter, the giving of gifts is still very much a matter for cultural prescription and rules (Douglas and Isherwood, 1978).

Morals, values and attitudes towards money

There is less emphasis on the importance of saving. And that makes a difference. When you and I were young it was very wrong to be in debt. It was regarded as a sin.

I do think that those of us of our generation that were poor, and most of us were, weren't we, our sense of values was different, wasn't it?

Many arguments about financial issues carry heavy moral overtones. Consumer choices invoke numerous basic moral judgements about, for example, what is a man, a woman, duty, family, self-worth. These judgements must be negotiated between the generations, over the decades, at family occasions (Douglas and Isherwood, 1978). Concern over the use or avoidance of credit raises underlying arguments about who is worthy, who is good or sinful, what actions are responsible or reckless and debates about consumer choices are often heated, tense, overladen with unstated meanings, hidden debates, old wounds.

Among our respondents, the retired group particularly endorsed an 'anti-debt' cluster of attitudes, seeing debt as a failure, as shameful, as to be avoided, while the single people, and to a lesser extent the couples, were 'pro-credit', seeing debt as normal, credit as a reasonable way of having what you want now, etc. The accounts given by each generation of the other seem to match the underlying attitudes of each, reflecting a generation gap in attitudes.

The groups also differed on a related issue: couples, and to a lesser extent single people, considered that although credit brings its own complications, none the less, debt is normal, part of everyday life and nothing to be ashamed of. They reflect, then, an ambivalence associated with their generally positive attitude towards credit. Older people, especially the empty nests, reject this position unambivalently, emphasizing instead that borrowing money simply reflects a failure to manage one's finances properly.

Attitudes to finances reflect more general underlying values which guide people's attitudes and behaviours in many life domains. We found that the generations differed here too. The younger generation (singles and couples) particularly valued achievement and self-direction, while families, empty nests and retired people, in contrast, emphasized social concern and security (Kamptner, 1989).

Social class

Just as there are popular images of different generations in relation to consumption, so too are there images of different social classes and consumption. These

Table 6.8   Percentage who believe parents should help their children financially, if needed, by social class

Class I	50
Class II	67
Class IIIN	76
Class IIIM	83
Class IV/V	53

connect with generation gaps to the extent that social class itself is changing, with the loss of unskilled jobs and the rise in white-collar and lower middle-class jobs. Are people becoming more middle class over the generations? Again, one can argue that these changes are illusory, with the relations between workers and bosses relatively unchanged. None the less, the question of social class differences is worth examining.

In our sample, there were in fact no differences between the social classes in the budgeting or managing of money. There were also no significant differences in ideas about parent–child influence or responsibility, no differences in possessions or in life events. The only exceptions were in relation to satisfaction or consumer sentiment, and in relation to helping children when they need help: higher social class was related to greater optimism about personal and general economic prosperity – clearly, this is also related to higher disposable incomes among the higher social classes. When asked if parents should help their children if they need it, the replies showed a general inverse relationship with class and income – those with more income, or of a higher social class, feel less responsibility to help, maybe because they feel that they have already invested in their children's education, while those with least feel most responsibility (Table 6.8). Finally, those in classes I, IIIN and IIIM generally felt they were doing better than their parents, whereas classes II, IV and V were less likely to feel that things were improving for them in comparison with their parents. Presumably, social mobility, or perceived social mobility, varies by social class.

Empirical differences across the generations and the life course

When we compare people at different stages in the life course and from different generations on a variety of consumption beliefs and practices, we can identify three distinct processes at work. First, people of all ages and stages broadly agree in their perceptions of mass consumption – they share a common social representation of what the younger and older generations do, they agree on what counts as a debt, and they agree on which goods are necessities and which are luxuries.

Secondly, clear age trends across the life course suggest evidence of generational differences. These age trends are seen in relation to values and attitudes towards everyday life and mass consumption, in relation to perceived control over finances, in the relations between spending, pleasure and identity, and in general trends in borrowing and debts. Here it seems that differing contexts of socialization have resulted in generational differences in mass consumption.

Thirdly, the specific demands and resources of different stages in the life course exert their own pressures on specific beliefs and actual practices, and so clear trends across the life course break down. This is evident in the frequency of actual borrowing to buy certain goods, perception and ownership of different types of goods and the perception and use of credit facilities. Thus there can be no simple translation of attitudes and perceptions into behaviour: some differences between the stages in the life course which are popularly attributed to generational differences (for example, beliefs about the use of credit cards or the definition of necessities) are better explained by stage in the life course. Moreover, while values and attitudes may vary as one's concerns change over the life course (Levinson, 1978), they are often limited in how far or how rapidly they can alter and adapt; hence discrepancies between attitudes and actions must add to the misunderstandings between generations. We should note, however, that people tell their stories from the point of view of their particular life stage: it may be that older people now value self-direction and ambition less than younger people, and so no longer recognize the ambition of their earlier years.

Families, at the mid-point of the life course, experience particular problems, for they are under greater economic stress, with more demands being made upon them, with less budgetary control and greater spending and borrowing, when compared to those who have no children or whose children have left home. To some extent, their life course commitments conflict with their generational identity. Maybe, like singles, they grew up during times of increased consumer durables and credit use, and yet unlike them, they have domestic demands which make consumption and debt more problematic.

Parents and children

Socialization, responsibility, dependency

> Attitudes are also parental, aren't they? I mean, my mum and dad, I am sure that despite the fact that times have changed, they are still influencing me now.

Where do people get their attitudes towards money and the consumption of goods from? What expectations and responsibilities bind the generations together in harmony or conflict? The great majority (88 per cent) of respondents felt that their parents were most responsible for their own attitudes towards money, with only a small minority identifying the government, school or TV. Similarly, 84 per cent of respondents consider that they, as parents, are most responsible for their children's attitudes towards money. Given that many parents consider that they manage their money better than their children, one wonders whether they feel they have done a poor job in influencing their children (Table 6.9, p. 126, shows that, on the contrary, people feel their children will do better because they, as parents, have passed on their valuable experience). Confused though parents may be in taking responsibility for the attitudes of the present younger generation, they often seem quite willing to blame other parents for other children:

> If they [children] were brought up correctly they would be responsible and would therefore act responsibly.

> I think that it all starts when you are very young with parents encouraging children if they want something to save for it, and then they realize what it is like to want something and not have it immediately, which is a problem today, they want it and they have it.

Their children are more ready to criticize or praise their parents directly:

> As far as instruction in financial matters, or setting an example, how one could think and behave and deal with money later in life, there was none of that, there were none of the hard examples, 'no you cannot have a new bicycle or football'.

> They taught me to be very very careful with money. They didn't have a great deal to go around, I suppose, when I was little, and in particular in their childhoods each of them was very hard up, so they've taught me to be careful. I don't think they've ever been in debt. I was encouraged to save my pocket money. I had a post office account opened at my Christening, and the best thing you could do with birthday money was go and put it in the post office account, so I was always encouraged to save, it was good to save.

If parents are responsible for their children's attitudes, are they also responsible for the finances? People at all life stages are agreed (94 per cent) that it is not the responsibility of parents to pay for their adult children's debts. Having none the less to pay these debts may cause resentment and distance between the generations:

> I think that parents like ourselves don't like the idea of children being in debt and themselves start paying off the children's debts because that is the way that we were brought up ourselves.

> I get accused of being rather old-fashioned by my children, who approve of credit and some of them live on credit. And I think that it should be discouraged because eventually they come back to me for money and I have to help them out.

In other respects, however, people differ on which role parents should adopt. For example, when asked whether parents should help their children set up home when young, a clear age trend emerges: 72 per cent of retired people believe that they should help their children set up home, 50 per cent of the 'empty nests' agree, 46 per cent of families, 36 per cent of couples, but only 21 per cent of single people. As each group is at a different life stage, we might hazard a guess that the majority of the retired people actually did help their children, as did some of the empty nests, and that half of the families received some help – or thought they should have done. Younger people either do not expect to receive much help, or think that they should not be thus helped. This may reflect decreased connectedness or increased independence between generations, and suggests that following the prospective increased inheritance of wealth following the housing boom of the late 1980s, those who least expect help might receive the most.

When asked whether parents should give their children financial help when needed, a similar trend is revealed: 44 per cent of single people think that parents should give this help, compared to 54 per cent of couples, 70 per cent of families, 90 per cent of empty nests and 87 per cent of retired people. To some extent, this may reflect a sympathy for the young on the part of older people, a recognition of the difficulties which young people face, as compared with their own lives:

> I don't know how anyone can get onto the housing ladder with the prices of houses, because the price of houses has gone way over what one earns in the last 20 years. If that is hanging over people's heads, then it is very worrying for young people.

> I wouldn't like to be a young person nowadays, no way.

> People no longer feel very secure in our society. Sooner or later the whole thing is going to go bust.

Remembering that the older people see the younger ones as managing badly, and further that they hold themselves responsible for their children's attitudes to money, one might further speculate that providing financial help when needed is one way in which parents ease their guilt as well as act from sympathy or duty. While acknowledging that they are not managing well, their children seem unlikely to regard this kind of help as appropriate, preferring to maintain independence from parents: 'But then, if you get parents sometimes who are interested in their kids to the extent where they will ask questions, the kids immediately become defensive and say the parents are being intrusive, don't they?' However, others do accept help: 'If they think I've got a lot of bills, they sometimes offer to help me out.'

Personal finances: Public knowledge or a private affair?

> My parents never really discussed money, money was just there.

How do the generations communicate about money? For those who have parents, around two-thirds of singles and couples report that their parents know what their financial situation is, as compared with only one-third of older people. For those who have spouses or partners, almost all say that their partners know of their financial situation, and for those who have children, roughly half of their children know of their finances (there are, however, questions about how much people know of their partner's finances, especially whether wives can be confident of knowing their husband's income). People differ in how much they tell their friends about their finances: singles feel that their friends know the least, families think friends know rather more, while for the retired, nearly four in five consider that most of their friends know of their financial situation. This may reflect varying sources of income. To ask someone their salary is to break a social taboo, based on the link between financial and moral worth, while pension levels are relatively public, and frequent public debates on benefits and pensions make them a social or policy issue rather than a personal one.

The generations report no differences in how often they think or worry about money. They do differ in how much they discuss financial matters with the 'significant others' in their lives. Singles, though they felt their friends knew least about their finances, discuss and argue about money more often with their friends than do older people: presumably for them money, or consumption, is seen as a public topic rather than a private problem. Families also report more arguments with their dependent children. Single people talk and argue more about money with both parents, especially as compared with families, while couples are the least likely to talk to their parents about money, especially to their fathers.

If knowing other people's finances, or talking about money with others, is a matter of personal privacy, then the public/private boundary is drawn differently for people at the different life stages. Theories of social support have consistently emphasized the importance of having other people who know of one's problems and can thus offer help when needed. Knowledge may bring not only practical support but also a sense of connectedness, of being part of a common experience. However, those who provide the support and those who need it may stand in equal or unequal relations to each other. Clearly, the parent–child relation is the least equal, that of partner may or may not be equal, while that of friends is the most equal.

Singles maintain a state of some tension, often knowing less of their parents' finances than their parents know of theirs, and certainly having fewer resources with which to support or intervene, while they actively discuss and argue about money with their peers, albeit on an impersonal level. Maybe this is part of the process of disengagement by which they make the symbolic transition from family of origin to the family they will construct themselves. Families seem the most private, keeping most knowledge and discussion within the nuclear unit, though couples also have few sources of support, as they have disengaged somewhat from parents but do not consider that their friends know of their situation, depending heavily on their own relationship. While retired couples talk and argue about money relatively infrequently except within the home and have lost their parents as possible confidantes, they seem less isolated in so far as their friends know of their situation without discussion being necessary because of common circumstances.

The belief in progress

Things are getting better all the time

I think that to some extent it is family background. Each generation wants to improve from the past generation. Well this is progress, isn't it? Things are bound to get better, irrespective of credit or anything else.

One of the most profound beliefs expressed by most of the people studied was in the concept of 'progress' (Katona, 1975). The many historical changes in the economy and social organization of everyday life are seen, in the main, as positive, as progressive, to be welcomed. This sense of 'progress' operates both as regards long-term generational trends and in the short term. Most people (69 per cent) feel better off than their parents when they were their age, and most (59 per cent) imagine that their children will be better off still when they reach the same age. In the short term, most believe they and their family are financially better off (47 per cent) or the same (33 per cent) as they were 1 year before, and most are optimistic about the year ahead: 41 per cent expect to be better off, 40 per cent expect to be the same, and only 19 per cent expect to be worse off. Maybe due to the boom in house prices or the weight of still unmade financial decisions looming, single people are the exception here, for 36 per cent expect to be worse off compared to only 14 per cent of the other groups.

We must not confuse personal and economic progress here. For while people are generally optimistic about the future, seeing a progressive improvement from parents to themselves, from themselves to their children, they are often pessimistic about the future of the economy in general. Only 10 per cent expect the next year to bring 'better times for the economy as a whole', and 53 per cent expect things to get worse. Thinking ahead to the next 5 years, they remain pessimistic, with 40 per cent expecting things to get worse and 33 per cent expecting an improvement. For the present, some 49 per cent think that the economy is doing either badly or very badly, again with younger people being more pessimistic than older people.

How can people maintain such optimism for themselves and their families in the face of a general pessimism about the economy in general? Does everyone think that they are the exception to the rule? One explanation may lie in the distinction between mediated and direct experience. The media continually tell stories of doom and gloom, for problems make better stories than contentment; indeed, problems are more worthy of public attention and concern than are satisfactory conditions. None the less, it seems that a social representation of gloom has resulted. People are dependent on the media for their understanding of 'the economy' (Ball-Rokeach, 1985; O'Guinn and Faber, 1991), but can judge their own financial well-being through direct experience which, for many but not all, is seen as positive. Tables 6.9 and 6.10 indicate the main reasons why people feel that they are better or worse off than their parents, and why they feel their children will be better or worse off when they reach their age.

The reasons why most people feel better off than their parents when they were the same age concern affluence, family commitments, lifestyle and social changes. Most particularly, nearly half of those who feel better off than their parents simply say they earn more: standards of living have improved, people have benefited from economic growth. This has various consequences: people think that they own more durable goods, they have benefited from increased home ownership, they have greater savings and more financial opportunities, compared to their parents. These are largely external economic attributions,

Table 6.9 Compared to your parents when they were your age, are you better off (69 per cent), worse off (18 per cent) or the same (13 per cent)? Why is this?

	Self better off (%)	Parents better off (%)
Affluence		
Higher incomes/better off	25	20
Improved living standards/economic growth	18	
Own more luxuries/consumer durables/cheaper goods	7	6
More savings/investments	7	2
Parental support	6	2
Bought own home	6	16
More opportunities/luck to acquire wealth	5	
Inheritance from parents/relatives	4	
Lower costs of living/inflation		12
Lower house prices relative to income		10
Not in debt	2	2
Family commitments		
No/fewer/later children	10	4
Single rather than married	4	
Married rather than single		4
Not divorced		6
Lifestyle		
Different lifestyle	9	10
Better education/more qualifications	9	6
Women work: have two incomes	7	
Better job/career	6	12
Manage finances better/more responsible	4	8
Upward mobility (in job/marriage/location)	4	
Studied for less time (earned sooner)		12
Social changes		
Better pensions	6	2
Regular employment (security, not unemployment)	6	6
No war and war after-effects	5	
Higher grants/welfare benefits/health	4	
Fewer consumer pressures and temptations	6	

from which they have benefited, but for which they take no credit. They also feel that their parents have directly supported them, passing on resources acquired later in life, through support and inheritance. Many feel they have gained by changed family commitments, particularly from delaying marriage – people do not think two can live more cheaply together – and from having fewer children or from having children later, clearly recognizing the increased expenses which children involve. Many feel that receiving more education than their parents has

Table 6.10 When your children are your age, do you think they will be better off (59 per cent), worse off (11 per cent) or the same (30 per cent)? Why is this?

	Children better off (%)	Self better off (%)
Affluence		
Improved living standards/economic growth	17	6
Higher incomes/better off	14	3
Parental support	8	3
Inheritance from parents/relatives	7	3
More opportunities/luck to acquire wealth	5	
Bought own home/bought earlier	3	
Lower house prices relative to income	1	3
Lower costs of living/inflation		19
Not in debt		3
Lifestyle		
Better education/more qualifications	14	3
Better job/career	10	
Manage finances better/more responsible	5	13
More ambitious		4
Gain parents' experience	4	
Different lifestyle	2	6
Women work: have two incomes	1	
Studied for less time (earned sooner)		3
Social changes		
Better pensions	2	
Regular employment (security, not unemployment)	2	3
Looming ecological crisis		10
Life getting harder		13
Fewer consumer pressures and temptations	3	

contributed to their greater incomes and better jobs (although as Halsey, 1978, notes in his discussion of social mobility, this education is unlikely to have changed their social class position, for those in the higher classes will have seen a comparable improvement in their own situations across the generations). They also point to changes in women's employment, resulting in dual income households. Somewhat less frequently, people also identified social changes such as improved pensions and benefits and lower unemployment, particularly compared with the pre-war generation. Finally, a number noted how their parents had suffered the lasting effects of a world war.

The reasons why people feel their parents were better off than they are when at the same age seem dependent on people's particular and diverse circumstances: maybe their parents earned more (20 per cent of those who feel worse off than their parents), or bought their own home whereas their children are renting (16 per cent), or had a better job or lived a different lifestyle. Some of the reasons indicate a sense of things more generally getting worse, the opposite of the belief in progress: their parents suffered fewer consumer pressures and temptations, or lived under conditions of lower inflation and cheaper living costs, particularly housing costs, or they didn't lose out by getting divorced. A few thought they had suffered by studying longer, thereby losing several years' income.

A similar picture emerges when people are asked whether their children will be better or worse off (Table 6.10). Again, most are optimistic, though rather more expect more stability into the next generation. The explanations for this picture, however, are less varied. In particular, people anticipate a continued growth in affluence, expecting further improvements in living standards and economic growth. They place considerable weight on their children's improved educational qualifications, anticipating better job prospects as a result:

And don't you think that with the working class, after the war, when educational opportunities came along, I don't know about other people, but I definitely wanted education for my children, the most important thing of all, which I had been deprived of, and I didn't care what happened as long as they had what I wanted.

Interestingly, they do not anticipate further changes in family commitments, with nothing being said about having children even later, about fewer or later marriages, or an increase in divorce – maybe such social changes are hard to imagine in advance. The significance of women working, better pensions, regular employment, and so forth is reduced: seemingly, the present generation of parents imagines that major social changes have taken place and that stability can be expected for the future, with the next generation simply increasing its qualifications, prospects and affluence. They anticipate a similar level of parental support and inheritance for their own children as that which they themselves received, but feel they have also benefited their children in other ways, by passing on their own experience of life, experience which they did not apparently receive from their own parents.

Those who are pessimistic about their children's prospects point to the increasing costs of living and rising inflation, to life getting generally harder, and to the looming ecological crisis, feeling that their children will be the ones to pay for present prosperity. Otherwise, a number feel that their children do not manage their money well, and so expect them to be worse off: 'I have a grandson who thinks that it is the right way to use other people's money rather than his own, and I can't make him understand that it really is his own money that he is spending in the end.'

While remaining proud of the ways they coped with financial problems in their lifetime, the post-war generation express the desire that their children should not suffer similarly or need to be compensated; thus they see themselves as attempting to break an inherited pattern. Ironically, they also recognize that this desire has created problems for their children:

A lot of parents, the post-war generation, can remember before the war when poverty meant starvation. And so when things did become better they wanted to give their children more. I wouldn't say that we spoilt them.

I think that perhaps that is when it started, just after the war, don't you, when children had been deprived, and parents said, oh we must give our children everything. And they overdid it. And children were then brought up to expect anything they wanted. Because they had had all they wanted, they thought that they could go on having all they wanted.

One of the trends is that the working class have got to some extent more wealth, and they look back to their parents who had to have second hand stuff and hand me downs, and the kids think well, we have a bit of money. It might be credit, but that is one reason why they want everything new, and they want to prove. It's a kind of rebellion. Whether they will go back to it when they have children of their own, I don't know.

They often seem ambivalent about how to judge the younger generation: are they irresponsible or ignorant, to be criticized or sympathized with, independent or greedy?

When you see some very sad programmes on the television, where parents have started to buy their own house and they are so proud of it, and then they are thrown out because they can't keep up with the mortgage, things, and then maybe I will go shopping and I see a young person putting things into the shopping trolley like biscuits and expensive cakes and things that can be made at home, I tend to lose sympathy, and yet on the other hand, they may not be able to cook.

My son was a bugger with money, he was always in debt. Credit wasn't available like that when we were teenagers. I think where we lived, there was always something to do down there, you didn't need money to go for a swim.

Golden age myths and the apocalyptic vision

Certainly we were not envious of people who had more than us at all. The people round about where we lived, they were very sympathetic towards each other. If somebody was ill, people would rally round. There was a community spirit certainly. In those days, families tended to live in the same area. Whereas, 1950-ish, housing estates were being built in this country and young married couples were being put on these housing estates from the slum areas and so they didn't have grandmother and mother round the corner did they? And I think this created a lot of tension and stress, a lot of problems.

People's understandings of their world depend on a story about historical change, often a story in which their own generation, rather than previous or subsequent ones, is at the pivot of change. The story takes one of two forms: the apocalyptic vision of the move from a golden age to a loss of values and standards, and the optimistic vision of a move from poverty to progress, often associated with the free market economy and technological innovation. These two modes of narrative have strong moral underpinnings – some claim that the world is getting better, as medicine develops and technology improves and welfare provision grows, others see a loss of faith, of traditional caring communities and the undermining of the family. Taking one's own generation as the pivot of change denies the doubts and anxieties of earlier times. For example, while many older people talked of their childhoods as stable and moral and poor, life then was changing rapidly. While at the beginning of the century, some 25 per cent of the population was estimated to be living in poverty, between the wars life for the majority of the working class improved:

> The First World War strengthened their pride and self-confidence, and, although the Depression affected many of them badly, the twenties and thirties were good decades of rising living standards for the workers employed in the new industries . . . and in the middle years of the twentieth century the majority of working people enjoyed a high degree of prosperity and a style of life which was very similar to that of the new-middle classes . . . gradually the mass of the people were collected and consolidated into a broad, modestly prosperous [and white collar] mainstream (Roebuck, 1973, p.9).

Going back further, the Edwardian years are often seen as years of confusion and contradiction – about the economy, the Empire, politics, women's suffrage, religion and the family. Moreover, the debate about mass consumption, materialism and personal identity, far from being new, was alive many years ago:

> The disillusion of the interwar years was thus tinged with irreligion and anti-establishment religion from the start . . . Some people sought relief from the problems of the world in amassing possessions and improving their material standard of living, while yet others began to maintain that materialism offered no cure for any ills, personal or social (Roebuck, 1973, p.111).

In historical and social analysis, the narrative of progress, and of history as a struggle between progressives and reactionaries, is now challenged. Modernity, modernization and the faith in science and the loss of religion, all are undergoing debate and reconsideration, provoked by, among other events, the role of science in Auschwitz and Hiroshima, by religious revivalist movements, and by the collapse of communism. Indeed, comparisons between present and previous times are extremely difficult to make. They often assume a purposive, moral view of social change, where social developments are intentional, where their results are foreseen, where some social plan is being enacted, or, on the apocalyptic view, where some moral force is punishing society for its selfishness and greed. The anti-nuclear campaign and the green movement seem to promote this fear of the apocalypse, and many traditions – liberal, socialist, communist – argue for the social benefits of putting grand and well-intentioned plans into practice. Certainly, much political propaganda exploits both hopes and fears concerning the future, the unknown.

A further problem is that popular historical comparisons in particular presume direct comparability of specific changes between one historical period and another. Thus one may castigate present society for its neglect of the elderly, compared to earlier, caring communities, without realizing that the present size of the elderly population is far greater, as a consequence of improved medicine and hygiene. Or one may welcome the increased availability of meat for one generation of children over an earlier one without noticing that this availability has its costs (chemical additives, intensive farming methods). The evaluation of social change depends on   the context of change and its unintended as well as intended consequences.

One way of understanding the generation gap as regards attitudes, under- standing and morality is through these twin narratives of the belief in progress and the apocalyptic vision. Thus intergenerational comparisons express either the belief in progress ('We only had an outside toilet, but my children have a dishwasher and a video, things are much better now, they are so lucky') or – or sometimes, and – the apocalyptic vision ('Young people nowadays expect to have everything given to them, they don't value things and just get into debt, expecting someone else to bail them out'). Certainly, people draw on both narratives in making sense of their lives, often being inconsistent or con- tradictory: motivation seems to depend on the feeling that things are getting better, and yet a recognition of mortality, disappointment and corruption cannot be avoided.

These narratives also provide a means of expressing profound emotions – envy, guilt, self-righteousness, fear, hope. When people are young, their material lackings are popularly justified in terms of necessity and frugality. When older, they must find a way of understanding why younger people have things they didn't have (assuming, once again, that the meaning of possessing a refrigerator in 1930 is comparable with its meaning today). It seems from many of our older discussants, that a sense of material injustice is made acceptable by the assertion of psychological or spiritual justice (they have the refrigerator but no community feeling or spiritual values). In this way, uncertainties are resolved and the sense of a just world is maintained (Lerner, 1980). Indeed, this is the justification offered by the Protestant work ethic; crudely, that material frugality leads to moral superiority. Thus they talk of the pleasure in saving up and waiting, finding fault with the otherwise obvious pleasure of immediate possession.

Political ideologies demand progress. Under capitalism, progress often trans- lates into a continued demand for new products (Forty, 1986), even though new products may not actually involve progress – consider the problematic case of labour-saving devices increasing rather than reducing housework (Davidson, 1982; Cowan, 1989) and, moreover, people are conservative, resisting change and novelty. This conservatism is partly fuelled by representations of what is being lost – classicism, the golden age, the glorious past – and may represent not a resistance to capitalism or market pressure, but the embedding of consumer products in everyday thinking and practice. Thus identities, pleasures, relationships and understandings may be as much bound up with the person–object relationship as they are with the person–person relationship, and may be as much constructed by economic and technological considerations as they are by interpersonal and social processes. The significance of change is itself problematic, for to be always changing has in itself become essential for modern identity.

It seems that 'in my day' serves as a cultural reference point for the rest of one's life, that point when, sometime in late adolescence or early adulthood, one becomes highly aware of contemporary ideas or practices but not yet aware of the relativity of those ideas and practices. A generation projects a sense of stability backwards onto the past and a sense of disjunction is experienced with the ideas and practices of that generation's children. So, for the generation which was brought up with radio, radio was normal and always in existence, while the TV represents a break between 'my children' and 'in my day'. Similarly, too, for the generation brought up without the car, that seems to introduce a great change in a stable way of life, and they forget that previous generations had themselves seen great changes – the toilet, electricity, and before that, the railway. The later adult's realization of different times and places seems not to dislodge that early confidence of knowing how things are and, more prescriptively, how things should be, or what is right. The relation between parents and children must exert its own influence across time, helping to explain why every generation has thought, ambivalently, both that things are 'going to the bad' and will never be the same again, and also that progress is happening before their eyes.

We can now add a further process to the three identified earlier, and conclude that four key factors determine how people of different ages differently relate to mass consumption processes, namely social representations of generations and of consumer culture, historical influences at the period of early adulthood, the demands and resources of one's stage in the life course, and the pressures and misunderstandings which exist at all stages between parents and children.

EVERYDAY ACCOUNTING FOR MASS CONSUMPTION

SEVEN

What do people think about the commodities they desire, purchase and own? How do they regard advertising or banking practices? Why do they think people get into debt? What possibilities do they see for resistance or alternative life-styles? In this chapter, we examine people's beliefs about, and accounts of, mass consumption. We begin by considering people's accounts of their relation to consumer society in the context of their life stories. We then focus on three related themes: general discourses about present consumer society; representations of luxury and necessity; and the ordinary explanation for personal debt.

Beliefs, accounts and representations

Most theories of consumption give some role to the beliefs, attitudes and opinions of the consumer, for the perceptions of the consumer mediate buying decisions, economic practices gain their meaning through their interconnections with belief systems, and beliefs play a role in appropriating goods into local and domestic cultures.

It is sometimes said that it doesn't matter what people think or understand, it's what they do that is important. We would argue that beliefs, and we use beliefs here to refer also to attitudes, explanations, representations, etc., are central to understanding social phenomena for several reasons. As symbolic interactionism has always argued, if people believe something to be the case, then that belief has real consequences because people act according to the world as they see it. This also relates to research showing that the ways in which people explain events affects their subsequent motivations – if they attribute failing an exam to personal inabilities rather than to their poor teacher, they will be less motivated to work for the next exam (Weiner, 1986). Similarly, beliefs can be seen to mediate the effects of social or economic factors through interpretative processes: how you react to a price increase or a new fashion depends partly on whether you perceive it as significant or as appropriate to your social group.

In other words, ordinary understandings, explanations and beliefs are semiotic, they make events meaningful, giving life to socially significant distinctions or judgements. They are inherently social, drawing on diverse forms of cultural representation and practice, but must often be negotiated anew for each person in the construction of social events. As beliefs gain their power through ideology and social difference, in the main, although the oppositions and subversions are important, they tend to be conservative, working to maintain and validate the status quo. For example, in the course of our interviews and discussions, many familiar clichés were quoted in explanation or advice:

- cut your garment according to your cloth;
- look after the pennies;
- make do and mend;
- the poor you have always with you;
- neither a borrower nor a lender be.

These clichés show not only that people do not always do their own thinking, but draw on socially given images and phrases, but also that such clichés tend to locate responsibility with the individual actor rather than with society, promising as a reward for accepting this view that 'the meek inherit the earth'. One of our interviewees began his life story with a host of such phrases:

> We didn't have much money, times were very hard when I was a child and the attitude was waste not want not, and save some money if you can for a rainy day and don't buy anything on credit, if you can't afford it do without it and try to save some money to buy what you want for cash and go through life like that. It was a question of being prudent and making things last. You don't throw anything away unless you have to. I accepted it.

Finally, beliefs are complex, first because they draw on multiple roots, encoding cultural oppositions, connecting to other beliefs and to everyday practices (de Certeau, 1984) and social structures. Secondly, they concern the explanation of complex social phenomena (Heider, 1958; Kelley, 1967, 1983): people understand societal phenomena, e.g. poverty or unemployment, through multiple interrelations among beliefs and explanations (Furnham, 1982; Lunt, 1988, 1989, 1991; Heaven, 1990). Finally, common sense can be viewed for its rhetorical as well as representational content: 'in indicating our attitudes, we do more than merely express our personal beliefs, and thereby something of ourselves as individuals. We also locate ourselves within a public controversy' (Billig, 1991, p.43). Thus to understand the nature of personal identity in an age of mass consumption, we must understand how people make sense of their world, how they explain the events around them, and how they locate themselves in relation to others.

Everyday beliefs and assumptions in personal biographies

We begin by considering how different understandings of one's relation to society can be seen in different personal biographies. When telling their life stories, people inevitably reveal their perspectives on many social, personal and moral matters. In so doing, they draw on commonsense understandings which may be shared by the culture, or may be specific to their class, gender or generation. They are also faced with the task of presenting a sensible account, one which makes sense to the interviewer and, more importantly, to themselves. Some use a narrative framework to show how their understandings developed, how their present beliefs are grounded in past events. Others use a thematic framework to show how key themes have from the beginning provided a structure for their lives. Each tells their story also to another, imaginary listener – the normal person, against whom distinctions are drawn or from whom normative approval is expected. This imaginary 'normal person' may be a representation of 'the younger generation' or the majority of one's own peers or the typical consumer or whatever. We present extracts from three of the biographical interviews here. Roughly speaking, they illustrate different positions – the engagement and conformity of living within the consumption system, the disengagement of dropping out of, or being unaware of, the system, and the oppositional position of alternative living.

Our first interviewee lived very much within the system. Muriel, now aged 67, has lived a 'traditional' life, consistent with the Protestant work ethic.

Family background

We were a large family. There were six children, and farming. So there wasn't a lot of money to spare. I was born in the 1920s, you see, so things were pretty tight. We had the essentials, but the luxuries we certainly had to save up money for and work for it, it wasn't just handed to us on a plate like today, you know.

Learning to budget: A jolly good upbringing

You were given pocket money. Children today are given a pound, two pounds a week. Nothing like that happened with us. We just had to either do jobs for our pocket money or we kept chickens or ducks or whatever and sold the produce. So we had to do budgeting because if the hens weren't laying we didn't get any pocket money. So it was really very good, it was a jolly good upbringing in a way, because it made you appreciate money and it made you realize that you just had to, well, one day you might have an awful lot and the next day you mightn't have anything at all if you didn't budget it out. We had a very, very happy childhood. It was absolutely super.

Learning to save, learning to value

I remember vividly wanting a particular doll and I had to save up for it and the doll was in the shop, and the shopkeeper said, 'Right, I'll keep it for you and you can come in each week and pay it off', and when I'd paid it, it was mine. That I think was tremendous. It stands you in good stead later on in life because you don't go out and buy things willy nilly when you want it today and forget about it tomorrow. The same happened at birthdays and Christmas, you had things that you really wanted, not a lot of unnecessaries. We didn't think we were deprived in any way at all. Of course, with the family, there was a lot of hand-me-downs. You accepted it, didn't you. I don't think there was so much keeping up with the Joneses then.

Treats and hardships

When I was a teenager I left school and did a commercial secretarial course. I was 17. That was in 1939, when I qualified, and I had a job for about 18 months, 2 years, I suppose, and then I was called up, I went into the forces. My first job, my salary was 15 shillings a week, paid by the month, which wasn't a fortune. When I went into the forces it was worse, it was 7s 6d a week. At least I was clothed and fed. Of course, as you went on and passed exams and things the pay went up. We basically spent it on food and entertainment. There wasn't any opportunity to get yourself dressed up, you had to be in uniform full time. So 7s 6d didn't go very far. If you had a day off, the biggest treat was to go into a restaurant and have something different from army food. There was no chance of saving anything. And after the war I came back and went back into the bank where I had been. You felt you had a fortune then, and that was only about three pounds a week I think. There again, there weren't the things to buy, the material things, immediately after the war, were there? I was in digs. The majority of your salary went on paying for accommodation. That was only from Monday to Friday, and I went home for the weekend, which was, of course, free for me. I used to cycle there and back, it saved the bus fare, it was about 17 or 18 miles. No one would do that nowadays would they?

Marriage: Getting sorted out

In 1948 I got married, and there again, when you got married, you had to leave your job, they didn't employ any married women in the bank in those days. You just had to go. Accommodation was a premium just after the war, and the only way we managed to get a flat was to know someone who was leaving it, and it happened to be a friend of my husband, and he said, 'Well, do you want it', and it was literally one room with a cupboard for a kitchen and you washed up over on a boiler with the bath. And the rent on that was two guineas a week. And that was jolly expensive. He was in the bank as well. Then we graduated to, it was all by word of mouth, and we moved to another place and we had the whole of the ground floor, and we were very lucky, there again, it was through my parents who knew the owner of the flat. It was less money than we were paying and about four times the accommodation, so we stayed there for quite some time, about 3 years.

Own home: Managing on our own

We bought our own house, which we still live in today, only that was a big struggle, it was expensive, but well worth the struggle. The bank set you up with a mortgage. They were very dictatorial in those days, because they considered that you should buy a house which is comparable to your salary. Anyway, we wanted one which was a bit more than that. So they were a bit nasty really. We certainly weren't helped in those times, like people are today, in their mortgages and things. If you move from A to B they'll pay your removal and all that kind of thing. If we had to move, you were on your own. I mean, you just had to sort it out yourself and hope it – I suppose you could always say your parents were in the background for a helping hand, but we never had to call on them, thank goodness. We managed on our own.

Setting up home: Things were different then

So then I got a part-time job and went back to work to the same firm where I got my first job. There was no way I could go back to the bank because they still did not or would not employ married women, so I went back to the insurance company until our son was born. Things were pretty tight. You didn't have much to spare at the end of the day. Having said that, there weren't the pressures put on people to buy things in those days. I mean, we were married 10 years before we had a fridge. That today is unheard of, nobody lives without a fridge. We didn't have a TV for a long long time, there wasn't all the advertising. We were happy in our situation. We didn't feel hard done by at all. You had to be careful. You budgeted for holidays and things like that. We didn't have money to throw around.

Joint finances: No worries

I was given so much housekeeping money to buy the general day-to-day requirements and he paid all the bills. If things became more expensive then I had more. Perhaps I was very lucky to have a bank manager for a husband because he's always helped with all the finances. I can honestly say I've never had any financial worries in my life, never, because he's always dealt with it all, so perhaps I've been very lucky, I don't know. I don't think we have bought anything we couldn't afford. We were very conscious of being careful. I think it all stems back to your upbringing, I'm sure it does. I think it starts right from the cradle, almost, whether you're a spender or a saver. I don't consider myself mean, but when I buy things for myself I don't just think I'll have that whether I need it or not. I don't part with my money easily. I think I'm far more generous if I'm giving it to someone else. I'm quite happy with what I've got.

Parenthood: Doing the right thing

As you progress and get promotion and so on, your salary goes up and it becomes easier. But then we had our son, and we decided that he should go to boarding school as he was an only child. When he was six I got a job again, a part-time job only, because I was able to be at home when he was at home and it was in a school so therefore I got all the school holidays, so that was ideal. Then he went to a prep school and then to a public school, away. And I continued to work, to do my part-time job. We worked it out that my husband paid for school fees and everything and I clothed him out of my salary and that worked very well indeed. And since then he has thanked us very much for what we did for him.

Repeating the pattern, breaking the pattern

We brought him up the same way that we had been brought up, that if he wanted to have anything luxurious then he'd got to save up for it. And it's stood him in excellent stead, I think. When he was at public school, he got a job every holiday and he did all sorts of things. Well, really, it's just part of his education, which was absolutely great. When he went to university, he still got a job in the holidays and he didn't expect us to give him money and he never got into debt either. He's now 32. When he left university he went to London. He lived in the YMCA for 3 years and then he said, I must buy a flat, I must get my feet on the ladder. We helped him buy the flat, not very considerably. It was far better to give him the money then than to wait till we're dead. He won't want it then, and he'll have struggled on, and so we felt it was far better to give it to him then than to wait till we'd died to have it. In retrospect, that's when we needed help and hadn't got any parents then to help us, both our parents had died, so we were really on our own, so we really knew what it was like not to have anyone to feel you know that if you are up against it really you had someone to fall back on.

The next generation: Parental influence

He's moved since then, and got something bigger. Mind you, he's in the world of finances, and maybe he knows what he's doing. He's now married with a child, and he's never come to us for money or anything or to bail him out in any way at all. I'm sure he's still got a mortgage. I don't know how he manages his money. I'm certain he uses credit cards, but, well, I would be very surprised if he got so in debt that he can't cope with it. I think that he's very careful. Perhaps it's all to do with his upbringing. I don't know, I do think that makes a lot of difference. If you've always been brought up to have what you like when you like whether or not you can afford it, you continue to do that. Myself to this day, you stop and think, well do I really want it? Is it really necessary, because it's been inbred in you, hasn't it? I know some friends of ours have got two daughters and they're everlastingly coming back and saying well, we need some help with this and that, mother will you shell out two or three hundred pounds a time. Well, it's never going to be any different for them, because they think, well, mother or father will pay up if we get into bother, but it shouldn't be, should it? At least, I don't think it should be.

Retirement: Keeping busy

I'm retired and so is my husband. After my son went off to boarding school, he didn't really come back home except for holidays, because he then went to university and then to the city. I mean, he used to come, he comes back quite frequently, but he was never living at home as such. So things were different then. But he's always there, anyway. We're working harder now than we did then, voluntarily. We do a lot of voluntary work. I think the general view is that when you're retired, everyone is calling on you to do this or that. But it's rather wonderful to be wanted still, and it certainly keeps your brain-box ticking over. I like to be busy doing things. There's so much to be done, and people to be helped, if you're willing to do it.

Our next interviewee pays little attention to normative assumptions when discussing her own life course, and appears to have dropped out of the economic/consumption scene. From a well-off, upper-middle class family, Margaret is now in her 60s. Her father 'made money from tobacco in Rhodesia', her mother 'was from Knightsbridge, Parisian everything'. Most of the family's money was lost when she was young, and her mother brought the children back to England where they just managed, with some family help, to send the children to private schools: 'a childhood of moving, moving, moving'. She learnt to draw and paint, married a man with a private income of four pounds a week who 'was very charming, but thought he was going to be a poet . . . he was an idealist, a dreamer, a pacifist' but he 'wasn't very good at getting jobs'.

Married life: Finding somewhere to live

Some friends offered us their flat for 2 months, so we got married. When I was pregnant, mother decided we should have a flat to have the baby, and then we moved to a flat for two pounds a week. And we had friends who were living on a sinking barge in the meadows, and they said they were going to Cornwall, would we like it for fifty pounds, so we moved down there. We had to bail it out every other day, and you went out to a little boat and collected a bucket of water and that was enough for bottles and cooking for a day unless people came and had coffee which they constantly did and we ran out of water. We weren't allowed to be in there either, and I used to push the pram around to collect firewood, and if we wanted to go out at night we moved the lock with a penknife and marched out, and invariably, the police would be coming up from the police station and we'd pretend we had a key. Anyway, then an artist who lived in St. Ives wanted to come here, so would we like his house and he could have the barge? So we said fine, and down we went to St. Ives, I suppose we were just living on the four pounds a week. Meanwhile, before we went to Cornwall, a friend of my husband's was selling a cottage for a thousand pounds, and he managed to get that money out of his trustee, so before we went to Cornwall, we knew we were coming back to a cottage, with two rooms upstairs, two down.

Where would the money come from?

You see, instead of getting a job, he started running a peace association. I was amazed, I mean, with my mother in the background saying where's the income, and obviously me sort of thinking what have I landed myself with. From teenage years I had a dress allowance of two pounds a week, so that added to the four pounds made six.

A second honeymoon

We came back from Cornwall and he wanted a second honeymoon, everyone wanted to go to the Continent. Funnily enough, he introduced me to a lovely woman, and she came to tea, and my daughter crawled all over her and this woman was desperately trying to become pregnant, and couldn't, and she said 'Oh some people say if you adopt a child you then become pregnant', so I said in desperation, 'would you like to borrow this one for a month', you see, oh and I had a fabulous charlady at the time, so she said yes, so we moved cot, highchair, child and charlady to her house, we let our cottage for 6 weeks, and we set off for Florence.

A lifetime of problems

[A good friend] had very blithely said to mother, well the only problem [preventing her husband getting a job] is that they've got too much money, six pounds a week, stop her dress allowance, my beastly husband exploded over this and said, well she can't see our daughter, and this went on for several months, meanwhile I said you must get a job . . .

This pattern continued, interrupted by sporadic crises. Margaret had a second child and her husband held a job for a while so they bought a house with help from her mother, putting the house in Margaret's name. He was soon sacked, started to study, and the house was furnished from junk shops and hand-me-downs: 'I would cook baked beans, I would cook sheep's heads'. When she was teaching painting part-time, he had a nervous breakdown, and afterwards he bought a share in a glider, and together they looked after groups of children, living in the marshes, teaching them ecology. She then had a breakdown and they lived apart for some years. Margaret comments on her present life: 'I am very careful, I pay my bills, I don't have holidays ... I don't want any more shocks ... It's a peculiar life, isn't it? I don't think I've fitted in anywhere ... '.

Finally, some of our interviewees were committed to alternative lifestyles lived out in conscious opposition to their perceptions of 'the normal'. From a middle-class family, Nick is now in his 30s. There was nothing out of the ordinary about the way his parents handled money, he got the normal amount of pocket money, his parents did not explicitly instruct him in financial matters and they themselves used credit to obtain material goods but were never in serious financial difficulties. Nick did paper rounds and Saturday jobs until he left school at 18.

An average background

When I was between the ages of 10 and 17, my parents' finances were very typical of their peer group. They were living largely on credit or in debt, they had a mortgage, company car, salaried rather than a waged job, a fairly good spread of the latest consumer durables bought often on credit. They were not in debt or suffering, but they were certainly stretched. But it was common of people of that kind to live in that way, live now pay later. So I would say thoroughly average.

The life of Riley

At the time I left school people were saying there was a recession. I hadn't had much experience of the working world. And I didn't look too strongly for a job and I claimed the popular state benefits, the dole, and led the life of Reilly for a while. That was what all my friends were doing, those that didn't go to university felt that that was actually a good way of doing it. To take a year off, couple of years off, and we all thoroughly enjoyed it and didn't feel we were over financially stretched.

Not settling down

Then I got several jobs in offices and things like that moving on out of my late teens and early twenties and beyond. But I've never gone into a job with a view to building a career within that particular area so I've never been settled in a particular job or particular career path. I've never, therefore, had foreseeable earnings and have never therefore got into the habit of using credit. Nothing in my childhood, as I've explained, was particularly conducive to teaching me how to handle or manage money. So I didn't get into the habit of using credit, although I've got nothing against credit *per se*. I wasn't establishing a home or any of that kind of thing which I think many people in that age group are nowadays thinking of doing. I was still playing like a child rather than being an adult. I had no need to go out and buy a fridge or buy a car and buy a suit and tie and collect about me all the icons of maturity. I had no investment in that at all.

Desiring and acquiring goods

I've never been acquisitive in any sense at all. If something becomes available to me, then I will look seriously at whether or not I want it, but I don't form ideas about wanting things and then go out seeking them. There isn't anything I'm thinking about now that I particularly want. There's nothing I would go into a shop and want to buy. The history of things I have acquired, a typical thing would be someone who by dint of the nature of their work acquired a load of surplus to their requirements trading stamps – they had become eligible to them, they didn't honestly want them. And that more or less describes the pattern of my acquisition of everything. My TV set I got in a jumble sale, my video I got because I saw it advertised in a newspaper. Prior to picking up that newspaper I hadn't intended to buy it. And all durable offers are more or less the same. Serendipity. That's what I call it. Things just appear. And when they appear I decide whether I'm the person they should go to or not.

Comparisons with others

I've acquired things very much later than my peers though. They've got themselves on a career path, got themselves some money and by the time they're 19 or 20 they've got everything I've got now. But they've worked for it and they've sweated and they've had nightmares about it. And maybe they haven't paid for it yet. At least everything I own, I haven't had to worry about it. I think that all the social pressures on them would divert them from wanting to acquire things second-hand. There's the pride of slapping your money or credit card on the counter and buying something new. And I think a lot of people working in a normal career path experience just that pride that they've been conditioned to operate on. We've all been conditioned to operate in some way by some thing. Or been influenced, should I say, to operate in a certain way.

My peers

I tend to imagine that my peer group are being less acquisitive or to whatever extent they are acquisitive that is less a prime feature of their outlook on life. I would just say that my peer group are more thinking people, you know? And I'm proud of it. Now they would all say, the career-orientated people, 'We may not be thinking people but we're doers, shapers and movers', and they'd be proud of that. And we each take our place on the rung of the ladder.

Values

They [ordinary people] are not very complicated people and it gives them pleasure to earn money and spend it. Now it gives people like myself pleasure to do a great many more complex and satisfying and interesting things. Along with earning money and spending it, that's got its place in this life. Let's be fair about that. But these other guys and women don't honestly have those higher concerns. In a nutshell, contemptuous of me though it may sound, without developing it any further, that's how I would briefly state it. I occasionally go round the museum. And I've gone round the museum with other people and the one comment I've heard from one person is 'I wish all these things had prices on them, you know'. Because he can understand what he's looking at if it's got a price on it. He can place it in its position in the world and in the hierarchy of things so the thing is not to be valued necessarily or specifically for its beauty as opposed to another thing but the thing with the £500 price tag has got to be valued more than the thing with the £100 price tag. And he's not actually sufficiently complex in his outlook, in the way he perceives his world, understands the things he encounters to take on board any kind of more subtle reasoning. You can't say to him 'Oh, it doesn't matter'. You've got two things that don't have price tags on them. You form an opinion about which one you prefer without that and he'd say, 'No, I wish they had price tags on them'. Now that's been my experience of these people, and that's how I formed my earlier expressed nutshell opinion.

Living differently from others

I'm not a hippy or a drop out, I've no great axe to grind against Thatcher's Britain or the consumer society or any of that kind of thing. I'm not standing outside consumer society as some kind of act of protest. I'm not trying to smash it or burn it or settle it in any way at all. And I'm not part of any group with a common aim to do something like that. I think I stand outside the alternative as much as I stand outside the straight world. I've kind of shunted outside the normal run of consumer living. It doesn't mean that I've made a step outside it. So having said that it's no big deal, the way it works is I've got an appreciation for the consumer durables, I like to be comfortable. I like to have options, using things chosen from a variety of choices rather than getting up and saying today I will wear my blue jeans because blue jeans are all I've got, it's nice to have a pair of black jeans to go with it, you know, and maybe ponder which ones will I wear today. It's nice to exercise options and therefore it's nice to acquire the goods to hold in readiness for a choice to be made.

Shopping

The places I tend to frequent are jumble sales or auctions, second-hand sales. I positively dislike shopping in a shop on the occasions when I've bought durable items brand new. First of all I feel a duty to rush around every shop selling the same one to see what the cheapest bargain is. And having rushed up and down in the town I always find that the cheapest one is the first one I went to, so I've got to rush back. And there is someone, I don't know, he's probably 19 years old and he's got an IQ way down here and he's very pleased with himself and he sees me coming in and he feels so smug because he saw me in the earlier part of the day and I asked him what seemed to him a lot of silly questions and wasted a lot of his time and now I'm coming back to buy something. So he's won and now I find that that's one reason why shopping at shops is often a flat and unpleasant experience.

Discourses on consumer society

I think that young people these days, they talk of buying houses, and that is one of the things that cause them to get into debt over small things, because they have to pay such a big mortgage, repayment and things, they have the opportunity to live on credit for the necessities that they require. This gets them further into debt, I think. They can't afford it, these house prices that are so terrific.

There was a considerable concern among our participants about recent changes in the way people conduct personal finances. Put crudely, there was a notion that traditional values of thrift, prudence and patience were replaced by increased personal debt, avarice and impatience. All these changes were seen as rooted in changes in the finance system (the growth of credit) and in the death of traditional communities.

People of all ages often referred to the time when one had to perform most or all financial transactions in cash. There was a nostalgic element to these recollections, in terms of the past having been a simpler age when personal accounting meant how much money you had left from the weekly wage, when it was wrong to use credit and if you wanted something you saved until you could afford it. The emphasis in the discussions was very much on being in control of finances, knowing what was the right thing to do and sticking to it. That these views were expressed in all discussion groups was surprising: younger people talked of their parents' times, people in their 40s and 50s sounded older than they really were, and older people talked as if the past was consistent and homogeneous. Most of the focus groups had been mixed in age, and the fact that the dominant representation was of the golden age of cash and saving up, suggests that, whatever people's personal experiences, this view is the generally accepted social and moral representation of everyday economic life (Moscovici, 1984). Of course, there were many disagreements, and many diverse opinions were expressed. People were not just expressing opinions in these discussions, they also argued, justified, explained, gave examples from their own lives, speculated and joked.

One key issue was the balance between personal and institutional control. In the idealized traditional, cash-based system, the financial institutions exercised considerable control over the availability of loans and credit: 'Banking has changed from all recognition, hasn't it? I mean, in the old days you didn't get a bank loan very easily, you had to have it guaranteed by your parents or god-father, or someone, but now it doesn't seem to matter. They go in and they can have it.' People are aware that the banks have now discovered the ordinary person as a market in which to make money by selling credit, moving away from the previous image of banks as advising and controlling:

> When we finished our mortgage we were told that it might be a good idea to get out another mortgage on another car, or you know, not to pay off, there was an actual sort of, don't finish your mortgage, because your money will be best left as a mortgage, we finished it last year and it was marvellous. But we were actually advised by one or two people not to finish our mortgage, it was extraordinary.

> I have heard people say how kind their bank managers have been because they have allowed them a good overdraft, but they don't seem to understand that that is why he is there, to make money out of them.

The new consumption system is seen as institutions giving up responsibility to the ordinary person, with the 'inevitable' consequence that some people will not be able to cope and that they will get into financial difficulty. These consider-ations mirror the concerns of pre-Keynesian economists with the lack of thrift in the working classes and the consequent notion that the answer to these problems is to educate people to handle their money:

> I think that before they leave school they should be given a lesson or two into finance and how to manage a bank account, or their money in any way at all. They don't do they?

> I would like to see children from the age of 5, when they start school, get education about handling money, because I know someone, who is perman-ently in debt and can never pay off the bills, and I think that credit is OK as long as people can handle the money.

The credit card was frequently attacked (although most people had one) because it cuts across the self-control and moral position of the cash system. Credit makes things instantly available without saving, so people lose the saving habit. Underlying these statements is a notion of lack of self-control, and indeed, as we saw earlier, in the study of savings and debt, people who save felt more in control of their finances and those who borrowed felt less in control. The credit system is seen as a major source of loss of individual control, satisfying the desire for ownership of possessions but leading to lack of self-discipline. Ford (1988) notes that credit cards in fact represent a very small proportion of personal credit; it is interesting, then, that they symbolize the new consumer society.

How are credit cards seen to lead to this degree of lack of control? Here people point to the properties of the credit card: essentially that it is not money, and that you do not need to have the money to acquire goods, you only have to be creditworthy. Goods are temptations, and with a credit card in our hands we think ourselves to be less capable of resisting this temptation. When we hand over cash we notice it. We are giving away our money in exchange for the goods. When we use credit we do not suffer the same loss. Money also induces more care: you can only buy what you can afford out of your pocket. There was also an awareness that credit is part of the sales techniques used in shops. The free availability of credit means that the shopper is deemed creditworthy by the shop – the person is allowed to participate. The expression of this belonging is through buying, and so, to express their legitimate consumer status, being sanctioned by the shop with credit, people buy. But then later they find they cannot meet the repayments. Thus credit introduces a crucial time lag into shopping: have now pay later means we have the fun part of consumption and delay payment. If we think of this as cost and gratification, instead of meeting the costs and delaying the gratification as in saving, with credit we gain the gratification and delay the cost.

However, the advantages of the credit card are also acknowledged. And again there is a debate as to whether the availability of credit is in itself a bad thing or whether it is an opportunity which people are not using properly or have not learned to use properly: 'It is easy I think to be lulled into dismissing credit completely as an unworthy and even evil thing. But I don't think that it necessarily is, it's being misused in the current age.' Many practical advantages were discussed, such as not having to carry money around, being able to make spontaneous purchases and having accounts sent for expenditure: 'I think that credit too, these days, it's easier to have a credit card and shop for various items, and then just pay one cheque at the end, this is very convenient.' Also, the system can be worked in a variety of ways. Some people reported investing their salaries at the beginning of each month in deposit accounts and using credit cards for most purchases with deferred payments. Others felt that the anonymity of borrowing using credit cards was an advantage, allowing one to avoid a potentially difficult and embarrassing encounter with a bank official.

These advantages and disadvantages did not come as separate lists but were linked. For example, not having to see a bank official about a loan was both an advantage in not having to justify expenditure and a disadvantage because having to justify oneself makes people think twice. Similarly, making spontaneous purchases was an advantage, but this increased the possibility of being tempted or seduced into buying:

> I don't think that there is anything wrong in living now and paying later, as long as you understand the necessity to pay later. Now it is very much the case that we are encouraged to buy things that we don't need and don't really want, and we are encouraged to forget about the fact that we are going to have to pay for them, or our parents, in the end. And I think that is where the fault lies.

Linked to this were notions of shopping as pleasure and seduction and the credit card as making self-discipline difficult. It was also understood that consumerism was the mode of participation in society for ordinary people and that consequently identities were linked to consumption. These changes were linked to broader moral changes in British society from a world where an elite group of middle class officials (e.g. the bank manager) made decisions for you, overseeing the morals of ordinary people, to a world where the individual has the responsibility for decision making. For many, the banks were going too far in offering inducements to borrow, undermining people's individual strengths and self-determination. The banking and credit system was thus seen to reflect the growing complexity as well as the growing freedoms of the individual in late capitalism:

> I accept that there are different standards of living, there are, you can't compare it, but I am talking about what people take as granted now, you wouldn't dream of having years ago. Free press, nearly every week, about people going to be sent to Florida or Disneyland because of the ticket. My first holiday was after I had got married. A week at Blackpool, and that was the highlight of my life then, spending bed and breakfast at Blackpool, and now they are talking about sending people to Florida, costing up to six hundred pounds each.

> But would you agree that, you would agree that the purchasing power of most people in our society today has considerably increased as compared to when we were young? Although the purchasing power has increased, in many very important respects, the actual standard of living has fallen. Everybody's standard of living has fallen.

Comments about the change in the nature of commodities were linked to changes in lifestyle; in particular, reference was made to women working which meant that convenience had become a very important dimension of commodities. The extra disposable income this generated along with the growth of pensions schemes and the rise in house prices and the spread of home ownership had all led to an increase in demand for consumer goods. Other changes in lifestyle were seen as generational, as we have discussed earlier, with a lot of talk about the way that young people were entering into the commercial culture, wanting everything now and everything new.

The second-hand market emerged as a significant arena in which opinions and disagreements were expressed. Many felt that second-hand goods used to be a basic feature of consumption, whereas now they were marginalized:

> It is almost unacceptable. You don't talk about things if you get them second-hand.

> We used to have second-hand stuff and not mind about it. But people nowadays must have new prams. When I was brought up as a child we had second-hand bicycles, and we had half the pocket money that most people do. It is just the way that I suppose I was brought up. I didn't mind second-hand clothes for my children in some cases. In fact I was jolly grateful if anyone offered me a hand-me-down dress for a child.

> It is easy to get locked into the idea that everything must be new, I have a
> friend who will never buy anything second-hand. I think that this is a
> terrible situation to get into. I actually feel a lot happier with second-hand
> things, for one thing they are cheaper, and the other thing is you don't feel
> that you have to look after them, you are not concerned if another scratch is
> added. It is not your responsibility. But this terrible thing when you get
> something brand new to try and preserve it which is a ridiculous situation.
> The only way you can preserve it is to put it in a museum.

The present devaluing of the second-hand was regarded both positively, for
the second-hand market had been a symbol of poverty, so its demise was a sign
of progress, and negatively, in terms of both the loss of the expertise and craft
culture of repair and of moral disapproval of desires for the latest and the new
being 'given in to'. People also acknowledged that it was more difficult to buy
second-hand now because of the changes in fashion and the built-in obsolescence
of modern consumer durables:

> But also things aren't built to last any more, are they? I mean things years
> and years ago, and it lasts for about 20 years, and now you will be lucky if it
> lasts 5. It's not built as well, it's a throw away society. You only have to look
> at the dustbins.

> It is the mechanism of fashion which conspires to prevent this passing on,
> and buying second-hand, because if we have bought something second-hand
> or are using it, we are instantly marked and everyone can see and we bear
> the shame of not being able to go into a shop and buy something. I think
> that's a shame.

Buying new things could be seen as a form of rebellion in the young against the
self-control of the older generation or as a pressure children apply to their
parents:

> I think parents are being got at by their children, because they are fashion-
> able at such a young age these days, they will not wear what you think they
> should, apparently, my grandchild is only 2, so he is toeing the line, but they
> demand certain clothes and toys and so on, and it is a strong parent who
> withstands the pressure.

Others describe an alternative lifestyle:

> I freely admit that I no way represent the mainstream, and when I have been
> involved in working in jobs with people who collect the wage packet at the
> end of the week and then go in and spend it in shops, I have always been
> confronted with their attitude that they would never do as I do – get things
> from skips, or jumble sales, or secondhand shops or whatever. They have
> none of the pride that I have in preserving something that would otherwise
> have gone to waste. Their pride is in having something produced for them,
> so to speak, brand new, untouched by human hands. They are almost eager
> to throw out what they bought last week in order that they can go and buy

something new this week, and they are keen to be doing it on credit, and they are keen to be, to be felt to be in the mainstream of this flow of credit of money and goods and services. And generally buy now and waste and throw away. I appreciate what you were saying about certain people preserving things and buying things second-hand, but I think that is very much the oddity. Which is something that I think is actually at the heart in the rise of credit in the last 10 years, because buying things new is particularly suitable for the credit system.

Second-hand goods were discussed as symbolic of the past, of poverty, of traditional class structures and the lack of consumer power. Buying only new goods was perceived as a form of social rebellion where the consumer will not accept the logic of their social class position by budgeting and buying second-hand. On the other hand, the people who did buy second-hand were using it to resist consumer culture. It seems that beliefs about second-hand goods act to justify buying them or not buying them. If we do buy second-hand goods, we valorize this as a form of resistance to advertising and consumption pressure. If we don't buy second-hand we characterize that market as the passive acceptance of an inferior material condition.

In general, these accounts link the personal, psychological world and the desire to buy with perceptions of the changing economic and financial position of the consumer. They centre on the negotiation of individual needs, rights and identity in relation to social processes. There is a set of oppositions which code these changes:

cash	credit
simplicity	complexity
budgeting	borrowing
control	loss of control
institutional control	individual responsibility
necessities	luxuries
being careful	having pleasure
second-hand	new

The changes in the social identity of the consumer are reflected in consumer experience: people emphasize that shopping has become a pleasurable activity, often a family activity; that buying with credit cards makes self-discipline difficult if not impossible and leads to people not being able to 'see' their financial position; that gratification is no longer delayed; and that we are moving away from once-valued traditions. People are also amazed and excited at the change in opportunities for working people. Not simply the increase in living standards and the invention of more and more sophisticated domestic products, but also the greater opportunities for travelling abroad, careers, education. The added value of consumerism is celebrated, while the loss of community and self-control is mourned. Among ordinary people, the basic debate about consumption and identity is ongoing – is involvement in material culture a liberation or an entrapment?

Drawing the line between luxury and necessity

They are luxuries because they are things you can do without.

A luxury is something extra, which gives my life something a bit more than
just having necessities.

How do people understand, explain and justify the distinction between luxury
and necessity? This distinction lies at the heart of economic ideologies: the claim
of necessity is used to justify expenditure or economizing, and social status is
marked materially through the display or absence of luxuries. Yet the definition
of necessity and luxury is contestable, and must be grounded in relation to other
societal and moral beliefs (Fraser, 1989). In everyday life, people must decide
what they need and want to consume. Equally important, they must account for
these decisions to themselves and others, in the context of their socioeconomic
circumstances and in conflict with alternative accounts or expectation. Thus they
must negotiate a personal interpretation in the context of the broader social
controversy over the distinction (Billig, 1991). As many goods may satisfy more
than one want, and as one want may be satisfied by a variety of goods, people's
choices gain meaning and may become predictable through their broader
theories of needs, wants and satisfiers.

There is disagreement in the social science literature about the meaning of
necessities and luxuries. In economics, early analyses of consumer behaviour
were conducted in terms of needs or wants (Baxter, 1988), forming the underpinnings for utility theory. Individuals maximize behaviours according to needs
and wants: as one moves up a hierarchy of needs (e.g. Maslow, 1970), more
goods are available to satisfy the need (Baxter, 1988). Individual mechanisms
of incentive value, reinforcement and utility are related to the perception of
goods as necessities or luxuries, generating discernible patterns of demand and
resources at the macroeconomic level. The Engel curve links income level to the
proportion of income occupied by particular goods: luxuries are goods that
occupy a small proportion of low incomes and an increasing proportion of larger
incomes; necessities take up a decreasing proportion of income as income
increases.

However, in the Marxist economic approach, 'the freedom promised by capitalism is an illusion, since it is wrested away by the capitalist from the people
and becomes merely the freedom of the wage labourer to be exploited by the
capitalist' (Miller, 1987, p.181). Thus the freedom to define and satisfy needs
and wants is denied to the individual, for the individual is seen as constructed
through the aims and practices of advertisers and producers. Further, in cultural
anthropology, goods cannot be reduced to their utility or competitive display
status but must be analysed in terms of their expressive, sociocognitive and ritual
functions: classifications of goods are thus related to classifications of people and
hence to social structures. The way a culture separates necessities from luxuries
reveals key cultural choices in the domains of morality, pleasure, desire, rights
and responsibilities (Douglas and Isherwood, 1978).

Lay understandings of the relation between needs/wants and necessities/luxuries

One conceptual problem which people must resolve is the relation between accounts of the motivation to consume (needs and wants) and accounts of the nature of goods (necessities and luxuries). When asking people to explain how they draw the line between necessities and luxuries, we observed three basic models of this relationship.[1]

In the first and simplest model, endorsed by half of our respondents, needs are split into basic and higher needs, and goods into necessities and luxuries. These are mapped onto each other so that luxuries serve higher needs and necessities serve basic needs: 'In general, necessities are food, water, warmth, shelter' and 'The basic necessities are food, warmth and shelter.' A variation proposes that basic needs are to be met by material goods, but that higher needs are to be met by non-material things:

> Necessities are: healthy food, adequate housing, suitable clothes and/or the income to provide them. Also a feeling of 'belonging' or 'being loved' or being a useful member of society which is not dependent on income but may be provided by the job which also provides the income.

> I believe that people in general have certain basic material needs – wholesome food, adequate housing, drinkable water, breathable air . . . They also have other non-material needs – love, a feeling of security in so far as society can provide this, meaningful work, social recognition quite independent of their bank balance.

Maybe luxuries are a substitute for spiritual, religious, or community-based needs. There is a common cultural theme concerning the decline of the spiritual in the elaboration of material culture. One might suggest that in the hierarchy of needs only some needs are directly satisfied by material goods, but that people have been misled into buying goods to satisfy higher needs. A further variant argues that the definition of basic and higher needs is a social one rather than a biological one. Thus some claim a universality for basic needs and others claim that basic needs are determined by culture and personal economic circumstances.

This basic view, with its variations, suggests a unified representation of the relationship between goods and human nature. Psychological theories, both scientific and lay, are given a specific role, justifying and accounting for the distinction between basic and higher needs and their satisfiers. It recognizes the many debates concerning physiology vs desire, the material vs the spiritual, and the universal vs the cultural, and the debate around whether a good satisfies a basic or a higher need.

The second model, suggested by one-third of our respondents, considers also how these needs, basic or higher, are satisfied – by necessities or luxuries? It thus introduces further areas for public debate, accounting and justification, through the various ways in which higher and basic needs can be satisfied. Here, needs are arrayed from basic to higher with a separate distinction drawn between necessities and luxuries, resulting in four categories of goods, for luxuries may satisfy either higher or basic needs and it is considered necessary to satisfy some higher-order needs in addition to satisfying basic needs. Thus, two new classes of objects emerge – luxuries which satisfy basic needs and necessities which satisfy higher needs:

> I think that people (and myself) actually *need* very little but, in a 'real world' situation, what others have actually does affect what we need. If a large number of people have a private car, it isn't just the luxury of having this possession that matters, it actually means they can look farther afield for jobs . . . someone without a car will not be able to do these things and will be disadvantaged as a result.

> All people need *more* than necessities such as food, clothing, warmth, each person needs enough of their choice to satisfy their inner needs.

In contrast to the first model, where luxuries simply satisfy higher needs and necessities satisfy basic needs, we now have a debate about how to satisfy each category of need which requires a further level of accounting or justification on the part of the consumer. The third model, offered by a few people, is a hybrid of the first two and identifies three classes of objects: necessities satisfying basic needs, necessities satisfying wants and luxuries satisfying wants (or desires). In this model, there is no class of luxuries which satisfies basic needs, for such items are deemed to be satisfying higher needs, thus retaining the notion that at the bottom end of the needs hierarchy there are basic needs that have a set of goods (necessities) with which they are satisfied. On this account, a luxury foodstuff, for example, would be deemed to be satisfying higher-order needs rather than basic physiological needs and the classy colour TV is not for ordinary entertainment but for self-aggrandisement:

> Clearly there are certain commonly accepted 'necessities' in life such as food, clothing and shelter. There are also certain desirable things which could only be described as luxuries, such as fast cars, holidays in exotic places, daily champagne and caviar, etc. The difficulty arises with the more mundane needs of life in the grey area . . . alcohol, tobacco, hairdo's, etc . . . for those to whom such things are important, their quality of life would be seriously diminished were they unable to afford those pleasures.

One respondent justifies retaining the luxury/higher need category by pointing to the difficulty of adequately satisfying both higher and basic needs without resorting to luxuries or excess. Acknowledging the difficulties of satisfying one's higher needs in everyday life with the range of material goods available is seen to mitigate against the possession of luxury goods – they represent failed attempts to satisfy one's higher needs: 'We all possess things which we don't really need. It is one of our basic human characteristics that we are forever demanding more of our environment. Satisfaction and contentment are very difficult states to achieve.'

People were acutely aware of the relativity of necessities and luxuries. They could not adopt the simple solution of explaining the differences between luxuries and necessities by just providing examples of each, for the same object may be a necessity under certain circumstances and a luxury under others. People wanted to retain some notion of 'real needs', and to discuss the things that were commonly called necessities as social constructions. They identified individual sources of relativity such as upbringing ('Luxury and necessity in the minds of people largely depends on their childhood upbringing'), personal circumstances ('Am disabled so have a car which I consider a necessity'; 'Video-recorders are also luxuries but I have heard "social workers" say that they are necessities for low income families "to entertain the children"'), individual differences ('Difficult to generalize about "people"'), personal preferences ('Clearly, there will be certain things which are near-necessities to one individual – alcohol, tobacco, hairdo's, etc. – which would be written off as mere luxuries by others without the inclination for such things').

They also identified social sources of relativity, such as generation differences ('Young friends seem to compensate for being out of work, etc., by indulging in spending and getting into debt . . . Older people seem to have learnt to manage better by having sorted out their priorities into "needs" and "wants"') and income differences ('I have found that luxuries become necessities as my income has increased, and in general it seems to me that the poor man's luxury is inclined to become the rich man's necessity').

They also made cultural comparisons with the Third World ('Compared to the Third World, we have so many needs which are luxuries by comparison') and with survival vs civilized life ('One has to distinguish between the most basic level of human subsistence – the minimum necessary for human survival – and what may reasonably be deemed "necessary" for civilized modern life').

Finally, they made historical comparisons with 20 years ago ('Twenty years ago what was considered a luxury is now considered a necessity') and with previous centuries:

> One might consider the evolution of the toilet which 100 years ago would be an out-house in the garden and which is now firmly placed inside the house. I don't think anyone would now regard this setting as a luxury, but in Victorian times it would almost certainly be thought of as such.

> Henry VIII was very rich but he didn't have a car or a TV or central heating so am I wealthier than the King of England?

The above examples suggest that certain artefacts are fluid with regard to being classified as luxury or necessity depending on a variety of cultural, historical, economic and personal factors. Further, people appreciate that notions of luxury and necessity are subject to similar influences:

> When I was a child, necessities were provided by my parents and for luxuries we were encouraged to save.

An individual's perceptions of luxury and necessity will vary according to his interests and character, as well as being reliant on his country's wealth.

Here people are hinting at relativity not only in the necessity/luxury boundary but also in the broader social belief systems which underpin this boundary. Either implicitly or explicitly, people do not feel they can answer the question of the distinction between necessities and luxuries without a broader consideration of socioeconomic life. Thus they include an analysis of why people might classify goods in the way they do as part of their understanding of the distinction itself. In other words, as argued above, the basis of distinction between luxuries and necessities is complex and social. Some of the accounts made this explicit. Here we consider one account (from Nick, see p.141) in some detail to exemplify this grounding of the economic understanding in a broader social belief system:

People need as much comfort in their lives as is necessary to reduce the background stress of living to a tolerable level. The point where individuals draw the line and their particular choice of comforts is due largely to peer group pressure which leads to in many cases people with lower incomes feeling that they need more of the latest brand-new and expensive hardware in their lives than is the case with people better placed to afford it. In fact all that we really need is food and shelter and all the rest may be held to be luxury. Then some will say we need food and shelter and provision for medical care. Then someone will say we need food, shelter, medicine and communication and things will be added to the list in greater numbers until the consensus view is reached that although a jacuzzi with variable bubble size and cocktail bar may be one of the bare essentials of a civilized life, having coloured disco lights in same would be utter and inexcusable decadence. For my own view, I do like a few gadgets, props and icons in my life, but I regard none of it as essential and seek to buy all durable items second-hand at a negotiated cash price. I do not oppose credit in principle – but administering my personal credit affairs would be an extra piece of work that I ain't prepared to do.

This account makes no attempt to list goods which are luxuries and necessities. The account immediately suggests that necessary goods are those which compensate us for the stresses of modern living, for individuals take sustenance from different goods. The comforts they choose are partly determined socially, according to those chosen by their peer group. The account then introduces a cautionary tale in which people choose comforts beyond their means, because of the social influence of the better off. The author then suggests that social influence over the choice of goods has resulted in people losing touch with an analysis of their basic needs. People are seen not to make decisions based on an objective analysis of their needs but rather they are seen to accept socially defined comforts as their goals. This process of social convention about the consumption of 'necessities' leads to an inflation of required goods. Here, interestingly, some goods are mentioned to illustrate the over-layering of commodities as the range of appropriate goods expands. The inflation of expectations proceeds by the upgrading of consensus as to what is an appropriate level of consumption – an essentially social process rather than one of individuals appraising their needs in isolation. The account then suggests that the only way around this is to detach oneself from the social influences by choosing second-hand goods over new ones. There is an interesting pairing here of second-hand with cash and new with credit – if we buy second-hand we avoid the credit system, and we step outside the social pressure for the new. A further strategy of resistance proposed is to personally resist the temptation to redefine luxuries as necessities.

This leads into a further aspect of the accounts offered, that of consequences for action and rhetorical advice concerning coping with consumption pressures. When asked to draw a distinction between classes of goods, people express some of their views as advice. Accounts are motivated in part by the desire for control over the social environment. The accounts also have a strongly rhetorical flavour. People do not just propose various criteria for distinguishing necessities and luxuries. They also, perhaps inevitably, indulge in a variety of moral prescriptions and recommendations for living in and coping with material culture. The necessity/luxury distinction has implications for many consumer decisions; for example, we reward ourselves by purchasing luxuries, we economize by restricting purchases to necessities. The following strategies or rules of resistance were offered:

1 *Make appropriate social comparisons:* do not think a good is a necessity for yourself just because someone else has it – they may have good reasons for having it. This rule stops people simply wanting what they see others possess. Before acquiring the good themselves, they would have to ask whether the person who owned it had a need for it which they did not have or had greater resources than they did:

> I think a washing-up machine [dishwasher] a luxury – but to others it is a necessity, e.g. large families, etc.

> I must compare myself to others actually living today and in my own country. However this makes it very easy to ignore people in other poorer countries whose situation seems very remote from our own.

> For a woman out at work a freezer is a necessity.

2 *Following guiding principles:* people offer abstract principles of consumption, which provide a framework for taking numerous specific decisions:

> Credit is not taken lightly.

> Having sorted out [their] priorities into 'needs' and 'luxuries'.

> More important to spend money on either major house work or charities or holidays.

> Non-material needs – love, a feeling of security in so far as society can provide this, meaningful work, social recognition quite independent of their bank balance.

[live] A fairly simple lifestyle.

Gandhi once said 'there's enough in the world for everyone's need, but not for everyone's greed'.

Learn to be content with the way things are: I've never known the life of Reilly but I've learned to be content with things as they are.

Freedom from stress can be more important than luxuries.

3 *Adopt coping actions:* people suggest specific actions to aid coping:

Choosing luxuries for oneself and one's friends which are within one's resources.

Use a credit card to your own advantage.

Buy all durable items second-hand at a negotiated cash price.

Much of the time I buy things second-hand.

If I can afford a luxury I want I will have it, if I can't I won't.

4 *Adopt cognitive coping strategies:* a variety of cognitive coping strategies are offered:

● Define necessities very conservatively:

I consider anything I cannot afford as a luxury.

All that we really need is food and shelter and all the rest may be held to be luxury.

Really the basics of living as absolute necessity and anything else I would regard as a luxury.

I believe these [basic] necessities have not changed much over the years.

● Know which luxuries you want:

I don't think of holidays as a luxury mainly as I feel I need them so badly.

Personally my 'luxuries' are I suppose very limited – some books, wine, entertaining friends, a visit to friends.

● Have to justify spending:

I find it difficult to buy things for myself which I consider to be luxury items, to justify spending that sort of money when there is so much poverty in the world.

● Distance yourself from spenders:

I firmly believe that people, mainly of the younger generation, want and expect everything that was a luxury years ago . . . Not necessarily having had to work for it!

● Adopt individualistic standards:

My ideas of needs and luxuries do not appear to have changed much, if at all.

Needs for myself include space, some solitude and being in contact with growing things.

Now I consider more abstract things important.

5 *Maintain self control:* the importance of having control over one's desires is often advocated:

Being able to say no to oneself or one's friends.

The running of two cars is a luxury and with careful planning could be avoided.

We used to have a car and it was greatly missed for a while, but we soon got used to being without.

6 *Warnings:* people also offer warnings about what they see happening around them:

Consumption of material for reasons other than what is contained in them, e.g. for perceived status value.

For some people they will only 'feel okay' when they and their family consume more and more!

These rules suggest a variety of views about the relationship between the individual and material culture. The point about specifying rules of personal behaviour is that a normal competent person should be able to carry them out. Therefore, stating a rule refers to a theory of how the individual can affect the way that economic factors affect them: people offer an implicit theory of the role of human action in the economic process. Since the prescriptions must be realistic, they reveal an implicit theory of practice, of people's competence, and personal control. The last quotation emphasizes the dynamic nature of the consumption process, the idea that pleasure in the act of consumption itself is the motivator which drives economic processes, and which therefore threatens to take society out of control.

When faced with the task of distinguishing luxury from necessity, people do not always offer an ostensive definition composed of categories of objects, nor do they offer the defining features of necessities or luxuries. They do not presume consensus, but discuss how they would make the distinction. To classify a good as either necessity or luxury involves general principles of classification, functional assessments of goods, lay theories of needs and wants, moral judgements of motivation or utility, an awareness of a variety of relativities, rhetorical and advisory implications of classification, and pragmatic rules of classification in particular behavioural contexts. The distinction between luxury and necessity is not an academic nicety but involves adopting positions on a variety of complex social issues. There is no choice here as regards adopting a position, though many choices lie behind the position adopted, for everyday life demands that people, in some way or other, come to a practical resolution of these consumption issues and this must be achieved in a manner consonant with their other social beliefs and everyday understanding.

Understanding why people get into debt

We now turn to a more detailed examination of one area of social beliefs – that of personal debt – to discover the ways in which beliefs are interconnected in systematic, or semiotic, ways. Debt is very much on the public agenda, a problem about which people have opinions, experiences and beliefs. Nor is debt an isolated problem, for it is part of a more general concern about the rise of consumerism and the changing moral climate of borrowing and spending. Thus, people's understanding of personal debt connects with their understanding of related processes, such as advertising or greed, and is conceived within more general frameworks of the relation between social and personal events which may also be used to explain other issues (such as unemployment or loneliness: Lunt, 1989, 1991). To explore the lay explanation of debt, allowing for its potential complexity and relations to other issues, we attempted to model perceived causal connections between causes of personal debt. The model is constructed in the form of a network, based on respondents' judgements of the likelihood that each cause brings about each of the other causes,[2] and is shown in Fig. 7.1.

The network represents a set of arguments about, or explanations for, the relations between various forces which cause debt. Different causal paths may be 'read off' the network when explaining different social processes, different people's circumstances or the role of different causes. For example, those with a fluctuating income are seen as not being able to save, and this results in stress. Similarly, those with children are seen as subject to demands for new purchases so as to keep up with peers, which also results in stress, but, importantly, children's demands are themselves seen as caused by advertising, peer pressure and the expectation of maintaining a high standard of living. The network is not so much a concretized set of beliefs as a model of contestable statements.

Clearly, the causes of personal debt form part of a system of causes, a system that is structured through causal time, differentiating among distal, mediating and proximal causes. Distal causes are those which do not affect any other causes in the system. Broadly speaking, external, commercial and economic pressures from advertising, product development, unexpected repairs and the high standard of living are seen to increase normative expectations, social comparisons, stress and greed. However, some distal causes, such as advertising, are seen to have a more limited role in that they have no direct influence over the economy but affect the social pressure to consume. Other distal causes, such as a high standard of living, have direct effects both on normative consumption patterns and on the credit system.

Proximal causes are mainly affected by other causes and do not themselves affect causes in the system (except for the central cause being explained, in this case, personal debt). For example, while not having any savings or a lack of self-discipline are seen as fairly direct causes of personal debt, the operation of

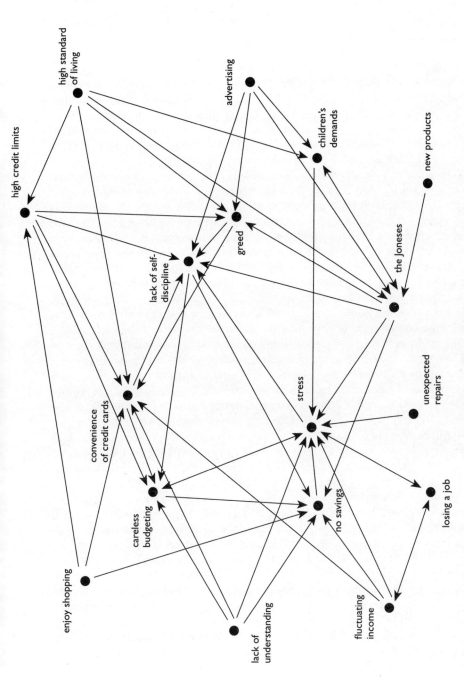

Figure 7.1 Network of perceived causal relations between causes of personal debt.

these causes is in turn seen to result from a wide range of other, distal and mediating causes. Mediating causes connect distal and proximal causes; for example, social comparisons (keeping up with the Joneses, children's demands) are believed to mediate the effects of economic factors on personal charact- eristics or states. Thus, social pressure translates economic pressure into stress, greed and lack of control over finances. Stress is the central mediating cause between external and internal causes. Its complex relations to other internal causes make the internal causes into a system: without stress, the internal causes would lead simply to not having any savings, but with stress we have a system with feedback and cycles of influence.

The system also varies in complexity: people believe that certain aspects of the process of getting into debt are more complex than others, involving the oper- ation of more causes in combination, while for other aspects of the process single causes may be effective. For example, unexpected repairs are seen to have a simple effect on debt by increasing stress, while the convenience of credit cards is complexly linked to other factors. Generally, the credit system (high credit limits, the convenience of credit cards) is seen as fuelled both by general econ- omic conditions (high standard of living) and by the pleasure people get from consumption (enjoy shopping). Both these factors are seen as having the same effects on the individual by influencing careless budgeting and lack of self- discipline: loss of control over one's budget is seen as part of the participation in the credit culture which arises from economic affluence and the pleasure of consumption. The convenience of credit cards has other links in the network: it is affected by fluctuating income, so that credit cards provide a convenient means of spreading repayments; by a lack of understanding, seeing people as not realizing how they will have to pay in the end at high rates of interest; and by greed, making a variety of goods instantly available. Maybe part of the attraction of credit cards is their multiple articulation in the economic sphere. Credit cards exemplify the complexity of relations between the person's psychology and a variety of external pressures in explaining personal debt.

A prominent role is given to people's understanding of finances: people who know and understand finances are seen as more likely to save, less likely to be under stress, better able to handle their budget and less likely to see credit cards as an easy option in financing. People identify four other personal factors to be avoided if one is to avoid debt – stress, careless budgeting, lack of self-discipline and not having any savings. Direct coping with these causes could include vari- ous ways of relaxing and defusing stress, taking more care over one's budget, controlling urges to spend and gradually building up savings. However, as the network suggests people believe that these personal causes of debt are influenced by a variety of other, often external, causes, to deal with these proximal causes directly would be like dealing with symptoms without attacking the underlying causes.

People see greed, a personal motivation, as under the direct influence of advertising and commercial pressures, which they believe persuade people about what to want. They see the result of this greed being a lack of self-discipline, which in turn leads to careless budgeting and no savings. The converse was not true: people did not subscribe to the view that advertising is a response to, or caused by, people's greed. Nor did people express the view that social comparison processes are driven by factors such as greed. Social comparisons and greed are instead seen as responses to economic expansion, commercial practices and advertising.

Commercial pressures are not seen simply as having a direct impact on individuals but rather as feeding into two social systems: the institutional operation of social norms and the provision of personal finance facilities, which then affect the individual's ability to cope with his or her finances. There is a balance between these two sources of control: if the banks, the government and other financial institutions make credit easier to obtain, they are seen to increase personal responsibility and ease the transformation of commercial pressures into personal pressures by providing the opportunity to obtain goods through credit.

The overall model operates as a series of knock-on effects which are elaborated at each stage. The system appears to gather momentum as it moves from the distal to the proximal causes, starting with market and advertising pressures, the expansion of credit facilities and social comparison pressures, and ending in a person in debt – with no savings, under stress, with a fluctuating income and careless budgeting. The collective representation of the causes of personal debt among ordinary people reveals a coherent and complex model of the interrelationships within a set of causes. This representation encodes a number of arguments, or a rhetorical position, which balances personal and social causes in a single, complex model. Doubtless similar representations could be discovered for explanations of other economic phenomena such as saving, and one might also expect to integrate perceptions of uncertainty, stress and ability with family and domestic concerns, all in the context of perceived socioeconomic developments. In lay understandings, personal control and responsibility are set against the background operation of a variety of commercial and institutional forces, and methods of coping are implied by the relations between societal and personal forces.

Learning from life

Finally, we reiterate that beliefs have a rhetorical or advisory function. When we asked people what they had learnt about managing their money during their lives, we obtained a long list of advice about finances, ranging from general advice such as 'live within your means' to specific strategies such as 'fill in your cheque book stubs'. The rhetorical nature of this general advice is apparent when we discover that while many say one should 'live within one's means', few actually do so. Moreover, to neither borrow nor save is certainly not encouraged by modern consumer society, which needs people both to take out loans or use credit and to invest, and which uses fluctuations in interest rates as a way of influencing consumer confidence and spending. Personal experiences generated several aphorisms ('you get into debt fast but getting out is slow') and many contradictions or disagreements ('easy to get into and out of debt'). People had learnt things about different aspects of finances – work, family, stress, needs and wants (Table 7.1).

Table 7.1   Describe anything which you feel that you have learnt from past financial difficulties or debts in your life

	No. of people to mention each
Budgeting	
Live within your means	44
Budget/plan/organize finances and stick to it	18
Be careful/sensible with money	16
Budget for unexpected/anticipate future events	9
Control your finances/don't let money master you	8
Look at finances regularly/know what you have	7
How to economize/manage on low income	7
Pay bills rather than put off payment	3
Face up to the reality of the situation	2
Appreciate costs of everyday extras	1
Look after the pennies, etc.	1
Avoid monthly repayments	1
Save a weekly sum for each fixed outgoing	1
Fill in your cheque book stubs	1
You can sort these problems out	1
Shopping	
Don't buy unless can pay cash/can afford it	18
Don't spend recklessly/control impulse to indulge	7
Check prices	1
Debts	
Avoid debts/don't borrow	22
A mortgage is an (the only) acceptable debt	5
Being in debt is unpleasant/lose self-respect	3
Borrow from the bank rather than credit/family	3
It is easy to get into debt	1
Only borrow if it brings more pleasure than worry	1
Debt is useful when income fluctuates	1
Only borrow for appreciating assets	1
Only borrow for essentials	1
Credit/debt can be advantageous, take advantage	1
Keep receipts for HP payments	1

Table 7.1   (cont'd)

	No. of people to mention each
Allow for interest on loans to increase	1
Only have one debt at a time	1
Don't borrow without savings as cushion	1
Deal with problems as soon as possible	1
Always take holiday, however much you owe	1
Credit	
Buying on credit is expensive because of interest	9
Credit cards are dangerous because they are easy to use	5
Don't take as much credit as possible/restraint	3
Keep check on amount building up on credit card	2
Don't have too many credit/store cards	1
Balance cost of credit against its convenience	1
Pay off bill before running up interest	1
Repayments	
Don't borrow more than you can afford to repay	10
Calculate and plan repayments before borrowing	5
Make repayments a priority	1
You get into debt fast but getting out is slow	1
Easy to get into and out of debt	1
Don't rely on having money to pay in the future	1
Credit cards are harder to pay off than they seem	1
Savings	
Savings are important for rainy day/reserve fund	18
Better to save up for purchase than to borrow	11
Saving up can be satisfying/achieving something	4
Savings bring peace of mind	3
Save as you earn, however little	2
Take a long-term insurance policy when adolescent	1
Property is the best investment	1
Don't rely on the stock market	1
Know about investments	1
Relationships	
Don't lend money to a friend	2
Co-operation between husband and wife is vital	2
Don't let others cause you problems	2
Friend/stranger is better in a crisis than family	2
Don't share house with people who don't pay bills	1
Put self before others	1

Table 7.1   (cont'd)

	No. of people to mention each
Both partners need to work to support family	1
Accept loans from friends/family	1
Lend money only to your family	1
Family needs are always changing	1
Neither a borrower nor a lender be	1
Better not to be dependent on spouse	1
Stress	
Don't panic/don't worry/relax	9
Debts are not worth the misery/guilt they cause	6
Debt is inconvenient but not worth worrying about	3
Shortage of money is a strain	2
Financial problems don't just go away	2
Being careful is as stressful as worrying	1
Worrying prevents you making a sensible decision	1
Debt, like alcohol, is depressive and habit-forming	1
No debts means no worries	1
When things go wrong, money is a further worry	1
Needs and wants	
One can manage on what you have and enjoy life	6
Moderation in wants	5
Don't try to keep up with the Joneses	3
Get what you really need now, borrow, don't wait	2
Accept lower standard of living if necessary	2
Recognize own weaknesses	2
Make the best of what you have	2
There are more important things than money	2
Having to save up tests if you really want it	1
Strive to improve your lot	1
Parents didn't need higher standard of living	1
Indulge yourself in other ways than spending	1
Never take no for an answer, go for what you want	1
Work	
Don't lend/be strict in business/have a contract	4
Be prepared to work hard to earn enough	3
Work hard to earn enough to avoid debts	1
Get qualifications to earn more	1
Steady income better than higher fluctuating one	1
Don't rely on overtime/extra money	1

Table 7.1   (Cont'd)

	No. of people to mention each
Large incomes bring complications	1
Better to work more hours than give up luxuries	1
Don't become self-employed	1
Need a secure salary before borrowing	1
Expert advice/creditors	
Talk honestly to your bank manager/those you owe	4
Finances are complex so take expert advice	3
Don't trust banks	2
Banks aren't as worried about debts as you think	1
Thoughts/advice about money	
Difficulties result from bad luck/disasters	4
Don't take money/situation for granted	3
Life is more expensive than you think	2
Financial difficulties are unavoidable	2
You can't win, they screw you for all they can	1
Consumerism and poverty go hand in hand in society	1
Society/adverts/fashion pressure us to overspend	1
Society encourages us all to be in debt	1
New problems arise as old ones are solved	1
No fun to be poor even if meek inherit the earth	1
Money is worth earning/having, nothing is free	1
People who talk and worry about money are boring	1

EIGHT | CONCLUSIONS

People are continually guided by moral and social issues in their economic choices. Their decisions to save, to spend, their orientation to shopping and possessions are all tied into a complex set of beliefs about their place in the economy, the 'proper' way in which to handle their finances and the relation between everyday economic activity and broader social concerns. However, people's conceptions of their place in the social and economic order are not fixed. Rather, people engage with lifestyle representations and expectations which are changing and often in conflict – addressing contradictions between the ways of different generations or different cultures or, within their own time and place, between the ways which are normative and those which are alternative or which resist social pressures. Economic practices are more than decision-based economic behaviours. Being involved in material culture is a way of locating oneself in a changing social and moral order.

Consumerism is popularly represented through two discourses, the regressive and the progressive. Together, these constitute a debate in society about the development of sociopsychological identities in terms of individuals' rights, responsibilities and resources within material culture. Many people endorse the dominant representation of recent and dramatic change, believing that we are moving away from old forms of social organization, with old moralities, towards the age of consumerism. Hence they express concern about advertising, financial organizations and the availability of credit. The widespread faith in progress tempers their otherwise gloomy vision. In short, people experience a contradiction between the desire to embrace the opportunities of modern consumer society and the fear of inevitable loss involved in the new social order. New developments – credit cards, shopping centres, compact disc players – are regarded with ambivalence.

It is popularly believed that since the end of the Second World War the material conditions of ordinary people have improved and that people are increasingly involved in consumer culture. This may be accounted for in terms of the strenuous efforts of retailers and manufacturers and a complementary relaxing of legislation restricting the availability of credit to ordinary people. These market and financial changes are themselves dependent on economic changes which reflect the move away from an economy rooted in mass production to a more consumer-led economy. In terms of personal identity, these changes are seen to increase both personal freedom and personal responsibility. Time and again, the contradictions of previous times being hard but secure, limited but moral, oppressive but authentic, emerged in our discussions.

Such representations and beliefs affect many aspects of everyday life, especially when socially shared: saying is doing, and, increasingly, what happens between people is action in the form of talk (Goffman, 1981; Moscovici, 1984). These representations of change affect personal and social relationships, influencing domestic identities and the relationship between expertise and the laity (Livingstone and Lunt, 1992). The banks, like other institutions such as the mass media, have changed their position in relation to their client groups or audiences, shifting responsibility onto the ordinary person, moving from a discourse of duty to one of choice. The ways in which people can officially borrow money are an example. Before the era of the credit card, if someone wanted to borrow in an agreed way, they had to apply to the bank for a loan in person, and legislation dictated that for durable goods the purchaser had to put down a proportion of the price before they could be given a loan. If credit was unavailable through these official means, then people turned to unofficial forms of credit. The credit card changed this: the client is free to 'spend' the allowed credit wherever and whenever they choose. He or she is also vulnerable to the temptation to spend, relatively unconstrained by having to possess, negotiate or account for the money. Underlying these changes are legislative changes reducing restrictions on borrowing and the change in orientation of financial institutions to extend their relations with business to their relations with lay people.

The discussions in which people are engaged – about social change, the role of the individual, and the nature of the economy – are, in part, the means by which these changes, roles and forms are made meaningful and by which resources and opportunities are negotiated in relation to duties and responsibilities (Fraser, 1989; Moore, in press). Notions of proper economic conduct and the place of material concerns in everyday life are constructed through such discussions. The looking back which is so much a part of the debate about personal responsibility in the face of increasing economic opportunity is not simply a form of nostalgia (Robertson, 1991) but is used to make sense of present events – setting up a contrast in order to conduct a debate. There are no right and wrong answers here, only a series of temporary positions adopted on the issue of how to spend, what to value, and so on. At different times and for different purposes, certain arguments are ruled in or ruled out, but they may be brought back later or used in different combinations for different effects. The discussions are rhetorical, concerned with opinions, and the oppositions between opportunity and danger, freedom and responsibility, pleasure and the moral order, form the dynamic around which this debate is played out (Mason, 1989; Billig, 1991).

The discussions are an attempt to locate the material world in a meaningful, human context. But this debate is not only a personal one; it is also a public debate, one which exercises the mass media and the major political parties. In 1991, both the Labour and Conservative parties produced citizens' charters which attempt to formalize the new relations between the active consumer and the state. While ordinary people are ambivalent about the opportunities and dangers of increased involvement in consumer culture, there is a parallel ambivalence for those in power giving up aspects of their control. We will attempt here to sketch the social context of this ambivalence.

Habermas (1984), among others, has examined changes in the institutionalization of societies in the modern period. He argues that the breakdown of broad religious world views at the beginning of the modern period involved the construction of expertise in the areas of science, politics and morals. The growing specialization of institutional control in society has always been linked to expertise, and the financial sector is no exception. In their turn, the experts manage the laity, determining the rights, resources and responsibilities – indeed, the identities – of ordinary people. As part of the development of the late modern period, identity has become a matter for public debate, as we saw continually in our discussions and interviews. The characterization of public influence on political processes has moved from the elite contribution of the café society to representation in the mass media, for mass consumption (Thompson, 1990).

The segmentation and specialization of modern life meant that important aspects of experience were seen as the legitimate domain of experts. For example, aesthetics was limited to high art, detached from everyday life, which was involved with the purely functional forms of mass-produced goods. Debates on the place of the citizen consumer have challenged the separation between different domains, different questions, which is central to modernism: science (concerned with truth), morality (concerned with norms and value) and art (concerned with aesthetics and taste). These separated elements of culture are being placed together (Holub, 1991), their boundaries are threatened (Featherstone, 1991). We have seen that people do regard recent times as characterized by an overwhelming diversity of goods, with new and exciting possibilities of involvement in consumer culture. At the same time, we have seen that people do have a sense of loss of the old life and of loss of continuity with the present and the future.

The passive role dictated by modernity for the ordinary person, that of receiving meanings articulated by experts in the fields of science, morality and art, is made palatable by the simplicity of living life according to established codes.

Mulgan (1991) suggests that governments are giving up central control over these questions because of three broad influences: the collapse of communism, the green movement and the development of consumer-led economies. In their different ways, these movements all involve questions about the balance between individual and state responsibility. For example, the green movement asks individuals to challenge the separation of local and global by taking responsibility for the global in their domestic consumption practices. The development of consumer-led economies depends upon a growing involvement in consumption and its associated values by ordinary people. These two developments are in many ways opposed. The picture of responsibility in the green movement requires a constraint which would hinder the development of consumerism. The changing political order cross-cuts this debate by increasing involvement through citizenship. Citizenship is linked to national movements, thus opposing global ecological considerations, and it links to personal identity through engagement in political action rather than through consumption. These developments and debates pose a challenge to existing political parties to formulate a balance between these apparently contradictory forms of social participation (national/global, political protest/consumer involvement, technological/environmental).

There are also problems with all these movements: the individual may be given more and more responsibility without the resources or power to act effectively (Mulgan, 1991). For example, the consumer is given the responsibility for generating wealth in the economy, for protecting the global environment and for the political and moral welfare of the community. But despite the implicit claims of much popular culture, it seems unlikely that people have the resources and power to manage this responsibility. Thus there are basic questions to be answered about how much power actually goes along with the new responsibilities given to ordinary people. Is the centre slimming itself down by contracting out various responsibilities while retaining strategic control at the centre? (Mulgan, 1991). This problem is reflected in people's ambivalence about their involvement in consumer culture and their fears about the direction and future of consumerism and their experienced lack of control over it.

Giddens (1991) discusses the notion of identity in late capitalism in terms of a movement away from the various forms of emancipatory politics towards what he terms 'life politics'. While emancipatory politics in its various forms was concerned with releasing people from the constraints of traditional social positions by dissolving fixed positions and hierarchies, life politics 'is a politics of self-actualisation in a reflexively organised environment, where that reflexivity links self and body to systems of global scope' (Giddens, 1991, p.214). Protest movements were an attempt to reveal the invasion and exploitation of daily life by social and political agencies. Life politics goes beyond this to encompass a level of involvement in social and political life of the ordinary person which enables them to challenge not through protest but through taking control of the shape of their own lives in the negotiation of their personal identities – the personal is political. As it has become possible to construct personal identities, so identity has become a social issue and a topic for public debate.

At the centre of the developments of late capitalism is the individual with personal rights, responsibilities and resources. The individual has choices to make which will influence economic, social and political life on a broad scale. The problem for the individual is to construct an authentic sense of identity in an unsupportive context, and to come to terms with the consequences of their choices. This is a social task, for it is conducted between individuals, groups and institutions, and because it concerns meanings, social representations and political ideologies. This struggle to construct a sense of identity by the citizen in the late twentieth century, is itself dependent on the negotiation of views of truth, beauty and morality.

If there has been a freeing of the individual to establish their 'own' identity through involvement in consumer culture, then the question of what constitutes self becomes problematic. If it becomes possible to construct ourselves, then it becomes possible to reconstruct ourselves or to construct diverse selves. How then do people maintain a sense of stability, of continuity across time and place? How do people negotiate their place in the reproduction of existing forms of social relationship if everything is transitory and open to reconstruction? This was a fundamental problem for people which emerged in our work on generations, where generational differences were constructed in relation to perceptions of changes in material conditions. People attempted to impose a notion of continuity by seeing life as a trade-off between security and freedom. They felt that the financial institutions and governments had given up too much responsibility, that the individual has too much opportunity, more than they can handle: the individual has greater freedom of choice through involvement in consumer culture but is also more vulnerable. There was a strong feeling that society was veering from one extreme to another when what was required was a more thoroughly worked-out relation between individual and institutional responsibility.

The development of identities in contemporary society allows for the reworking of issues which had been encoded into traditional cosmologies and usurped by the fragmentation of modernism. The contemporary era replaces the expert segmentation of life with the valorization of everyday life as the site where moral, political and aesthetic questions are worked through in the context of the practical choices open to people when negotiating their identities. Influenced by Bourdieu's (1984) work on the social dimensions of taste, Featherstone (1991) argues that the discourse of freedom and personal control operates within social space rather than outside it: the growing class of the petit bourgeoisie asserts its views of identity through involvement in consumer culture:

> The new petit bourgeois is a pretender, aspiring to more than he is, who adopts an investment orientation to life; he possesses little economic or cultural capital and therefore must acquire it . . . An approach to life which is characterized by . . . quests for both security *and* adventure. The new narcissism where individuals seek to maximise and experience the range of sensations available, the search for expression and self expression the

fascination with identity, presentation and appearance make the new petit bourgeois a 'natural' consumer (Featherstone, 1991, pp.90–1).

Identity and mass consumption are related through discourse, the arguments and rhetorical positions promoted by the rising lower middle class and to justify their particular tastes, resources allocations and social position. Those in the higher class positions have then to discover more exclusive products and practices, 'positional' goods, which will mark them out as different. Intellectuals oppose the spread of cultural capital by staying one step ahead of the super-market shopper in their discovery of exotic products and practices. Thus the changes in material conditions express continuing social class divisions rather than the breakdown of structure.

The people we have talked to during our research for this book are engaged in a debate concerning the nature of identity in consumer culture. The dynamic of the debate is a natural milieu for them, there is no resolution offered, merely layers of discourse which play with a series of oppositions concerning tradition and modernity, freedom and determinism, opportunity and danger. Big issues played out in a domestic setting.

APPENDIX

The original research reported in this book is based on an empirical project on consumption. The data were collected in 1989 and consist of an in-depth postal survey questionnaire from 279 respondents, a series of nine focus group discussions, a series of 20 individual in-depth interviews on life histories, and additional paper-and-pencil tasks given to subsamples of these respondents. Some of this empirical research has been described in more detail in the original reports listed in the References.

In this Appendix, we describe the questionnaire and additional data collection techniques, the sample of respondents and its representativeness, and the statistical methods used throughout the book.

The questionnaire

Range of issues

The 20-page questionnaire contained nearly 400 open-ended and fixed-choice questions which covered a wide range of issues:

- demographic details;
- income and expenditure, financial arrangements;
- strategies, judgements and expectations about budgeting;
- definitions of debt;
- satisfaction judgements;
- consumer possessions, judgements of necessities and luxuries;

- consumer desires and pleasures;
- attitudes towards debt and credit;
- patterns of shopping, spending and credit use;
- locus of control scale;
- thinking, worrying and talking about money;
- coping strategies for general and financial problems;
- life events in the past three months;
- values; and
- attributions about the causes of own financial problems.

Instructions to respondents

The following instructions preceded the questionnaire:

This questionnaire is concerned with the way people manage their personal finances. It asks some general questions about your finances and your attitudes towards saving, borrowing, spending and debt. Following the recent consumer boom, and the increased use of credit facilities, we are interested in people's opinions about financial matters and in their experiences of credit and debt. This questionnaire is being filled out by a large number of people and everybody's answers will be pooled together to tell us about different opinions and experiences in relation to money. Your answers will be very useful, and we are grateful for your participation in this survey. The questionnaire is completely anonymous and all replies will be kept confidential. We make no record of your name. Please make sure that you answer all the questions. However, if there are any questions which you would prefer not to answer, leave them blank. Some of the questions are addressed to you personally and others concern your household. Some of the questions are quite detailed, but do not worry too much about accuracy. Please do not consult anybody else as you fill in the questionnaire. Try to answer the questions by yourself as well as you can. There are several possible answers provided for each of the questions and for each question you should put a circle around the appropriate answer. The questionnaire should take about one hour to complete. When you have finished it, please check once more that you have answered all the questions and then return it to us using the prepaid envelope. Thank you for your help.

Sampling procedure

The questionnaires were sent to 241 people living in or around Oxford during September 1989. They were mainly contacted through the University Subject Panel, and approximately 91 per cent of those contacted returned a completed postal questionnaire ($n = 219$). Each was paid a nominal £2 for their time and the questionnaire took $1-1\frac{1}{2}$ hours to complete. As this sample contained insufficient working people, the sample was supplemented using a snowballing technique through workplace contacts. A further 60 completed questionnaires were thus obtained (47 per cent response rate), making a final total of 279 questionnaires for analysis.

Sample representativeness

In the following description of the sample, percentages are rounded, so some totals may vary slightly from 100 per cent. Where appropriate and where information is available, the figures given below are compared with those from *Social Trends* (1991), which were based on representative large-scale social surveys carried out in 1989.

Demographic information

Of the 279 respondents in the sample, 62 per cent were women and 38 per cent were men. Their ages ranged from 18 to 82, with an average age of 44 years. The Registrar General's classification of occupations was used to classify respondents by social class, where professional and managerial occupations comprise class I (e.g. doctor, lecturer), semi-professional occupations form class II (e.g. nurse, teacher), other non-manual occupations (e.g. secretary, clerk) form class IIIN, skilled manual workers (e.g. foreman, supervisor) are classified as class IIIM, semi-skilled manual work (e.g. bricklayer, hairdresser) forms class IV and, finally, class V comprises unskilled manual work (e.g. porter, shop assistant). When all respondents were classified according to their own occupation, the sample was as follows:

1 People in paid work (61 per cent of sample; of these, 83 per cent work full-time):
   - 8 per cent social class I,
   - 28 per cent social class II,
   - 17 per cent social class III (non-manual),
   - 2 per cent social class III (manual),
   - 3 per cent social class IV,
   - 3 per cent social class V.
2 People not in paid work (41 per cent):
   - 17 per cent retired,
   - 7 per cent housewives (may include some pensioners),
   - 3 per cent unemployed,
   - 14 per cent students.

If we classify the retired and unemployed according to their stated previous occupation, the housewives according to their partners' occupation, and the remainder (mainly students) according to their fathers' occupation, we can classify the whole sample by social class as follows:

   - 17 per cent class I,
   - 43 per cent class II,
   - 25 per cent class III (non-manual),

- 9 per cent class III (manual),
- 3 per cent class IV,
- 3 per cent class V.

The sample contains a moderate bias towards the middle class, with few very poor or very rich respondents, and an underrepresentation of lower social classes. In 1989, 7.8 per cent of men and 4.2 per cent of women were unemployed (*Social Trends*, 1991).

Education

On average, the sample completed their education around 19 years old, with some 27 per cent having few or no qualifications and some 41 per cent being educated to degree level. In 1989, 71 per cent of men and 64 per cent of women below retirement age had a recognized qualification (*Social Trends*, 1991).

Tenure

A total of 64 per cent of our respondents were home owners, with 19 per cent private tenants, 4 per cent council tenants and 4 per cent in lodgings (9 per cent lived in some other arrangement). In 1989, some two-thirds of dwellings were owner-occupied (*Social Trends*, 1991).

Family type

Many of the sample were married (47 per cent), with 32 per cent being single, 10 per cent cohabiting, 7 per cent divorced, 3 per cent widowed and 2 per cent separated. The sample can be classified by household type (see Table A.1). From this it can be seen that the sample is representative for the categories of single parents, families and couples with non-dependent children (empty nests), but that it is somewhat biased towards single people and against couples without dependent children. The pensioner households are difficult to compare, but do not seem too dissimilar when the different classification schemes are allowed for.

Political vote

When asked if there was a general election tomorrow, which party would you be most likely to vote for, the following was the result: 31 per cent Labour, 29 per cent Conservative, 10 per cent SDP/Liberal, 18 per cent Green and 11 per cent no vote.

Financial resources and arrangements

Real household disposable income per head increased by one-third between 1981 and 1989 (*Social Trends*, 1991). Approximately 60 per cent of household

Table A.1   Demographic characteristics of sample

	Sample (%)	Social Trends (1991) (%)
Single people under pensionable age (includes adults sharing)	32	13
Member of couple[a] under pensionable age (no children)	8	27
Member of a family (couple with dependent children)	21	26
Single parent of dependent children	3	5
Member of couple with non-dependent children[b]	11	13
Pensioners[c]	25	16
Total	100	100

[a] In our sample, couple includes cohabitees.
[b] In our sample, these were all under pensionable age, while the *Social Trends* figure includes pensioner couples.
[c] In our sample, this includes couples where one partner was a pensioner; in the *Social Trends* figures, only single pensioners are included.

Table A.2   Sources of income for respondents

	Self (%)	Partner (if applicable) (%)
Salary/wages	61	68
Child benefit	20	5
Pension	24	13
Interest on savings	52	28
Unemployment benefit	1	0
Maintenance	5	0
Income support	4	0

income comes from employment (*Social Trends*, 1991). Respondents in our sample reported receiving the sources of income shown in Table A.2. Households were classified into the following types:

- 19 per cent pension(s), no wages;
- 3 per cent benefit(s), no wages;
- 45 per cent one wage (possibly in addition to pension/benefits, etc.);
- 33 per cent dual wage (possibly in addition to pension/benefits, etc.).

Total annual gross income was reported as averaging £8585 for the respondents (ranging between £0 and £50,000) and averaging £11,158 for their partners (ranging between £0 and £60,000). Disposable income (after tax and other stoppages) averaged £7176 p.a. for respondents and £9394 p.a. for partners. Household disposable income (combining all household types) averaged £12,002 p.a. Breaking down the respondents' data another way, the average annual disposable income was £6322 for women and £8520 for men.

Comparing this to *Social Trends* (1991), the gross annual wages of full-time employees in 1989 averaged £14,014 for men and £9480 for women. Bearing in mind that gross income is greater than disposable income, and that the figures for the sample include all sources of income (including those for part-time workers or those only supported by benefits), it seems that the incomes of the respondents are fairly representative. The figures reflect in part the greater number of women than men in the sample as a whole.

Household expenditure

Estimates of the average weekly amounts spent by the household on basic items (with the range over households in rounded brackets and the equivalent figures where available from *Social Trends*, 1989, in square brackets) were as follows:

Rent/mortgage	£50	(0–540)	[£29.9]
Fuel (electricity, etc.)	£13	(0–60)	[£10.5]
Food	£39	(0–200)	[£34.9]
Travel (petrol, fares)	£14	(0–100)	[£25.5][a]
Insurance	£12	(0–100)	
Clothes	£10	(0–120)	[£13.5]

[a] This figure includes the costs of running a car.

Total consumer expenditure rose 70 per cent in real terms from 1971 to 1989, this rise being most marked in the category of consumer durables, which rose by 160 per cent, especially TVs, videos and washing machines. The fastest growing category of expenditure is spending abroad, i.e. holidays, the costs of housing have grown steadily, and spending on food, alcohol and books has fallen slightly (*Social Trends*, 1991). Some 16 per cent of total expenditure was spent on leisure in 1989, mainly on holidays, alcohol consumed away from the home, TV and radio, and meals consumed out, and the number of overseas holidays increased by three-quarters between 1981 and 1989 (*Social Trends*, 1991).

Debts and savings

A total of 94 per cent of the sample had at least one bank account, 74 per cent had one or more credit cards, and 86 per cent had one or more savings accounts. When measured either personally or jointly, debts did not differ significantly between men and women, either in terms of the absolute amounts owed or as a percentage of disposable income.

Financial management strategies

People with a spouse or partner reported the following mutual household arrangements:

- you manage most of the money coming into the household (12 per cent);
- your spouse/partner manages most of the money coming into the household (11 per cent);
- the man manages most of the family finances, but gives the woman a house-keeping allowance (11 per cent);
- you both put your money into a common pool and both manage the family finances from this pool (30 per cent);
- each of you keeps your own income separate and both contribute towards household expenditure (27 per cent);
- other (9 per cent).

Additional samples

Interviews

Twenty individual in-depth taped interviews lasting approximately 1 hour were held with a subsample of those who completed the main questionnaire. Each interview was very open-ended in approach, but began by saying that 'we are interested in your attitudes towards money, in the decisions you have made in your life about borrowing, saving and spending, and in your experiences, if any, of credit and debt'. The interviews began by asking participants to talk of their upbringing, their parents' attitudes to money, and then discussed their first and subsequent jobs, relationships and marriages, children and so forth in relation to issues of expectations, decisions, resources, necessities, social relations, family dynamics and specific financial experiences. Where these interviews are quoted in depth, names and identifying details have been changed to preserve anonymity. When needed for clarification, the interviewer's question is included in square brackets.

Focus group discussions

Nine focus group discussions were held (Morgan, 1988). Each lasted approximately 1 hour and was audio-taped. The groups contained between 3 and 7 people (average = 5), totalling 47 people in all. The participants were selected randomly from the Oxford Subject Panel. There were 18 men and 29 women, with an average age of 56 years. Of those in debt, they owed on average £407, with the overall average debt being £139. Groups 3 and 4 were all over 60 years old, groups 7 and 8 were all women, and the remaining five groups were mixed by age and sex. The group leader aimed for a fairly free-flowing discussion, offering mainly open-ended questions and neutral prompts. The groups generally covered the following issues: what do people think about the present use of credit; how might things develop; are credit and debt different; should individuals or society be responsible; what historical and social changes, if any, do they see; how should we understand the boundary between luxury and necessity; why might people save; how might people budget; what contribution was made by the housing boom; is there a stigma of debt; how is spending linked to pleasure; attitudes towards the second-hand market; and what expectations do – or should – people have of their standard of living. All unattributed quotations in the text of this book are taken verbatim from this series of focus group discussions held on issues regarding consumption.

Accounting for mass consumption

For the studies reported in Chapter 7 (see Lunt and Livingstone, 1991b, for full details) the subjects were as follows. For the network task: 45 subjects (17 men, 28 women) were recruited from the Oxford University Subject Panel. They ranged in age from 18 to 79 years (average = 55 years). Their social class, as classified through their occupations (former or present) according to the Registrar General's scheme, was 3 from class I, 17 from class II, 12 from class IIIN, 2 from class IIIM, 4 from class IV and 1 from class V. One of the remaining subjects was a student, and the social class of five was unknown. Of this sample, 18 were now retired, 4 were unemployed and 9 were housewives. The subjects also varied in political affiliation (14 Labour, 12 Conservative, 11 Green, 7 SDP/SLD and 1 unknown). Some 28 had no debts. The remaining 17 owed on average £433. For the necessity/luxury task (also discussed in Chapter 4): the respondents comprised 30 people recruited from the Oxford University Subject Panel, of both sexes, differing ages, and a range of occupations and social classes (see Livingstone and Lunt, 1991, for full details).

Statistical analyses

Throughout the reporting of findings in this book, statistical details are kept to a minimum. Where indicated, analyses have been reported in more detail in other articles (see References).

Statistical comparisons

Analysis of variance was used for all comparisons between groups using continuous variables; where categorical variables are compared, chi-square tests were used; where associations are reported, Pearson's correlations were calculated. All analyses were conducted using the statistical package for the social sciences, SPSSx. For factor analyses and discriminant function analyses, all factors or functions with eigenvalues greater than 1 were retained. Discriminant function analysis was used to provide the best, most parsimonious description of the underlying differences between categorical groups. Multiple regression analysis was used to determine the best combination of predictors for a continuous variable.

Size of samples

Occasionally, the numbers of respondents or respondent subgroups used in different analyses varied slightly as different statistical analyses deal with missing data differently.

Significance level

In all cases, every reported finding is statistically significant at or beyond the 5 per cent level ($P < 0.05$). Conversely, all comparisons discussed as showing no differences are statistically insignificant ($P > 0.05$). Variance explained measures (R^2) are reported adjusted for degrees of freedom.

Hierarchical ordering of variables

Where stepwise hierarchical multiple regression or discriminant function analysis are reported, the independent variables were entered in the following order. First, demographic measures (such as age, social class, educational qualifications, marital status, family size and home ownership) were entered into the analysis. Secondly, a variety of economic measures were entered, including disposable income, total amount of savings, amount of regular saving, possession of consumer durables, and expenditure on basic items such as housing, food, travel, and so forth. After these demographic and economic variables, the psychological variables were entered, some of which had been constructed through factor analysis of specific items (see below), using a hierarchical stepwise procedure in the following order: general value factors followed by specific value questions; locus of control factors followed by individual items on the locus of control scale; attitude to money factors followed by the specific items on attitudes to money; general coping strategies; life events; attributions for financial problems; satisfaction ratings; economic coping factors and perceived control over finances; a range of specific economic beliefs and behaviours (e.g. budgeting, shopping, talk about finances, consumer sentiment, social comparisons with peers and family). The variables were entered in this order to ensure that variance associated with demographic or economic measures was accounted for first, so that any significant psychological variables could not be explained away as due to such measures. In stepwise multiple regression procedures, the possibility of multicolinearity was avoided by dropping significant predictors from the final equations and checking for changes in Betas of the remaining predictors.

Factor analyses

A number of the questionnaire items were designed to reference common themes, identified by factor analyses. Details of these analyses are presented below, as the factors are frequently used as predictors of key dependent variables throughout the book.

Locus of control

Items were selected or adapted from Rotter's (1966) locus of control scale designed to differentiate those who feel events are largely under their personal control from those who feel events depend on external circumstances or fate (Table A.3). These factors were interpreted thus:

- factor 1: personal control *vs* fatalistic;
- factor 2: things going wrong *vs* drifting;
- factor 3: just world *vs* intervention.

Attitudes towards saving, credit and debt

Based on interviews and pilot questionnaires, an eight-item scale was constructed concerning attitudes towards saving, credit and debt, where respondents rated each item on a 5-point scale from 'strongly agree' to 'strongly disagree'. The eight items together with their factor loadings (>0.3) on three factors are shown in Table A.4. These factors were interpreted thus:

- factor 1: anti-debt *vs* pro-credit;
- factor 2: ambivalence – credit useful but problematic;
- factor 3: credit as failure *vs* credit as normal.

Coping strategies for general and financial problems

Separate factor analyses were conducted for eight items concerning people's coping strategies in everyday life – first for general problems and then for money problems. In each case, a three-factor solution was found. The items were adapted from research on coping by Ray *et al.* (1982) and were rated by respondents on a 5-point scale from 'nearly always' to 'rarely' as shown in Table A.5. These factors were interpreted thus:

- factor 1: emotional coping *vs* cognitive coping;
- factor 2: cool/positive coping;
- factor 3: active *vs* passive coping.

For financial coping, the same items as in Table A.5 (abbreviated in Table A.6) were used. These factors were interpreted thus:

- factor 1: active/expressive/negative coping;
- factor 2: cool/positive coping;
- factor 3: active *vs* passive coping.

Values

Adapted from Rokeach (1973), seven items, rated on a 9-point scale, were devised to index values or general principles according to how people lived their lives. A three-factor solution was produced as shown in Table A.7. These factors were interpreted thus:

- factor 1: general factor;
- factor 2: social responsibility *vs* personal ambition;
- factor 3: quality of life *vs* standard of living.

Attributions for financial problems

Eighteen items covering a range of financial problems were offered to respondents who rated each on a 4-point scale, from 'very important' to 'not at all important', as a cause of any financial problems they might have had. A three-factor solution was found as shown in Table A.8. These factors were interpreted thus:

- factor 1: general factor;
- factor 2: hedonism *vs* external disasters;
- factor 3: economic constraints *vs* social pressures.

Table A.3   Factor loadings for locus of control items

	Factor			
	1	*2*	*3*	*4*
Variance explained by factor	18%	14%	10%	10%
Item:		*Factor loading*		
In the long run, people get the respect they deserve in this world (mean = 2.73)	0.57		0.36	
Usually when I plan to do something, I can carry it out (mean = 1.88)	0.57		−0.40	
Becoming a success is a matter of hard work, luck has little or nothing to do with it (mean = 2.98)	0.53			0.33
Many of the unhappy things in people's lives are due to bad luck (mean = 2.87)	−0.48	0.34		
In general, I think about a decision before taking action (mean = 1.60)	0.43	0.32	−0.35	
I often find myself drifting along according to old habits (mean = 2.71)	−0.40	−0.30	0.36	0.39
Unfortunately, an individual's worth often passes unrecognized no matter how hard he or she tries (mean = 2.35)	−0.45	0.56		

Table A.3 (cont'd)

	Factor			
	1	2	3	4
Getting a good job depends mainly on being in the right place at the right time (mean = 2.42)		0.49		0.30
The best laid plans often go astray (mean = 2.22)	−0.41	0.49		
People's misfortunes result from the mistakes they make (mean = 3.07)	0.41	0.43		0.37
There will always be wars, no matter how hard people try to prevent them (mean = 2.52)		0.49	0.56	
One of the major reasons why we have wars is because people don't take enough interest in politics (mean = 3.56)			−0.48	0.65

Table A.4 Factor loadings for attitude items

	Factor		
	1	2	3
Variance explained by factor	45%	12%	11%
Item:		*Factor loading*	
It is better to save up for something and buy it only when you have the money to pay (mean = 2.05)	0.79		
Getting into debt is wrong and should be avoided (mean = 2.14)	0.75		
It is better to borrow money so as to have possessions now, when you want them (mean = 4.03)	−0.71	0.43	
It is better to borrow money so as to have possessions now, when you need them (mean = 3.18)	−0.69	0.46	
Being in debt shows that you cannot manage your finances properly (mean = 3.04)	0.67		0.42
Being in debt is part of everyday life nowadays and is nothing to be ashamed of (mean = 3.01)	−0.61		−0.59

Table A.4   (cont'd)

	Factor		
	1	*2*	*3*
On the whole, credit facilities make life easier because they can solve financial problems (mean = 3.49)	−0.54		
On the whole, credit facilities make life complicated because they can bring their own problems (mean = 1.87)	0.55	0.62	−0.38

Table A.5   Factor loadings for general coping items

	Factor		
	1	*2*	*3*
Variance explained by factor	30%	17%	13%
Item:	*Factor loading*		
You tend to feel threatened and you try to avoid dwelling upon or dealing with the situation (mean = 3.87)	0.72		
You tend to feel that others are better at dealing with the situation than you are and you rely on them to sort things out (mean = 3.74)	0.71		
You tend to feel that there is not much that you can do about the situation and to accept whatever happens (mean = 3.50)	0.62		−0.35
You tend to blame yourself for the situation and to feel that you are an unworthy person (mean = 3.47)	0.62		0.53
You tend to try and obtain information about the situation so that you can resolve the problem without getting upset (mean = 2.15)	−0.52	0.52	
You tend to concentrate on calming yourself down and trying to feel relaxed in the situation (mean = 2.67)		0.75	0.37
You tend to reassure yourself and argue that the problem is not so bad and that really little needs to be done about it (mean = 3.40)	0.60		
You tend to see yourself as the victim of an unjust situation and become frustrated, demanding or angry (mean = 3.78)	0.53		0.58

Table A.6 Factor loadings for financial coping items (items abbreviated)

	Factor		
	1	2	3
Variance explained by factor	30%	16%	15%
Item:		*Factor loading*	
Threat (mean = 3.92)	0.82		
Accept (mean = 3.62)		0.71	
Others (mean = 3.76)	0.64		
Blame (mean = 3.87)	0.58		0.49
Calm (mean = 2.74)		0.82	
Not bad (mean = 3.49)	0.51	0.53	−0.30
Victim (mean = 3.84)	0.35		0.67
Info (mean = 2.12)		0.42	0.59

Table A.7 Factor loadings for value items

	Factor		
	1	2	3
Variance explained by factor	33%	18%	15%
Item:		*Factor loading*	
Social concern (e.g. helpfulness, forgiveness, being loving, honesty, equality) (mean = 7.95)	0.71	−0.33	
Maturity (e.g. wisdom, mature love, standing up for one's own beliefs, a world of beauty) (mean = 7.75)	0.70		−0.41
Self-discipline (e.g. obedience, politeness, cleanliness, self-control) (mean = 7.33)	0.56		
Security (e.g. inner harmony, family security, a world at peace, responsibility) (mean = 8.12)	0.51	−0.44	0.46
Achievement (e.g. being capable, ambition, getting social recognition, having a sense of accomplishment) (mean = 6.76)	0.46	0.71	
Self-direction (e.g. imagination, being intellectual, independence, being logical) (mean = 7.32)		0.58	0.61
Enjoyment (e.g. pleasure, being cheerful, happiness, having a comfortable life) (mean = 7.97)	0.43		0.71

Table A.8 Factor loadings for attribution items

	Factor		
	1	2	3
Variance explained by factor	34%	9%	8%
Item:		*Factor loading*	
Not having any savings (mean = 2.7)	0.69		
Stress (mean = 3.0)	0.68		
High credit limits (mean = 3.2)	0.64		−0.36
Not understanding finances (mean = 3.2)	0.62		
Greed (mean = 3.4)	0.60	−0.33	
Convenience of credit (mean = 3.4)	0.60	−0.33	
High standard of living (mean = 3.1)	0.59		0.30
Unexpected repairs (mean = 2.7)		0.57	0.33
Fluctuating income (mean = 2.8)		0.56	0.41
Losing a job (mean = 3.2)		0.56	0.48
Demands from children (mean = 3.2)		0.56	0.37
Development of new products (mean = 3.7)	0.52		0.52
Enjoying shopping (mean = 3.2)		0.52	−0.41
Bad luck (mean = 3.3)		0.48	0.37
Advertising (mean = 3.7)	0.48		0.65
Keeping up with the Joneses (mean = 3.8)	0.30		0.54
Careless budgeting (mean = 2.8)			
Lack of self-discipline (mean = 2.8)			

NOTES

Chapter 1: Everyday experiences of mass consumption

1 This book does not pretend to offer comprehensive coverage of the many issues relating to everyday economic experience. Sometimes intentionally and other times accidentally, a number of issues were omitted, including certain economic activities such as gambling, certain economic structures such as pensions and insurance, or certain social groups such as the very rich or the very poor. Interested readers are referred to Douglas and Isherwood (1978), Featherstone (1991), Furnham and Lewis (1986) and Lea *et al.* (1987) among others.

Chapter 3: Saving and borrowing

1 Various researchers have studied the problems which personal debt causes for poor families (Mack and Lansley, 1985; Hartropp *et al.*, 1987), students (Bryant and Noble, 1989), consumers generally (Berthoud and Kempson, 1990), the banks (Leigh-Pemberton, 1989) and creditors (Lawson, 1989).

2 Those identified as in debt all owed money personally to one or more sources (except house mortgage). If they were married or cohabiting, they might or might not also owe money jointly, so those not in debt (44 per cent) were defined as people who did not owe money either personally or jointly. Respondents were also divided into three groups according to their pattern of saving: those who did not save money regularly and who had no savings, either personally or jointly (17 per cent); those who personally both saved a certain sum of money on a regular basis and had personal savings (37 per cent); and those who did not save regularly, either personally or jointly, but who did have personal savings, possibly saved up previously or inherited or received as gifts (46 per cent).

3 To discriminate among those with personal debts ($n = 101$) and those who were not in debt ($n = 140$), either personally or jointly, a stepwise hierarchical discriminant function analysis was conducted, entering first demographic, then financial, and finally psychological variables. The resultant discriminant function was highly significant and could correctly classify 95 per cent of the cases (see Livingstone and Lunt, in press b, for further details). Table 3.6 shows variables listed in order of predictive value.

4 People who owed money (personal debts greater than zero) were selected for analysis ($n = 107$). Multiple regression analysis was used to determine the best combination of predictors of amount of debt, using a stepwise hierarchical procedure which entered first demographic, then financial and, finally, psychological predictors (Cohen and Cohen, 1975). The final regression equation was highly significant, explaining 66 per cent of the variance in amounts of money owed (see Livingstone and Lunt, in press b, for further details).

5 Using the same hierarchical stepwise procedure for multiple regression as before, we attempted to predict respondents' reported willingness to use credit cards. The final regression equation was highly significant and explained 42 per cent of the variance.

6 Multiple regression analysis was carried out on the same sample as was used to predict amount of debt and using the same stepwise procedure as above in order to predict the amount of regular debt repayment. The final regression equation was highly significant, explaining a total of 60 per cent of the variance in amounts of debt repayments each month (see Livingstone and Lunt, in press b, for further details).

7 A discriminant function analysis was conducted, as before, to discriminate among those who do not save regularly and have no savings (non-savers, $n = 39$), those who save regularly and have savings (savers, $n = 82$) and those who do not save regularly but do have savings (non-savers with savings, $n = 109$). Two discriminant functions emerged from the analysis which were highly significant and which classified 88 per cent of the respondents into the correct saving group. Using only the first function, 72 per cent were correctly classified, with non-savers being confused with non-savers with savings. However, a very similar profile of variables distinguished savers from non-savers and, within the non-savers, those with and without savings, so only the first function was used, that which discriminated savers from non-savers (see Lunt and Livingstone, 1991a, for further details). The variables in Table 3.7 are listed in order of predictive value.

8 For those who saved on a regular basis ($n = 92$), stepwise hierarchical multiple regression analysis was used to determine why some save more than others by finding the best combination of predictors of recurrent saving. The final regression equation was highly significant, explaining a total of 65 per cent of the variance (see Lunt and Livingstone, 1991a, for further details).

9 Stepwise hierarchical multiple regression analysis was carried out on those with savings (n = 162) with the dependent variable of total savings in the same way as that for recurrent savings, in order to determine why some people have more savings than others. The final regression equation was highly significant, explaining a total of 57 per cent of the variance (see Lunt and Livingstone, 1991a, for further details).

10 Using a stepwise hierarchical discriminant analysis as before, all six groups were discriminated successfully, correctly classifying 94.93 per cent of respondents with five functions, of which the first two correspond to those which separate debtors from non-debtors and savers from non-savers, as discussed above. The remaining functions reveal the interaction between saving and borrowing, as shown in Tables 3.8, 3.9 and

3.10 (Livingstone and Lunt, in prep.). In each table, variables are listed in order of predictive value.

Chapter 4: The meaning of possessions

1 All quotes attributed to family members A to P are taken from Livingstone (in press; see also Silverstone et al., 1989), which reports a series of personal construct interviews conducted separately with husbands and wives, in their homes, on the subject of their domestic information and communication durables (video, washing machine, telephone, etc.). All names have been changed.

Chapter 5: Shopping, spending and pleasure

1 Consumer researchers produce complex and elaborate models for these decisions, using a variety of social and psychological predictors (see Nicosia, 1966; Howard and Sheth, 1969; Engel et al., 1972). The field of consumer research is vast and we can only refer to a few examples in this chapter.

2 This list of motives resembles the uses and gratifications frequently shown in relation to the mass media (Blumler and Katz, 1974), suggesting that a more general theory of 'what people do with' the texts of mass consumption (whether TV programmes or the supermarket), in contrast to 'what these texts do with' the consumer, could be developed.

3 Many other classifications exist. Moschis (1976) studied consumers of cosmetics and identified six groups: special-sales shoppers, brand-loyal shoppers, store-loyal shoppers, problem-solving shoppers, socializing shoppers and name-conscious shoppers. Zikmund (1977) found three kinds of consumers: comparative shoppers, neighbourhood shoppers and outshoppers. Westbrook and Fornell (1979) classified people in terms of the frequency and intensity of information search and found four groups: objective shoppers who made many visits to various shops to consider alternatives; moderate shoppers who tended to visit just one retail outlet; store-loyal shoppers; and store-intensive shoppers who visit four or more retailers and rely on personal sources of information.

4 The 279 respondents were clustered on their responses to 17 shopping items using Ward's method of hierarchical analysis (based on the Euclidean distance measure). The five-cluster solution was selected for interpretation. In order to interpret the shopping groups from the cluster analysis, an internal (i.e. descriptive, not explanatory) discriminant analysis was conducted using the same 17 shopping items to discriminate among the five clusters. The resultant analysis generated four significant functions which together correctly classified 83.87 per cent of cases.

5 A stepwise hierarchical discriminant function analysis was performed to differentiate among the five shopping groups, entering first sociodemographic, then economic and, finally, psychological predictors from the questionnaire. This produced four significant functions which together correctly classified 75.63 per cent of the cases (71.33 per cent of cases correctly classified with three functions).

Chapter 6: Generational and life course influences on economic beliefs

1 Caution is needed in so far as the notion of life course or cycle is inevitably a normative one, implying that everybody passes through a fixed sequence of stages –

growing up, finding a partner, settling down, having children, retiring – with little room for alternative paths. By omitting alternative life courses, the descriptive may be taken for the prescriptive, while the alternative becomes deviant or invisible. However, most people are in the process of passing through one of the basic stages of anticipating, forming, living within and then dissolving or dispersing a nuclear family structure. Ideologically, alternative household structures are often construed in distinction to the normative model. Pragmatically, when mapping our sample into categories defined by life stages, nearly 80 per cent fitted well, though this need not presume that those placed earlier in the life course will necessarily follow those later in the life course, nor that those placed in the same category are identical in attitudes or experiences, nor indeed that the remaining 22 per cent of the sample are in any way deviant. Caution is also needed with regard to the inevitable confounding of life course and generation: for example, those now retired would have had their children in a particular period, namely after the war; those who are now starting families are doing so during a consumer boom and widespread use of credit; and so on.

2 Much of the following analysis is given in greater detail in Livingstone and Lunt (1991).

Chapter 7: Everyday accounting for mass consumption

1 See Lunt and Livingstone (1990) and Livingstone and Lunt (in press a) for further details.

2 Several researchers have recently studied the knowledge people have of complex causal processes by assuming that ordinary people's knowledge can be represented as a network of causal interconnections or *perceived causal structure* (e.g. Kelley, 1983; Antaki, 1985; Lunt, 1988, 1989, 1991, Livingstone *et al.*, in press). In this study, we analysed asymmetric judgements of the perceived likelihood of cause–effect relationships between all pairs of causes using network analysis (Knoke and Kuklinski, 1982). All links endorsed by two-thirds of respondents were drawn onto the network shown in Fig. 7.1 (for further details, see Lunt and Livingstone, 1991).

REFERENCES

Adorno, T. and Horkheimer, M. (1973). *Dialectics of Enlightenment*. London: Allen Lane.

Althusser, L. (1971). *Lenin and Philosophy and Other Essays*. London: New Left Books.

Antaki, C. (1985). Ordinary explanation in conversation: Causal structures and their defence. *European Journal of Social Psychology*, 15, 213–30.

Appadurai, A. (1986). Commodities and the politics of value. In A. Appadurai (Ed.), *The Social Life of Things: Commodities in Cultural Perspective*. Cambridge: Cambridge University Press.

Ball-Rokeach, S. J. (1985). The origins of individual media-system dependency: A sociological framework. *Communication Research*, 12, 485–510.

Barty-King, H. (1991). *The Worst Poverty: A History of Debt and Debtors*. Stroud: Sutton.

Baudrillard, J. (1988). Consumer society. In M. Poster (Ed.), *Jean Baudrillard: Selected Writings*. Cambridge: Polity.

Baxter, J. L. (1988). *Social and Psychological Foundations of Economic Analysis*. New York: Harvester-Wheatsheaf.

Bem, S. L. (1991). The lenses of gender: The social construction of gender and sexuality. Seminar presented at London School of Economics and Political Science, July.

Berthoud, R. and Kempson, E. (1990). *Credit and Debt in Britain*. Report of first findings from the PSI survey. London: Policy Studies Institute.

Billig, M. (1991). *Ideology and Opinions*. Sage: London.

Blumler, J. G. and Katz, E. (Eds) (1974). *The Uses of Mass Communications: Current Perspectives on Gratifications Research*. Beverly Hills, Calif.: Sage.

Bohannan, P. (1959). The impact of money on an African subsistence economy. *Journal of Economic History*, 19 (4), 491–503.

Bourdieu, P. (1984). *Distinction: A Social Critique of the Judgement of Taste* (translated by R. Nice). London: Routledge and Kegan Paul.

Brown, G. and Harris, T. (1978). *The Social Origins of Depression.* London: Tavistock.

Bruegel, I. (1983). A feminist view. In A. Horrox and G. McCredie (Eds), *Money Talks: Five Views of Britain's Economy.* London: Thames Methuen.

Bryant, R. and Noble, M. (1989). Education on a shoestring: A survey of the financial circumstances of students at the long-term residential colleges. Occasional Paper No. 2. Applied Social Studies Course, Ruskin College, Oxford.

Byng-Hall, J. (1978). Family myths used as defence in conjoint family therapy. *British Journal of Medical Psychology,* 40, 239–50.

Cameron, S. and Golby, D. (1990). Correlates of over-commitment in a sample of crisis debtors. In S. E. G. Lea, P. Webley and B. M. Young (Eds), *Applied Economic Psychology in the 1990s.* Exeter: Washington Singer Press.

Campbell, C. (1987). *The Romantic Ethic and the Spirit of Modern Consumerism.* Oxford: Blackwell.

Carsten, J. (1989). Cooking money: Gender and symbolic transformations of means of exchange in a Malay fishing community. In J. Parry and M. Bloch (Eds), *Money and the Morality of Exchange.* Cambridge: Cambridge University Press.

Caughey, J. L. (1984). *Imaginary Social Worlds: A Cultural Approach.* Lincoln, Nebraska: University of Nebraska Press.

Cohen, J. and Cohen, P. (1975). *Applied Multiple Regression/Correlation Analysis for the Behavioral Sciences.* New York: John Wiley.

Cohler, B. J. and Grunebaum, H. U. (1981). *Mothers, Grandmothers and Daughters.* New York: John Wiley.

Coshall, J. T. (1985). Urban consumers' cognitions of distance. *Geografiska Annaler,* 67B, 107–19.

Cowan, R. S. (1989). *More Work for Mother: The Ironies of Household Technology from the Open Hearth to the Microwave.* London: Free Association Books.

Coward, R. (1984). *Female Desire.* London: Paladin.

Csikszentmihalyi, M. and Rochberg-Halton, E. (1981). *The Meaning of Things: Domestic Symbols and the Self.* Cambridge: Cambridge University Press.

Curwen, P. (1990). *Understanding the UK Economy.* London: Macmillan.

Davidson, C. (1982). *A Woman's Work is Never Done: A History of Housework in the British Isles 1650–1950.* London: Chatto and Windus.

de Certeau, M. (1984). *The Practices of Everyday Life.* Los Angeles, Calif.: University of California Press.

Deem, R. (1982). Women, leisure and inequality. *Leisure Studies,* 1, 29–46.

Desai, M. (1986). Drawing the line: On defining the poverty threshold. In P. Golding (Ed.), *Excluding the Poor.* London: Child Poverty Action Group.

Dittmar, H. (1989). Gender identity-related meanings of personal possessions. *British Journal of Social Psychology,* 28, 159–71.

Dittmar, H. (1991). Meanings of material possessions as reflections of identity: Gender and social-material position in society. In F. W. Rudmin (Ed.), To have possessions: A handbook on ownership and property. *Journal of Social Behaviour and Personality,* 6 (6), 165–86 (spec. issue).

Douglas, M. and Isherwood, B. (1978). *The World of Goods: Towards an Anthropology of Consumption.* Harmondsworth: Penguin.

Drury, A. C. and Ferrier, C. W. (1984). *Credit Cards.* London: Butterworths.

Duesenberry, J. S. (1949). *Income, Saving and the Theory of Consumer Behavior.* Cambridge, Mass.: Harvard University Press.

Eliot, T. S. (1948). *Notes Towards a Definition of Culture.* London: Faber and Faber.

Engel, J. F., Kollat, D. T. and Blackwell, R. D. (1972). *Consumer Behavior*, 2nd edn. Hinsdale, Ill.: Dryden.

Featherstone, M. (1991). *Consumer Culture and Postmodernism*. London: Sage.

Fishbein, M. and Ajzen, I. (1975). *Belief, Attitude, Intention and Behavior: An Introduction to Theory and Research*. Reading, Mass.: Addison-Wesley.

Fisher, I. (1930). *The Theory of Interest*. London: Macmillan.

Ford, J. (1988). *The Indebted Society: Credit and Default in the 1980s*. London: Routledge.

Forty, A. (1986). *Objects of Desire: Design and Society, 1750–1980*. London: Thames and Hudson.

Fraser, N. (1989). *Unruly Practices: Power, Discourse and Gender in Contemporary Social Theory*. Cambridge: Cambridge University Press.

French, M. (1985). *Beyond Power: On Women, Men and Morals*. Harmondsworth: Penguin.

Frieden, B. (1965). *The Feminine Mystique*. Harmondsworth: Penguin.

Friedman, M. (1957). *A Theory of the Consumption Function*. Princeton, N.J.: Princeton University Press.

Friedman, R. and Zimmer, M. R. (1988). The role of psychological meaning in advertising. *Journal of Advertising*, 17 (1), 31–40.

Furby, L. (1978). Possessions: Towards a theory of their meaning and function throughout the life cycle. In P. B. Baltes (Ed.), *Life-span Development and Behavior*. New York: Academic Press.

Furnham, A. (1982). Explanations for unemployment in Britain. *European Journal of Social Psychology*, 12, 335–52.

Furnham, A. (1990). *The Protestant Work Ethic: The Psychology of Work-related Beliefs and Behaviours*. London: Routledge.

Furnham, A. and Lewis, A. (1986). *The Economic Mind: The Social Psychology of Economic Behaviour*. Brighton: Harvester-Wheatsheaf.

Galbraith, J. K. (1970). *The Affluent Society*, 2nd edn. Harmondsworth: Pelican.

Gardner, C. and Sheppard, J. (1989). *Consuming Passion: The Rise of Retail Culture*. London: Unwin Hyman.

Gergen, K. J. (1973). Social psychology as history. *Journal of Personality and Social Psychology*, 26, 309–20.

Giddens, A. (1991). *Modernity and Self-identity: Self and Society in the Late Modern Age*. Cambridge: Polity.

Goffman, E. (1961). *Asylums: Essays on the Social Situation of Mental Patients and Other Inmates*. Harmondsworth: Penguin.

Goffman, E. (1981). *Forms of Talk*. Oxford: Blackwell.

Goldman, A. (1977). Consumer knowledge of food prices as an indicator of shopping effectiveness. *Journal of Marketing*, 41, 67–75.

Goldthorpe, J. H., Lockwood, D., Bechhofer, F. and Platt, J. (1969). *The Affluent Worker in the Class Structure*. Cambridge: Cambridge University Press.

Gramsci, A. (1971). *Prison Notebooks*. London: Lawrence and Wishart.

Gray, A. (1987). Women and video. In H. Baehr and G. Dyer (Eds), *Boxed in: Women on and in Television*. London: Routledge and Kegan Paul.

Habermas, J. (1984). *The Theory of Communicative Action*. Cambridge: Polity.

Hall, S. (1988). *The Hard Road to Renewal*. London: Verso.

Halsey, A. H. (1986). *Change in British Society*, 3rd edn. Oxford: Oxford University Press.

Hartmann, H. (1981). The family as the locus of gender, class and political struggle: The example of housework. *Signs*, 6 (3), 366–94.

Hartropp, A., Hanna, R., Jones, S., Lang, R., Mills, P. and Schluter, M. (1987). Families in debt: The nature, causes and effects of debt problems and policy proposals for their alleviation. Jubilee Centre Research Paper No. 7. Cambridge: Jubilee Centre Publications.

Heaven, P. C. L. (1990). Human values and suggestions for reducing unemployment. *British Journal of Social Psychology*, 29, 257–64.

Hebdige, D. (1979). *Subculture: The Meaning of Style*. London: Methuen.

Hebdige, D. (1988). Towards a cartography of taste, 1935–1962. In *Hiding in the Light*. London: Comedia.

Heider, F. (1958). *The Psychology of Interpersonal Relations*. New York: John Wiley.

Held, D. (1980). *Introduction to Critical Theory*. London: Hutchinson.

Held, D. (1991). Between state and civil society: Citizenship. In G. Andrews (Ed.), *Citizenship*. London: Lawrence and Wishart.

Henwood, M., Rimmer, L. and Wicks, M. (1987). Inside the family: The changing roles of men and women. Occasional paper No. 6. London: Family Policy Studies Centre.

Hepworth, M. (1987). The mid life phase. In G. Cohen (Ed.), *Social Change and the Life Course*. London: Tavistock.

Hoggart, R. (1957). *The Uses of Literacy*. Harmondsworth: Penguin.

Holub, R. C. (1991). *Jurgen Habermas: Critic in the Public Sphere*. London: Routledge.

Horton, D. and Wohl, R. R. (1956). Mass communication and parasocial interaction. *Psychiatry*, 19, 215–29.

Howard, J. A. and Sheth, J. N. (1969). *The Theory of Buyer Behavior*. New York: John Wiley.

James, W. (1890). *Principles of Psychology*. New York: Holt, Rinehart and Winston.

Jansen-Verbeke, M. (1987). Women, shopping and leisure. *Leisure Studies*, 6, 71–86.

Kamptner, N. L. (1989). Personal possessions and their meanings in old age. In S. Spacapan, and S. Oskamp (Eds), *The Social Psychology of Aging*. Newbury Park: Sage.

Katona, G. (1975). *Psychological Economics*. New York: Elsevier.

Kelley, H. H. (1967). Attribution theory in social psychology. In D. Levine (Ed.), *Nebraska Symposium on Motivation*, Vol. 15. Lincoln, Nebraska: University of Nebraska Press.

Kelley, H. H. (1983). Perceived causal structures. In J. Jaspars, F. D. Fincham and M. Hewstone (Eds), *Attribution Theory and Research: Conceptual, Developmental and Social Dimensions*. London: Academic Press.

Keynes, J. M. (1936). *The General Theory of Employment, Interest and Money*. London: Macmillan.

Knoke, D. and Kuklinski, J. H. (1982). *Network Analysis*. Beverly Hills, Calif.: Sage.

Kopytoff, I. (1986). The cultural biography of things: Commoditization as process. In A. Appadurai (Ed.), *The Social Life of Things: Commodities in a Cultural Perspective*. Cambridge: Cambridge University Press.

Lawson, R. (1989). Problems with debt: A survey of creditors' perceptions and practices. Occasional Paper. London: National Association of Citizens Advice Bureaux.

Lea, S. G., Tarpy, R. M. and Webley, P. (1987). *The Individual in the Economy: A Survey of Economic Psychology*. Cambridge: Cambridge University Press.

Leigh-Pemberton, R. (1989). Personal credit problems. *Bank of England Quarterly Bulletin*, 29 (2), 243–5.

Lerner, M. J. (1980). *Belief in a Just World: A Fundamental Delusion*. New York: Plenum Press.

Levinson, D. J. (1978). *The Seasons of a Man's Life*. New York: Ballantine.

Lindqvist, A. (1981). A note on determinants of household saving behaviour. *Journal of Economic Psychology*, 1, 39–57.

Livingstone, S. M. (1988). Talk about technology: Domesticity, gender and control. Paper presented to the BPS Social Section Conference, University of Kent, September.

Livingstone, S. M. (1990). *Making Sense of Television: The Psychology of Audience Interpretation*. Oxford: Pergamon Press.

Livingstone, S. M. (in press). The meaning of domestic technologies: A personal construct analysis of familial gender relations. In R. Silverstone and E. Hirsch (Eds), *Consuming Technologies*. London: Routledge.

Livingstone, S. M. and Lunt, P. K. (1991). Generational and life cycle differences in experiences of ownership. In F. W. Rudmin (Ed.), To have possessions: A handbook on ownership and property. *Journal of Social Behaviour and Personality*, 6 (6), 229–42 (spec. issue).

Livingstone, S. M. and Lunt, P. K. (1992). Expert and lay participation in television debates. *European Journal of Communication*, 7 (1), 9–35.

Livingstone, S. M. and Lunt, P. K. (in press a). Everyday conceptions of necessities and luxuries: Problems of cultural relativity and moral judgment. In P. Webley, S. Lea and B. Young (Eds), *New Directions in Economic Psychology: Theory, Experiment and Application*. London: Edward Elgar.

Livingstone, S. M. and Lunt, P. K. (in press b). Predicting personal debt and debt repayment: Psychological, social and economic determinants. *Journal of Economic Psychology*.

Livingstone, S. M. and Lunt, P. K. (in prep.). Savers and borrowers: Strategies of personal financial management. Unpublished manuscript.

Livingstone, S. M., Lunt, P. K. and Slotover, M. (in press). Debating drunk driving: The construction of causal explanations in television discussion programmes. *Journal of Community and Applied Social Psychology*.

Lunt, P. K. (1988). The perceived causal structure of examination failure. *British Journal of Social Psychology*, 27, 171–9.

Lunt, P. K. (1989). The perceived causal structure of unemployment. In K. G. Grunert and F. Olander (Eds), *Understanding Economic Behaviour*. Amsterdam: Kluwer.

Lunt, P. K. (1991). The perceived causal structure of loneliness. *Journal of Personality and Social Psychology*, 61 (1), 26–34.

Lunt, P. K. and Livingstone, S. M. (1990). Drawing the distinction between luxury and necessity. In S. E. G. Lea, P. Webley and B. M. Young (Eds), *Applied Economic Psychology in the 1990s*. Exeter: Washington Singer Press.

Lunt, P. K. and Livingstone, S. M. (1991a). Psychological, social and economic determinants of saving: Comparing recurrent and total savings. *Journal of Economic Psychology*, 12, 621–41.

Lunt, P. K. and Livingstone, S. M. (1991b). Everyday explanations for personal debt: A network approach. *British Journal of Social Psychology*, 30, 309–23.

McDowell, L. (1983). Urban housing and the sexual division of labour. In M. Evans and C. Ungerson (Eds), *Sexual Divisions: Patterns and Processes*. London: Tavistock.

Mack, J. and Lansley, S. (1985). *Poor Britain*. London: Allen and Unwin.

McKendrick, N., Brewer, J. and Plumb, J. H. (1982). *The Birth of a Consumer Society: The Commercialisation of Eighteenth-century England*. Bloomington, Indiana: Indiana University Press.

McRobbie, A. (Ed.) (1989). *Zoot Suits and Second-hand Dresses*. Basingstoke: Macmillan.

Madigan, R. and Munro, M. (1990). Ideal homes: Gender and domestic architecture. In T. Putnam and C. Newton (Eds), *Household Choices*. London: Futures Publications.

Marcuse, H. (1964). *One Dimensional Man*. London: Routledge and Kegan Paul.

Martineau, P. (1952). *Motivation in Advertising*. New York: McGraw-Hill.

Marx, K. (1976). *Capital*. Harmondsworth: Penguin.

Maslow, A. H. (1970). *Motivation and Personality*. New York: Harper and Row.

Mason, J. (1989). *Philosophical Rhetoric: The Function of Indirection in Philosophical Writing*. London: Routledge.

Mauss, M. (1966). *The Gift: Forms and Functions of Exchange in Archaic Societies*. London: Cohen and West.

Mead, G. H. (1956). *On Social Psychology*. Chicago: University of Chicago Press.

Mennell, S. (1985). *All Manners of Food: Eating and Taste in England and France from the Middle Ages to the Present*. Oxford: Blackwell.

Miller, D. (1987). *Material Culture and Mass Consumption*. Oxford: Blackwell.

Miller, D. (1990). Bacchanal as a mode of domestic consumption of the media in Trinidad. Paper presented to ESRC/PICT Workshop on Domestic Consumption and Information and Communication Technologies, Brunel University, May.

Modigliani, F. (1970). The life-cycle hypothesis and inter-country differences. In W. Eltis (Ed.), *Inflation, Growth and Trade*. Oxford: Clarendon Press.

Moles, A. A. (1972). *Theorie d'Objets*. Paris: Editions Universitaires.

Moore, H. L. Household and Gender Relations: The Modelling of the Economy. In S. Ortiz (Ed.), Economic Anthropology. Boulder, Coler.: Westview Press.

Morgan, D. L. (1988). *Focus Groups as Qualitative Research*. Newbury Park, Calif.: Sage.

Morley, D. (1986). *Family Television: Cultural Power and Domestic Leisure*. London: Comedia.

Moschis, G. P. (1976). Shopping orientations and consumer uses of information. *Journal of Retailing*, 52, 61–70.

Moscovici, S. (1981). On social representation. In J. P. Forgas (Ed.), *Social Cognition: Perspectives on Everyday Understanding*. London: Academic Press.

Moscovici, S. (1984). The phenomenon of social representations. In R. M. Farr and S. Moscovici (Eds), *Social Representations*. Cambridge: Cambridge University Press.

Moyal, A. (1990). Women and the telephone in Australia: Study of a national culture. Paper presented at the Annual Conference of the International Communications Association, Dublin, June.

Mulgan, G. (1991). Citizenship and responsibilities. In G. Andrews (Ed.), *Citizenship*. London: Lawrence and Wishart.

Murray, R. (1988). Life after Henry (Ford). *Marxism Today*, October.

Nava, M. (1991). Consumerism reconsidered: Buying and power. *Cultural Studies*, 5 (2), 157–73.

Nicosia, F. M. (1966). *Consumer Decision Processes*. Englewood Cliffs, N.J.: Prentice-Hall.

Oakley, A. (1974). *Housewife*. Harmondsworth: Penguin.

O'Guinn, T. C. and Faber, R. J. (1991). Mass communication and consumer behavior. In T. S. Robertson and H. H. Kassarjian (Eds), *Handbook of Consumer Behavior*. Englewood Cliffs, N.J.: Prentice-Hall.

Olson, D. H., McCubbin, H. I., Barnes, H. L., Larsen, A. S., Muxen, M. J. and Wilson, M. A. (1983). *Families: What Makes Them Work*. Beverly Hills, Calif.: Sage.

Ortner, S. (1974). Is female to male as nature is to culture? In M. Rosaldo and L. Lamphere (Eds), *Woman, Culture, and Society*. Stanford, Calif.: Stanford University Press.

Oskamp, S. (Ed.) (1988). *Television as a Social Issue*. Newbury Park, Calif.: Sage.

Oumlil, A. B. (1983). *Economic Change and Consumer Shopping Behavior*. New York: Praeger.

Packard, V. (1957). *The Hidden Persuaders*. Harmondsworth: Penguin.

Pahl, J. (1989). *Money and Marriage*. London: Macmillan.

Parker, G. (1988). Credit. In R. Walker and G. Parker (Eds), *Money Matters: Income, Wealth and Financial Welfare*. London: Sage.

Parker, G. (1990). *Getting and Spending: Credit and Debt in Britain*. Aldershot: Avebury.

Parry, P. and Bloch, M. (1989). Introduction: Money and the morality of exchange. In J. Parry and M. Bloch (Eds), *Money and the Morality of Exchange*. Cambridge: Cambridge University Press.

Perring, C. (1991). The use of life histories in social research. Seminar presented at the Methodology seminar series, London School of Economics, May.

Piachaud, D. (1982). Patterns of income and expenditure within families. *Journal of Social Policy*, 11 (4), 469–82.

Prentice, D. A. (1987). Psychological correspondence of possessions, attitudes and values. *Journal of Personality and Social Psychology*, 53, 993–1003.

Radway, J. (1984). *Reading the Romance*. London: Verso.

Ray, C., Lindop, J. and Gibson, S. (1982). The concept of coping. *Psychological Medicine*, 12, 385–95.

Reiss, D. (1981). *The Family's Construction of Reality*. Cambridge, Mass.: Harvard University Press.

Robertson, R. (1991). After nostalgia? Wilful nostalgia and the phases of globalisation. In G. Andrews (Ed.), *Citizenship*. London: Lawrence and Wishart.

Roebuck, J. (1973). *The Making of Modern English Society from 1850*. London: Routledge and Kegan Paul.

Rokeach, M. (1973). *The Nature of Human Values*. New York: Free Press.

Rotter, J. B. (1966). Generalized expectancies for internal versus external control of reinforcement. *Psychological Monographs*, 80 (1).

Schneiderman, L. (1988). *The Psychology of Social Change*. New York: Human Sciences Press.

Segal, J. (1985). *Phantasy in Everyday Life: A Psychoanalytical Approach to Understanding Ourselves*. Harmondsworth: Penguin.

Silverstone, R., Morley, D., Dahlberg, A. and Livingstone, S. M. (1989). Condemned to the family: The household context of information and communication technologies. Working paper, Centre for Research into Innovation, Culture and Technology, Brunel University.

Simmel, G. (1990). *The Philosophy of Money*. London: Routledge.

Social Trends (1989). Vol. 19, Government Statistical Service Publication. London: HMSO.

Social Trends (1991). Vol. 21, Government Statistical Service Publication. London: HMSO.

Stone, G. P. (1954). City shoppers and urban identification: Observations on the social psychology of city life. *American Journal of Sociology*, 60, 36–45.

Tajfel, H. (1982). *Social Identity and Intergroup Relations*. Cambridge: Cambridge University Press.

Tauber, E. M. (1972). Why do people shop? *Journal of Marketing*, 36, 46–9.

Thompson, J. B. (1990). *Ideology and Modern Culture*. Cambridge: Polity.

Townsend, P. (1979). *Poverty in the United Kingdom*. Harmondsworth: Penguin.

Turkle, S. (1984). *The Second Self: Computers and the Human Spirit*. New York: Simon and Schuster.

Warneryd, K. (1989). On the psychology of saving: An essay on economic behavior. *Journal of Economic Psychology*, 10, 515–41.

Weiner, B. (1986). *An Attributional Theory of Motivation and Emotion*. New York: Springer-Verlag.

Westbrook, R. A. and Fornell, C. (1979). Patterns of information source usage among durable goods buyers. *Journal of Marketing Research*, 16, 303–12.

Whitehead, A. (1981). I'm hungry mum: The politics of domestic budgeting. In K. Young (Ed.), *Of Marriage and the Market*. London: CSE Books.

Williams, J. and Watson, G. (1988). Sexual inequality, family life and family therapy. In E. Street and W. Dryden (Eds), *Family Therapy in Britain*. Milton Keynes: Open University Press.

Wilson, G. (1987). *Money in the Family: Financial Organisation and Women's Responsibility*. Aldershot: Avebury.

Winship, J. (1987). *Inside Women's Magazines*. London: Pandora.

Zeithami, V. A. (1988). Consumer perceptions of prices, quality, and value: A means–end model and synthesis of evidence. *Journal of Marketing*, 52, 2–22.

Zikmund, W. G. (1977). A taxonomy of Black shopping behaviour. *Journal of Retailing*, 53, 61–72.

INDEX